The Book Of The Secrets-2

The Book Of The Secrets-2

Discourses on "Vigyana Bhairava Tantra"

Bhagwan Shree Rajneesh

Compilation:
Ma Yoga Astha
Swami Amrit Pathik

Editing:
Ma Ananda Prem

HARPER COLOPHON BOOKS
Harper & Row, Publishers
New York, Hagerstown, San Francisco, London

THE BOOK OF THE SECRETS 2. Copyright © 1975 by Rajneesh Foundation, Poona, India. All rights reserved. Printed in the United States of America. No part of this book may be used or reproduced in any manner whatsoever without written permission except in the case of brief quotations embodied in critical articles and reviews. For information address Harper & Row, Publishers, Inc., 10 East 53d Street, New York, N.Y. 10022. Published simultaneously in Canada by Fitzhenry & Whiteside Limited, Toronto.

First HARPER COLOPHON edition published 1979

ISBN: 0-06-090668-5

83   10   9   8   7   6

Editor's Note

A newcomer to the literature of Bhagwan Shree Rajneesh would be surprised to know, when reading this volume on "Vigyana Bhairava Tantra", that Bhagwan never prepares for any of his lectures. A sutra is merely read by him or a question is put to him, and with superb spontaneity his Divine wisdom flows forth in response.

All the books of Bhagwan's that are being published are the transcribed, edited, verbatim transcriptions of these spontaneous lectures with hardly a word altered. The editor's function is merely to punctuate, paragraph and set in grammatical sentence structure that which has its source in the wisdom of the Divine — a divine task indeed for the one who is editing.

Bhagwan never writes anything except letters. The spoken word has always been his medium. Thus, the reader will find a great aliveness in these discourses, as they were originally presented through an alive medium.

We are fortunate in this age to have the invention of the modern tape recorder. Imagine if the tape recorder had existed at the time of Buddha, Christ, or Mahavir and we had been able to preserve their actual words, voice intonations and language dialects for posterity! What a blessing it would have been to have their original words rather than the partialized interpretations handed down by their disciples!

But with Bhagwan future posterity will know what a rare living Enlightened Master once walked the earth. It will know the wisdom he has spoken, the *sadhanas* (spiritual practices) he has taught and even the soothing quality of his voice, since tapes as well as books will be preserved.

So, we are not only indebted to modern inventions as well as to ancient teachings like those in "Vigyana Bhairava Tantra" (herewith presented in this volume), but especially to Bhagwan for showering his grace upon us by taking so much trouble to awaken and teach such a distressed, tense, overanxious civilization as ours is.

Ma Ananda Prem

Contents

The Book Of The Secrets—II

Eighty discourses on "Vigyana Bhairava Tantra"
(Lord Shiva's 112 Methods of meditation)
in five volumes

Given by
Bhagwan Shree Rajneesh

From October 1972 to November 1973
in Bombay, India

1
Several "Stop" Techniques

December, 8, 1972, Bombay, India

SUTRAS:

1. *Just as you have the impulse to do something, stop.*
2. *When some desire comes, consider it. Then, suddenly, quit it.*
3. *Roam about until exhausted and then, dropping to the ground, in this dropping be whole.*

Life has two balances: one is of being and the other of doing. Your being is your nature. It is with you always; you have not to do anything to get it. It is already the case. You are it. It is not that you possess it. Not even that distance exists between you and it. You are it. You are your being. Doing is an achievement. Whatsoever you do is not already the case. If you do it, it will happen. If you do not do it, it will not happen. All that is not already the case is not your being.

To exist, to survive, you have to do much. And then, by and by, your activity becomes a barrier to know your being. Your activity is your circumference. You live on it; you cannot live without it. But it is only the circumference. It is not you; it is not the center. Whatsoever you have is the achievement of your doing. Having is the result of doing, but the center is surrounded, engulfed, by your doing and your having.

The first thing to note before we proceed into these techniques is that whatsoever you have is not your being, and whatsoever you do or can do is not your being. Your being precedes all doing. Your being precedes all your possessions, all your having. But the mind is constantly involved in doing and having. Beyond mind or below mind exists your being. How to penetrate into that center is what religions have been seeking. This is what has always been the search of all those who are interested in knowing the basic reality of human existence, the ultimate core, the substance of your being. Unless you understand this division between the circumference and the center, you will not be able to understand these sutras which we are going to discuss.

So note the distinction. Whatsoever you have — money, knowledge, prestige, whatsoever you have — it is not you. You have them. They are your possessions; you are different from them. Secondly, whatsoever you do is not your being. You may do it or you may not do it. For example, you laugh, but you may laugh or you may not laugh. You run, but you may run or you may not run. But you are and there is no choice. You cannot choose your being. You are already there.

Action is a choice. You may choose, you may not choose. You may do "this", you may not do "this". You may become a saint or you may become a thief, but your sainthood and your thiefhood are both doings. You can choose, you can change. A saint can become a thief and a thief can become a saint. But that is not your being: your being precedes your sainthood, your thiefhood.

Whenever you have to do something, you have to be there already; otherwise you cannot do it. Who runs ? Who laughs ? Who steals ? Who becomes a saint ? The being must precede all activity. The activity can be chosen, but being cannot be chosen. Being is the chooser, not the chosen, and you cannot choose the chooser. He is already there. You cannot do anything about him. Remember this — having, doing, are with you just as a circumference is with the center. But you are the center.

This center is the Self, or you may call it the *Atman* or whatsoever name you like. This center is your innermost point. How to reach it ? And unless one reaches it, knows it, unless one Realizes it, one cannot reach to a blissful state which is eternal, one cannot know the deathless, one cannot know the Divine. Unless one Realizes this center, one will remain in misery, anguish and suffering. The circumference is the hell.

These techniques are the means to enter into this center. The first technique: *"Just as you have the impulse to do something, stop."*

All these techniques are concerned with stopping in the middle. George Gurdjieff made these techniques very well known in the West, but he was not aware of "Vigyana Bhairava Tantra". He learned these techniques from Tibet, from Buddhist Lamas. He worked on these techniques in the West, and many, many seekers came to Realize the center through these techniques. He called them "stop exercises", but the source of these exercises is "Vigyana Bhairava Tantra".

Buddhists learned from "Vigyana Bhairava". Sufis also have such exercises. They are also borrowed from "Vigyana Bhairava". Basically, this is the source book of all techniques which are known all over the world.

Gurdjieff used it in a very simple way. For example, he would tell his students to dance. A group would be dancing, a group of, say, twenty people would be dancing, and suddenly he would say, "Stop!" And the moment Gurdjieff would say stop, they would have to stop totally. Wherever the pause would fall, they have to stop then and there. No change could be made, no adjustment could be made. If your one foot was above the earth and you were just standing on one, you would have to remain that way. If you fell that was another thing, but you were not to cooperate with the fall. If your eyes were opened, they had to remain opened. Now you could not close them. If they closed by themselves, that was another thing. But as far as you were concerned, consciously you have stopped. You have become just like a stone statue.

Miracles happened because in activity, in dance, in movement, when suddenly you stop a gap happens. This sudden stoppage of all activity suddenly divides you into two: your body and you. Your body and you were in movement. Suddenly you stop. The body has the tendency to move. It was in movement, so there is momentum. You were dancing, and there is momentum. The body is not ready for this sudden stop. Suddenly you feel that the body has the impulse to do something, but you have stopped. A gap comes into existence. You feel your body as something distant, far away, with the impulse to move, with momentum for activity. And because you have stopped and you are not cooperating with the body and its activity and its impulse, its momentum, you become separate from it.

But you can deceive yourself. A slight cooperation and the gap will not happen. For example, you feel uncomfortable, but the teacher has said, "Stop!" You have heard the word, but still you make yourself comfortable and then you stop. Then nothing will happen. Then you have deceived yourself, not the teacher, because you missed the point. The whole point of the technique is missed. Suddenly, when you hear the word "Stop!" instantly you have to stop, not doing anything now.

The posture was inconvenient. You were afraid you might fall down, that you might break a bone. Whatsoever happens, now it is not your concern. If you have any concern, you will deceive. This suddenly becoming dead creates a gap. The stopping is at the body and the stopper is the center. The circumference and the center are separate. In that sudden stopping you can feel yourself for the first time: you can feel the center.

Gurdjieff used this technique to help many. This technique has many dimensions; it can be used in many ways. But first try to understand the mechanism. The mechanism is simple. You are in activity, and when you are in activity you forget yourself completely. The activity becomes the center of your attention.

Someone has died, and you are weeping and crying, and tears are falling down. You have forgotten yourself completely. Someone who has died has become the center, and around that center this activity is happening — your weeping, your crying, your sadness, your tears. If I suddenly say to you, "Stop!" and you stop yourself completely, you will be totally taken away from your body and the realm of activity. Whenever you are in activity, you are in it, deeply absorbed in it. Sudden stoppage throws you off balance; it throws you out of activity. This being thrown leads you to the center.

Ordinarily, what are we doing? From one activity we move to another. We go on from one activity to another, from A to B and from B to C. In the morning the moment you are awake activity has started. Now you will be active the whole day. You will change many activities, but you will not be inactive for a single moment. How to be inactive? It is difficult. And if you try to be inactive, your effort to be inactive will become an activity.

There are many who are trying to be inactive. They sit in a Buddha posture and they try to be inactive. But how can you try to be inactive? The very effort is again an activity. So you can convert inactivity also into activity! You can force yourself to be quiet, still, but that forcing is an activity of the mind. That is why so many try to go into meditation but never reach anywhere: because their meditation is again an activity. They can change. If you were singing an ordinary song, you can now change to a *bhajan* — to a devotional song. You can sing slow now, but both are activities. You are running, you are walking, you are reading: these are activities. You can pray: that too is an activity. From one activity to another you can move, and with the last thing in the night, when you are falling into sleep, you are still active. The activity has not stopped. That is why dreams happen — because the activity goes on. You have fallen asleep, but the activity continues. In the subconscious, you are still active — doing things, possessing things, losing things, moving. Dreaming means you have fallen asleep because of exertion, but the activity is still there continuously.

Only sometimes, for a few moments (and these have become more and more rare for the modern man), only for a few moments, dreaming stops and you are totally asleep. But then that inactivity is unconscious. You are not conscious: you are fast asleep. The activity has ceased; now there is no circumference. Now you are at the center, but totally exhausted, totally dead, unconscious.

That is why Hindus have always been saying that *sushupti* (dreamless sleep) and *Samadhi* (the Ultimate ecstasy) are both similar, the same, with only one difference. But the difference is great: the difference is of awareness. In *sushupti*, in dreamless sleep, you are at the center of your being — but unaware. In Samadhi also, in the ultimate ecstasy, in the ultimate state of meditation also, you are at the center — but aware. That is the difference, but a great difference, because if you are unaware, even if you are at the center it is meaningless. It refreshes you; it makes you more alive again; it gives you vitality. In the morning you feel fresh and blissful, but if you are unaware, even if you are at the center your life remains the same.

In Samadhi you enter yourself fully conscious, fully alert. And once you are at the center fully alert, you will never be the same again. Now you will know who you are. Now you will know that your possessions, your actions, are just on the periphery: they are just the ripples, not your nature.

The mechanism of these techniques of stopping is to throw you suddenly into inactivity. The point must come suddenly, because if you "try" to be inactive you will turn it into activity. So do not try, and suddenly be inactive. That is the meaning of "Stop!" You are running and I say, "Stop!" Do not try; just stop! If you try, you will miss the point. For example, you are sitting here. If I say stop, then stop immediately then and there. Not a single moment is to be missed. If you try and adjust, and you settle down and then say, "Okay, now I will stop," you have missed the point. "Suddenly" is the base, so do not make any effort to stop. Just stop!

You can try it anywhere. You are taking your bath: suddenly order yourself to "Stop!" and stop. Even if only for a single moment, you will feel a different phenomenon happening within you. You are thrown to the center and suddenly everything stops — not only the body: when the body stops totally, your mind stops also. When you say, "Stop!" do not breathe then. Let everything stop. No breathing, no body movement. For a single moment remain in this stop, and you will feel you have penetrated suddenly, in rocket speed, to the center. And even a glimpse is miraculous, revolutionary. It changes you, and by and by you can have more clear glimpses of the center. That is why inactivity is not to be practised. Use it suddenly, when you are unaware.

So a teacher can be helpful. This is a group method. Gurdjieff used it as a group method because if you say "Stop!" you can deceive easily. First you make yourself comfortable and then you say stop. Or even if consciously you have not made any preparation for it, unconsciously you may be prepared. Then you may say, "Now I can stop." If it is done by the mind, if there is a planning behind it, it is useless. Then the technique will not be of any help. So in a group it is good. A teacher is working with you, and he says, "Stop!" And he will find moments when you are in a very inconvenient posture, and then a flash happens, a sudden lightning.

Activity can be practised, inactivity cannot be practised. And if you practise it, it becomes just another activity. You can be inactive only suddenly. Sometimes it happens that you are driving a car, and suddenly you feel there is going to be an accident, that another car has reached near yours and in just a moment there will be a crash. Suddenly your mind stops, breathing stops, everything stops. So many times in such accidents one is thrown to the center. But you may miss the point even in an accident.

I was in a car and there was an accident, and one of the most beautiful accidents possible. Three persons were with me, but they missed the whole thing completely. They missed the whole thing completely! It could have been a revolution in their lives, but they missed. The car went down in a river bed, into a dry bed, from a bridge. The car was totally upside down, and the three persons with me began crying; they began weeping.

One woman was there and she was crying. She was just beside me and she was crying, "I am dead! I am dead!" I told her, "If you were dead, then no one would be here to say this." But she was trembling, and she said, "I am dead! What will happen to my children!" Even after we carried her out of the car she was trembling and saying the same thing: "What will happen to my children! I am dead!" It took at least half an hour for her to calm down.

She missed the point. It was such a beautiful thing: suddenly she could have stopped everything. And one couldn't do anything. The car was falling from the bridge, so her activity was not needed at all. One couldn't do anything! But still the mind can create activity. She started thinking about her children, and then she began crying, "I am dead!" A subtle moment was missed. In dangerous situations the mind stops automatcially. Why? Because mind is a mechanism and it can work with only routine things — that which it has been trained to do.

You cannot train your mind for accidents; otherwise they would not be called accidents. If you are ready, if you have passed through rehearsals, then they are not accidents. "Accident" means that the mind is not ready to do anything. The thing is so sudden, it leaps from the unknown. Mind cannot do anything. It is not ready; it is not trained for it. It is bound to stop unless you start something else, unless you start something for which you are trained.

This woman who was crying about her children was not at all attentive to what was happening. She was not even aware that she was alive. The present moment was not in her focus of consciousness. She had moved away from the situation to her children, to death and to other things. She had escaped. As far as her attention was concerned, she had escaped from the situation completely.

But as far as the situation was concerned, nothing could be done. One could only be aware. Whatsoever was happening was happening. One could only be aware! As far as the present moment is concerned, in an accident what can you do? It is already beyond you, and the mind is not prepared for it. The mind cannot function, so the mind stops.

That is why dangers have a secret appeal, an intrinsic appeal: they are meditative moments. If you race a car and it goes beyond 90 miles per hour, and then beyond 100 and then beyond 110 and beyond 120, then a situation comes in which anything can happen and you will not be able to do. Now, really, the car is beyond control, going beyond control. Suddenly the mind cannot function; it is not ready for it. That is the thrill of speed: because a silence creeps in; you are thrown to the center.

These techniques help you to move to the center without any accidents, without any danger. But remember, you cannot practise them. When I say you cannot practise them, what do I mean? In a way you can practise them; suddenly you can stop. But the stopping must be sudden; you must not be prepared for it. You should not think about it and plan about it and say that "At twelve o'clock I will stop". Let the unknown happen to you when you are unprepared. Move in the unknown, the uncharted, without any knowledge. This is one technique: "Just as you have the impulse to do something, stop." This is one dimension.

For example, you have the impulse to sneeze. You are feeling that the impulse is coming, you are feeling the sneeze coming. Now a moment comes when you cannot do anything: it will happen. But in the very beginning of the feeling, when you feel the sensation of a sneeze coming to you, the moment you become aware, "Stop!" What can you do? Can you stop the sneeze? If you try to stop the sneeze, the sneeze will come sooner, because stopping will make your mind more conscious about it and you will feel the sensation more. You will become more sensitive, your total attention will be there, and that attention will help the sneeze to come out sooner. It will become unbearable. You cannot stop the sneeze directly, but you can stop yourself.

What can you do? You feel the sensation that the sneeze is coming: Stop! Do not try to stop the sneeze. Just you yourself stop. Do not do anything. Remain completely unmoving, with not even your breath going in and coming out. For a moment stop, and you will feel that the impulse has gone back, that it has dropped. And in this dropping of the impulse, a subtle energy is released which is used in going toward the center, because in a sneeze you are throwing some energy out — in any impulse.

"Impulse" means you are burdened with some energy which you cannot use and cannot absorb. It wants to move out, it wants to be thrown out. You want a relief. That is why after you sneeze you will feel good — a subtle well-being. Nothing has happened. You have simply released some energy which was superfluous, a burden. Now it is no more there; you are relieved of it. Then you feel a subtle relaxation inside.

That is why physiologists, particularly Pavlov, B. F. Skinner and others, they say sex is also like sneezing. They say physiologically there is no difference, and sex is just like sneezing. You are overburdened with energy; you want to throw it out. Once it is thrown, your mechanism relaxes. You become unburdened. Then you feel good. That goodness is just a release according to physiologists, and as far as physiology goes they are right. They are right! Whenever you have some impulse, just as you have the impulse to do something, stop! Not only with a physiological impulse: any impulse can be used.

For example, you were going to drink a glass of water. You have touched the water, the glass, and suddenly stop. Let the hand be there, let the desire to drink, the thirst, be there inside, but you stop completely. The glass is outside, the thirst is inside, the hand is on the glass, the eyes are on the glass: stop suddenly. No breathing, no movement — as if you have become dead. The very impulse, the thirst, will release energy, and that energy is used for going to the center: you will be thrown to the center. Why? Because impulse is a movement outward. Remember, "impulse" means energy moving outward.

Remember another thing: energy is always in movement — either going out or coming in. Energy can never be static. These are the laws. If you understand the laws, then the mechanism of the technique will be easy. Energy is always movement. Either it is moving out or moving in. Energy can never be static. If it is static it is not energy, and there is nothing which is not energy. So everything is moving somewhere.

When impulse, any impulse, comes to you, it means energy is moving out. That is why your hand goes to the glass. You have moved out. A desire has come to do something. All activities are movements toward that which is without from that which is within — movements from within to without. When you stop suddenly, the energy cannot be static in you. You have become static, but the energy cannot be static in you, and the mechanism through which it was moving out is not dead: it has stopped. So what can the energy do? The energy cannot do anything other than move inward. Energy cannot be static. It was going out. You have stopped, the mechanism has stopped, but the mechanism which can lead it toward the center is there. This energy will move inward.

And you are converting your energy and changing its dimension every moment without knowing. You are angry, and you feel to beat someone or to destroy something or to do something violent: try this. Take someone — your friend, your wife, your children, anyone — and hug, kiss or embrace him or her. You were angry. You were going to destroy something; you wanted to do some violent thing. Your mind was destructive; the energy was moving toward violence. Love someone immediately.

In the beginning you may feel that this is just like acting: You will wonder, "How can I love? I am angry! How can I love in this moment? I am angry!" You do not know the mechanism. In this moment you can love deeply because the energy has been aroused, it has arisen. It has come to a point where it wants to be expressed, and energy needs movement. If you just start loving someone, the same energy will move into love and you will feel a rush of energy that you may not have ever felt.

There are persons who cannot go into love unless they are angry, unless they are violent. There are people who can only go into deep love when their energy is moving violently. You may not have observed, but it happens daily: couples will fight before they make love. Wives and husbands fight, become angry, become violent, and then they make love — and they may not have understood what was happening. Then it becomes a mechanical habit. Whenever they fight, they will love, and the day they do not fight they will not be able to love.

Particularly in Indian villages where wives are still beaten, if a certain husband stops beating his wife it is known that now he has stopped loving her. And even wives understand that if the husband has beome totally non-violent toward them, it means the love has stopped. He is not fighting, so it means he is not loving.

Why ? Why is fight so associated with love ? It is associated because the same energy can move, the same energy moves, in different dimensions. You may call it love or hate. They look opposite, but they are not so opposite: because the same energy is moving. So a person who becomes incapable of hate becomes incapable of love according to your definitions of love. A person who cannot be violently angry becomes incapable of the love which you know. He may be capable of a different quality of love, but that is not your love. A Buddha loves, but that love is totally different. That is why Buddha calls it compassion; he never calls it love. It is more like compassion, less like your love, because your love implies hate, anger, violence.

Energy can move, can change directions; it can become hate, it can become love — the same energy. And the same energy can move inward also, so whenever you have the impulse to do something, stop ! This is not suppression. You are not suppressing anything. You are just playing with energy — just playing with energy and knowing the working of it, how it works inwardly. But, remember, the impulse must be real and authentic; otherwise nothing will happen.

For example, there is no thirst. You move to a glass and then suddenly you stop. Nothing will happen because there is nothing to happen: the energy was not moving. You were feeling love toward your wife, your husband, your friend. You wanted to hug, to kiss. Stop ! But the impulse must be there authentically. If the impulse is not there and you were just going to console someone, to kiss because the kiss is expected, and then you stop, then nothing will happen because nothing was moving inside.

So first, remember, the impulse must be authentic, real. Only with a real impulse does energy move, and when a real impulse is suddenly stopped the energy becomes suspended. With no dimension from where to move out, it turns in. It has to move. It cannot remain there.

But we are so false that nothing seems real. You eat your meal because of the clock, because of the time, not because of hunger. So if you stop, nothing will happen, because there was really no hunger behind it, no impulse. No energy was moving there. That is why, if you take your meal at one o'clock, at one o'clock you will feel the hunger. But the hunger is false. It is just a mechanical habit, just a dead habit. Your body is not hungry. If you do not eat you will feel something is missing, but if you can remain for one hour without eating you will forget it. The hunger will have subsided.

A real hunger will grow more; it is bound to grow. If your hunger was real, then at two you will feel more hungry. If the hunger was false, then at two you will have completely forgotten. Really, there will be no hunger at two. Even if you want to eat, now you will not feel hungry. The hunger was just a false mechanical feeling. No energy was moving. It was just mind saying to you that now this is the time to eat, so eat.

If you are feeling sleepy, stop, but the feeling must be real; that is the problem. And that is the problem for us. It was not so in Shiva's time. When the "Vigyana Bhairava Tantra" was for the first time preached, it was not so. Man was authentic, humanity was real — pure. Nothing was false about it. With us everything is false. You pretend that you love; you pretend that you are angry. You go on pretending and then you forget yourself whether you are pretending, or whether anything real is left. You never say what is in you; you never express it. You go on expressing what is not there. Watch yourself and you will come to know it.

You say something, but you feel something else. Really, you wanted to say quite the contrary, but if you say the real thing you will become totally unfit because the whole society is false, and in a false society you can exist only as a false person. The more adjusted, the more false, because if you want to be real you will feel a maladjustment.

That is why renunciation came into existence. It came because of a false society. Buddha had to leave not because it had any positive meaning, but only a negative meaning — because with a a false society you cannot be real. Or, at every moment you are in a constant struggle unnecessarily and dissipating energy. So leave the unreal, leave the false, so that you can be real: that was the basic reason for all renunciation.

But watch yourself how unreal you are. Watch the double mind. You are saying something, but you are feeling quite the contrary. Simultaneously, you are saying one thing in your mind and something else without. Thus, if you stop anything which is not real, the technique will not help. So find something authentic about yourself and try to stop that. Everything has not become false. Many things are still real. Fortunately, sometimes everyone is real; in some moment everyone is real. Then stop it.

You are feeling angry, and you feel it is real. You are going to destroy something, beat your child, or do something: stop! But do not stop with a consideration. Do not say that "anger is bad, so I should stop" — no! Do not say; "This is not going to help the child, so I should stop." No mental consideration is needed, beause if you consider, then the energy has moved into consideration. This is an inner mechanism. If you say, "I should not beat my child because it is not going to do anything good for him, and this is not good for me also, and this is useless and this never helps," the same energy which was going to become anger has become consideration. Now you have considered the whole thing, and the energy has subsided. It has moved into consideration, into thinking. Then you stop; then there is no energy to move in. When you feel angry, do not consider it, do not think "good" or "bad"; do not think at all. Suddenly remember the technique and stop !

Anger is pure energy — nothing bad, nothing good. It may become good, it may become bad: that will depend on the result, not on the energy. It can become bad if it goes out and destroys something, if it becomes destructive. It may become a beautiful ecstasy if it moves within and throws you to the center. It may become a flower. Energy is simply energy — pure, innocent, neutral. Do not consider it. You were going to do something: do not think. Simply stop and then remain stopped. In that remaining you will have a glimpse of the inner center. You will forget the periphery and the center will come to your vision.

Just as you have the impulse to do something, stop. Try it. Remember three things: One, try it only when a real impulse is there. Secondly, do not think about stopping: just stop. And, thirdly, wait ! When you have stopped — no breathing, no movement — wait and see what happens. Do not try. When I say wait, I mean do not try now to think about the inner center. Then you will again miss. Do not think of the Self, of the *Atman*. Do not think that now the glimpse is there, now the glimpse is coming. Do not think. Just wait. Let the impulse, the energy, move itself. If you start thinking about the Brahman and the *Atman* and the center, the energy will have moved into this thinking.

You can waste this inner energy very simply. Just a thought will be enough to give it a direction, then you will go on thinking. When I say stop, it means stop totally — fully. Nothing is moving, as if the whole time has stopped. There is no movement. Simply you are ! In that simple existence, suddenly the center explodes.

The second technique: *"When some desire comes, consider it. Then, suddenly, quit it."*

This is a different dimension of the same technique. "When some desire comes, consider it. Then, suddenly, quit it." You feel a desire — a desire for sex, a desire for love, a desire for food, anything. You feel a desire: consider it. When the sutra says consider it, it means do not think for or against it. Just consider the desire — what it is.

A sexual desire comes to the mind: you say, "this is bad." This is not consideration. You have been taught that this is bad, so you are not considering this desire. You are consulting the scriptures, you are consulting the past — the past teachers, the *rishis* (sages). You are not considering the desire itself: you are considering something else. And because of that something else — your conditioning, your upbringing, your education, your culture, your civilization, your religion — you are considering many things, but not the desire.

This simple desire has come. Do not bring in the mind, the past, the education, the conditioning; do not bring in values. Just consider this desire — what it is. If your mind could be washed completely from all that has been given to you by the society, from all that your parents have given to you, the education, the culture, if your total mind could be washed out, the desire for sex will arise. It will arise, because that desire is not given to you by the society. That desire is biologically built in; it is in you.

For example, if a child is born and no language is taught, the child will not learn any language. He will remain without language. A language is a social phenomenon; it has to be taught. But when the right moment comes, the child will feel sexual desire. That is not a social phenomenon. It is biologically built in. The desire will come at the right mature moment. The desire will come! It is not social: it is biological — deeper. It is built into your cells.

Because you were born out of sex, every cell of your body is a sex cell. You consist of sex cells. Unless your biology can be washed out completely, washed off, the desire will be there. It will come; it is already there. When a child is born the desire is already there, because the child is a by-product of a sexual meeting. He comes through sex; his whole body is built with sex cells. The desire is there; only a time is needed before his body becomes mature to feel that desire, to enact that desire. The desire will be there whether you are taught that sex is bad or good, whether you are not taught that sex is hell or heaven, whether you are taught this way or that way, for or against — because both are teachings.

The old traditions, the old religions, Christianity particularly, they go on preaching against sex. The new cults of hippies and yippies and others have started the opposite movement. They say sex is good, sex is ecstatic, sex is the only real thing in the world. Both are teachings. Do not consider your desire according to some teaching. Just consider the desire in its purity, as it is — a fact. Do not interpret it.

Consideration here means not interpreting it, just looking at the fact as it is. The desire is there: look at it directly, immediately. Do not bring in your thoughts or ideas, because no thought is yours and no idea is yours. Everything has been given to you, every idea is a borrowed thing. No thought is original, no thought can be original. Do not bring in thinking. Just look at the desire — at what it is, as if you do not know anything about it. Face it ! Encounter it ! That is what is meant by "consider it".

When some desire comes, consider it. Just look at the fact — at what it is. Unfortunately, it is one of the most difficult things — one of the most difficult things to do. Compared to this, reaching to the moon is not so difficult or reaching to the peak of Everest is not so difficult. It is highly complicated: reaching to the moon is highly complicated, infinitely complicated, a very complex phenomenon. But compared to living with a fact of the inner mind it is nothing, because the mind is so subtly involved in everything you do. It is always there. Look at the word: if I say "sex", the moment I say it you have decided for or against. The moment I say "sex", you have interpreted: "This is not good. This is bad." Or, "This is good." You have interpreted even the word.

Many persons came to me when the book "From Sex to Superconsciousness" was published. They came and they said, please change the title "From Sex to Superconsciousness". The very word "sex" makes them disturbed. They have not read the book, and those who have already read the book also say change the title.

Why? The very word gives you a certain interpretation. Mind is so interpretive that if I say "lemon juice" your saliva starts flowing. You have interpreted the words. In the words "lemon juice" there is nothing like lemon, but your saliva starts flowing. If I wait for a few moments, you will become uneasy because you will have to swallow it. The mind has interpreted; it has come in. Even with words you cannot remain aloof without interpreting. It will be very difficult, when a desire arises, to remain aloof, to remain just a dispassionate observer, calm and quiet, looking at the fact, not interpreting it.

I say, "This man is a Mohammedan": the moment I say, "This man is a Mohammedan", the Hindu has thought that this man is bad. If I say, "This man is a Jew", the Christian has decided that this man is not good. The very word "Jew", and in the Christian mind comes the interpretation. The traditional, conventional idea flares up. This Jew is not to be considered. Now the interpretation is old and will have to be imposed on this Jew.

Every Jew is a different Jew. Every Mohammedan is a different, unque individual. You cannot interpret him because you "know Hindus". You may come to conclude that all the Hindus you have known are bad. Then too this Hindu is not in your experience. You are interpreting this Hindu according to your past experience. Do not interpret. Interpretation is not consideration. Consideration means consider THIS fact — absolutely this fact. Remain with this fact.

Rishis have said that sex is bad. It may have been bad for them; you do not know. You have the desire, a fresh desire, with you. Consider it; look at it; be attentive to it. Then, suddenly, quit it.

Two parts are in this technique. First, remain with the fact — aware, attentive of what is happening. When you feel a sexual desire, what is happening in you? See how you become feverish, how your body begins to tremble, how you feel a sudden madness creeping in, how you feel as if you are possessed by something else. Feel it, consider it, do not exercise any judgement. Just move into this fact — the fact of sexual desire. Do not say it is bad!

If you have said that, the consideration has stopped. You have closed the door. Now your face is not toward the desire: your back is. You have moved away from it. You have missed a deep moment in which you could have gone down into your biological layer of being. You are clinging to the social layer which is the uppermost.

Sex is deeper than your *shastras* (scriptures) because it is biological. If all the *shastras* can be destroyed (and they can be destroyed: many times they have been), your interpretation will be lost. But sex will remain; it is deeper. Do not bring superficial things in. Just consider the fact and move within, and feel what is happening to you. What happened to particular *rishis*, to Mohammed and Mahavir, is irrelevant. What is happening to you this very moment? This alive moment, what is happening to you?

Consider it; observe it. And then the second part: this is really beautiful. Shiva says, "Then, suddenly, quit it." "Suddenly" — remember. Do not say, "This is bad, so I am going to leave it. I am not going to move with this idea, this desire. This is bad, this is sin, so I will stop it, I will suppress it." Then a suppression will happen, but not a meditative state of mind. And suppression is really creating by your own hands a deceived being and mind within.

Suppression is psychological. You are disturbing the whole mechanism and suppressing energies which are going to burst any day. The energy is there; you have simply suppressed it. It has not moved out, it has not moved in. You have simply suppressed it. It has simply moved sideways. It will wait and it will become perverted, and a perverted energy is the basic problem with man.

And the psychological diseases are by-products of perverted energy. Then it will take such shapes, such forms which are not even imaginable. And in those forms it will try again to be expressed, and when it is expressed in a perverted form, it leads you into a very, very deep anguish, because there is no satisfaction in any perverted form. And you cannot remain perverted. You have to express it. Suppression is creation of perversion. This sutra is not concerned with suppression. This sutra is not saying control, this sutra is not saying suppress. The sutra says, "Suddenly, quit it."

What to do ? The desire is there; you have considered. If you have considered it, it will not be difficult. The second part will be easy. If you have not considered it, look at your mind. Your mind will be thinking, "This is good. If we can quit sexual desire suddenly, this is beautiful." You would like to do it, but your liking is not the question. Your liking may not be your liking, but just the society's. Your liking may not be your own consideration, but just tradition. First consider; do not create any liking or disliking. Just consider, and then the second part becomes easy: you can quit the desire.

How to quit it ? When you have considered a thing totally, it is very easy; it is as easy as dropping this paper from the hand. "Quit it": What will happen ? A desire is there. You have not suppressed it, and it is moving out, it is coming up, it has stirred your whole being. Really, when you consider a desire without interpretation your whole being will become a desire.

When sex is there and if you are not against it or for it, if you have no mind about it, then just by looking at the desire, your whole being will be involved in it. A single sex desire will become a flame. Your whole being will be concentrated in the flame, as if you have totally become sexual. It will not only be at the sex center: it will spread all over the body. Every fiber of your body will be trembling. The passion will have become a flame. Now, quit it. Don't fight with it: simply say, "I quit it."

What will happen ? The moment you can simply say, "I quit," a separation happens. Your body, your passionate body, your body filled with sex desire and you, become two. Suddenly, in a moment, they are two poles apart. The body was writhing with passion and sex, and the center is silent, observing. No fight is there — just a separation, remember this. In fight you are not separate. When you are fighting you are one with the object. When you have just quit it, you are separate. Now you can look at it as if someone else is there, not you.

One of my friends was with me for many years. He was a constant chain smoker, and he tried and tried, as smokers do, not to smoke. One day suddenly in the morning he would decide, "Now I am not going to smoke," and by the evening he would be smoking again. And he would feel guilty and he would defend it, and then for a few days he would not gather courage again to decide not to smoke. Then he would forget what happened. Then one day, again he would say, "Now I am not going to smoke," and I would just laugh because this had happened so many times. Then he himself became fed up with the whole thing — with this smoking and then deciding not to smoke and this constant vicious circle.

He wondered what to do. He asked me what to do. So I told him, "Do not be against smoking: that is the first thing to do. Smoke, and be with it. For seven days do not be against it; do this thing." He said, "What are you telling me? I have been against it, and then too I could not leave it. And you are saying not to be against it. Then there is no possibility of leaving it." So I told him, "You have tried with the inimical attitude and you have been a failure. Now try the other — the friendly attitude. Do not be against it for seven days."

Immediately he said, "Then will I be able to leave it?" So I told him, "Then again, you are still inimical toward it. Do not think about leaving it at all. How can one think about leaving a friend? For seven days just forget. Remain with it, cooperate with it, smoke as deeply as possible, as lovingly as possible. When you are smoking, just forget everything; become smoking. Be totally at ease with it, in deep communion with it. For seven days, smoke as much as you like and forget about leaving it."

These seven days became a consideration. He could look at the fact of smoking. He was not against, so now he could face it. When you are against something or someone you cannot face it. The very being against becomes a barrier. You cannot consider. How can you consider an enemy? You cannot look at him. You cannot look into his eyes; it is difficult to face him. You can look deeply only in the eyes of one you love; then you penetrate deep. Otherwise eyes can never meet.

So he looked into the fact deeply. For seven days he considered it. He was not against, so the energy was there, the mind was there, and it became a meditation. He had to cooperate with it; he had to become the smoker. After seven days he forgot to tell me. I was waiting for him to say, "Now the seven days have ended, so now how can I leave it?" He forgot completely about the seven days. Three weeks passed and then I asked him, "Have you forgotten completely?" He said, "The experience has been so beautiful, I do not want to think about anything else now. "It is beautiful, and for the first time I am not struggling with the fact. I am just feeling what is happening to me."

Then I told him, "Whenever you feel the urge to smoke, simply quit." He didn't ask me how to quit it. Simply, he had considered the whole thing. And the whole thing became so childish, and there was no struggle. So I said, "When you feel again the urge to smoke, consider it, look at it, and leave it. Take the cigarette in your hand, stop for a moment, then leave the cigarette. Let it drop, and as the cigarette drops let the urge also drop inside."

He didn't ask me how to do it, because consideration makes one capable. You can do it, and if you cannot do it, remember, you have not considered the fact. Then you were against it, all the time thinking how to leave it. Then you cannot quit it. When suddenly the urge is there and you quit it, the whole energy takes a jump inward. The technique is the same; only the dimensions differ: "When some desire comes, consider it. Then, suddenly, quit it."

Third: *"Roam about until exhausted and then, dropping to the ground, in this dropping be whole."*

The same! The technique is the same! Roam about until exhausted. Just run in a circle. Jump, dance, and run again until exhausted — until you feel that now not a single step more can be taken. But you will have to understand that your mind will say that now you are completely exhausted. Do not pay any attention to the mind. Go on running, dancing, jumping. Go on! Do not pay any attention. The mind will say that now you are exhausted, now you cannot go on any more. Continue until you "feel" — not think, until you feel — that the whole body is tired, that "A single step more has become impossible, and if I move I will fall down".

When you feel that you are falling down and now you cannot move, that the body has become heavy and tired and completely exhausted, "then, dropping to the ground, in this dropping be whole." Then drop! Remember, be so exhausted that dropping happens of itself. If you continue, you will drop. The verge point has come; you are just going to drop. Then, the sutra says, drop, and in dropping be whole.

That is the central point in the technique: When you are dropping, be whole. What is meant? Do not drop just according to the mind — that is one thing. Do not plan it; do not try to sit; do not try to lie down. Drop as a whole, as if the whole body is one and it has dropped. And you are not dropping it, because if you are dropping it, then you have two parts: you who is dropping it, and the body which has been dropped. Then you are not whole. Then you are fragmentary — divided. Drop it as a whole; drop yourself totally. And remember, drop! Do not arrange it. Fall down dead. "In this dropping be whole": if you can drop in this way, you will feel for the first time your whole being, your wholeness. You will feel for the first time your center — not divided, but one, unitary.

How can it happen? The body has three layers of energy. One is for day-to-day affairs that is very easily exhausted. It is just for routine work. The second is for emergency affairs; it is a deeper layer. When you are in an emergency, only then is it used. And third is the Cosmic energy which is infinite. The first can be easily exhausted. If I say to you run, you will take three or four rounds and you will say, "I am feeling tired." Really, you are not feeling tired: the first layer is exhausted. In the morning it will not be so easily exhausted; in the evening it will be exhausted very easily because the whole day you have been using it. Now it needs a repair. You will need a deep sleep. From the Cosmic reservoir it can again get energy, enough to work. This is the first layer.

If I tell you to run just now, you will say, "I am feeling sleepy; I cannot run." And then someone comes and says, "Your house is on fire." Suddenly the sleepiness has gone. There is no tiredness; you feel fresh; you start running. What has happened so suddenly? You were tired, and the emergency has made you connected with the second layer of energy, so you are fresh again. This is the second layer. In this technique, the second layer has to be exhausted. The first layer is exhausted very easily. Continue. You will feel tired, but continue. And within a few moments a new surge of energy will come, and you will feel again renewed and there will be no tiredness.

So many people come to me and they say, "When we are in a meditation camp, it seems miraculous that we can do this much in the morning — for one hour, meditating actively, chaotically, going completely mad. And then in the afternoon we do an hour, and then in the night also: three times a day, we can go on meditating chaotically." Many have said that they feel that this is impossible, that they cannot continue and they will be dead tired, and the next day it will be impossible to move any limb of the body. But no one gets tired. Three sessions every day, doing such exertions, and no one is tired. Why? Because they are in contact with the second layer of energy.

But if you are doing it alone (go to a hill and do it alone), you will be tired. When the first layer is finished, you will feel, "Now I am tired." But in a big group, five hundred people doing meditation, you feel no one is tired, so "I should continue a little more". And everyone is thinking the same: "No one is tired, so I should continue a little more. If everyone is fresh and doing, why should I feel tired ?"

That group feeling gives you an impetus, and soon you reach the second layer. And the second layer is very big — an emergency layer. When the emergency layer is also tired, finished, only then are you in contact with the Cosmic, the source, the infinite.

That is why much exertion is needed — so much, that you feel, "Now it is going beyond me." The moment it is going beyond you, it is not going beyond you: it is just going beyond the first layer. And when the first layer is finished, you will feel tired. When the second layer is finished, you will feel, "If I do anything now, I will be dead." So many come to me, and they say that whenever they reach deep in meditation, a moment comes when they become afraid and scared and they say, "Now I am afraid. It seems as if I am going to die. Now I cannot penetrate any further. A fear grips, as if I am going to die. Now I will not be able to come out of meditation."

That is the right moment — the moment when you need courage. A little courage, and you will penetrate the third — the deepest, infinite layer.

This technique helps you very easily to fall into that Cosmic ocean of energy: "Roam about until exhausted and then, dropping to the ground, in this dropping be whole." And when you drop to the ground totally, for the first time you will be whole, unitary, one. There will be no fragments, no divisions. The mind with its divisions will disappear, and the Being that is undivided, indivisible, will appear for the first time.

2
Remaining With The Facts

December 9, 1972, Bombay, India

QUESTIONS:

1. Is permissiveness in expression a growth toward authenticity?

2. Why does one sometimes feel uneasy when stopping anger, sex, etc.?

3. If there is unawareness during an authentic impulse, how to "stop"?

4. Isn't initiation and grace of guru more important than techniques, and how to become capable of receiving?

The first question: *"You said last night that modern man has become inauthentic in expressing anger, violence, sex, etc. You say that in India students and the younger generation are less violent in their emotional expressions than are Western youth. Does this mean that Western youth are becoming more authentic in their expressions? Is permissiveness in the expression of sex and anger a growth toward being authentic in emotional expressions?"*

Many things have to be considered. One, to be authentic means to be totally factual. Ideologies, theories, isms, they distort you and they give a false "persona". You cultivate faces, then whatsoever you show you are not. The reality is missed and you are suddenly acting and acting. Your life becomes less alive and more a game in which you are enacting something — not your real soul, but the culture, the education, the society, the civilization. Man can be cultivated — and the more you are cultivated, the less real you are.

The reality is your uncultivated self untouched by society. But that is dangerous. A child, if left to himself, will be just an animal. He will be authentic, but he will be an animal; he will not become a man. So that is not possible: that alternative is closed. We cannot leave a child to himself. We have to do something, and whatsoever we do will disturb the real self. It will give clothings, it will give faces and masks to the child. He will become a man, but then he will become an actor. He will not

28

be real. If you leave him to himself he will be like an animal — authentic, real — but not man. So it is a necessary evil that we have to teach him; we have to cultivate and condition him. Then he becomes man, but unreal.

The third possibility opens with these techniques of meditation. All techniques of meditation are really "unconditionings". Whatsoever society has given to you can be taken again, and then you will not be an animal. Then you will be something more than man. You will be a superman — real, but not an animal.

How does it happen? A child has to be given culture, education. There is no possibility of leaving him to himself. If you leave him to himself, he will never become a man: he will remain an animal. He will be real, but he will miss the world, the dimension of consciousness which opens with man. So we have to make him a man, and he becomes unreal.

Why does he become unreal? Because this man is just imposed from without. Inside he remains the animal. From outside we impose humanity on him. He is divided; he is split in two. Now the animal goes on living within, and the man without. That is why whatsoever you do and say is a double bind. You have to maintain a face which has been given to you, and you continuously have to satisfy your animal also. That creates problems, and everyone becomes dishonest. The more you are idealistic, the more you will have to be dishonest, because the ideal will say, "do this," and the animal will be quite the contrary: he would like to do something else that is quite opposite.

Then what can one do? One can deceive others and oneself; then one can maintain a face, a false face, and go on living the life of the animal. That is what is happening. You live a life of sex, but you never talk about it. You talk about *bramacharya* (celibacy). Your sex life is just pushed into the dark — not only from society, not only from your family, but even from your own conscious mind. You push it into the dark as if it is not a part of your being. You go on doing things which you are against because your biology cannot change just by education.

Remember, your inheritance, your biological cells, your structure, cannot be changed just by ideological education. No school, no ideology can change your inner animal. Only a scientific technique can change the inner being. Just moral teachings will not help unless you have a scientific technique to change your total inner consciousness. Only then will you not be double: you will become single.

The animal is single, unitary; the saint too is single and unitary. Man is double because man is just between the two, the animal and the saint — or, you can say between God and dog. Man is just in between. Inside he remains the dog; outside he pretends to be God. That creates a tension, anguish, and everything becomes false. You could fall down and become an animal; then you will be more authentic than man. But then you will miss much: you will miss the possibility to become God.

The animal cannot become God because the animal has no problems to transcend. Remember, the animal cannot become God because there is nothing to be transformed. The animal is at ease with himself. There is no problem, no struggle, no transcendence. The animal is not even conscious. He is simply unconsciously authentic, but the animal is authentic although the authenticity is unconscious. No animal can lie; that is impossible. But not because animals maintain a morality: they cannot lie because they are not aware of the possibility that one can be false.

They are bound to be true, but that truth is not their choice. It is their slavery. An animal is bound to be true — not because he has chosen to be true, but because he cannot choose the other alternative. There is no alternative for him; he can only be himself. There is no possibility to be false because he is unconscious of possibilities.

Man is conscious of possibilities. Only man can be untrue. That is a growth! That is evolution! Man can be untrue and that is why he can be true. Man can choose. Animals are bound to be true. That is their slavery, not their freedom. If you are true, that is an achievement because you could always be untrue.

The possibility is open, but you have not chosen it. You have chosen the other. It is a conscious choice.

Of course, then man is always in difficulties. Choosing is always difficult, and the mind wants to choose something which is easy to do. The mind wants to have something with the least resistance. To lie is easy; to be false is easy. To appear loving is easy; to be loving is very difficult. To create a façade is easy; to create a being is difficult. So man chooses the simple, the easy, which can be done without any effort and without any sacrifice.

With man freedom comes into existence. Animals are just slaves. With man, freedom comes into existence, choice comes into existence, then difficulties and anxieties. With man, the untrue, the false, enters. You can deceive. Up to this point it is a necessary evil.

Man cannot be simple and pure in the same way as animals, but he can be more simple and pure, and he can be more impure and more complex. He can be more simple and more pure and more innocent, but he cannot be simple and pure and innocent just like animals. That innocence is unconscious, and man has become conscious. Now he can do two things: he may go on with his falsities, with his falseness, and constantly remain a divided being in conflict with himself. Or, he may become conscious of the whole phenomenon of what has happened and what is happening to him, and he may decide not to be false. He may leave all that is false. He may sacrifice, he may choose to sacrifice, whatsoever can be gained by being false. Then he becomes again authentic.

But this authenticity is different — qualitatively different — from the authenticity of an animal. The animal is unconscious. He cannot do anything; he is forced by nature to be authentic. Now a man decides to be authentic. No one is forcing him; on the contrary, everything is forcing him to be inauthentic — the society, the culture, all that exists around, is forcing him to be inauthentic. He "decides" to be authentic. This decision makes you a self, and this decision gives you a freedom which no animal can attain and no false man can attain.

Remember, whenever you lie, deceive, are dishonest, you are forced to do that. That is not your choice, not a real choice. Why do you lie ? Because of the consequences, because of the society: you will suffer if you say the truth. You lie and you escape suffering.

Really, the society has forced you to lie; it was not your choice. If you say the truth, it is your choice. No one is forcing you to say the truth. Everything is forcing you to say a lie, to be dishonest. That is more convenient, safe, secure. Now you are entering danger, insecurity, but this is your choice. With this choice, for the first time you attain a Self.

So animal authenticity is one thing, and man's authenticity is qualitatively different: it is a conscious choice. So a Buddha is one again. He is like an animal, with only one difference: he is simple, pure, innocent like an animal, but unlike an animal because he is conscious. Now everything is a conscious choice. He is alert, aware.

The question is, "Does this mean that Western youth is becoming more authentic ?" In a sense, yes. It is becoming more authentic because it is falling toward the animal. It is not a choice. Rather, again, it is the easiest course — to fall down. Western youth is more authentic than Eastern youth in the sense that they are now falling deeper down toward the animal. Eastern youth is false. Their behaviour looks like a façade — not real, but phony. But both of these are not really the alternatives.

Eastern youth is false, cultured, cultivated, forced to be something which is not real. Western youth has revolted against this, revolted toward the authenticity of the animal. That is why sex and violence have taken more and more of a grip on the Western youth. In a way, they are more authentic, but in a way the greater possibility is lost. A Buddha is in revolt and a hippie is also in revolt. But the revolts are different; the quality differs. A Buddha is also revolting against the conditioning, but he is going beyond it — toward a unity which is higher than man and higher than the animal. You can revolt and go down toward the animal. You are also going toward a unity, but that is going down, below man.

But in a way, revolt is good — because once revolt comes into the mind, the day is not far off when you will come to understand that this revolt is just going backwards. A revolt is needed which must go forward. So Western youth may come to understand sooner or later that their revolt is good, but the direction is wrong. Then it will become possible in the West for a new humanity to be born.

In this sense, the Eastern phoniness is not worth anything. It is better to be authentic, to be revolting, because a revolting mind will not take much time to see that the direction is wrong. But a phony youth may continue for millennia, may not be even aware that there is a possibility to revolt and to go beyond. But nothing is worth choosing between the two. The third alternative is the way.

Man must revolt against conditioning and go beyond. If you fall below then you may have the pleasure of revolting, but the revolt has become destructive: it is not creative. Religion is the deepest revolt, but you may not have thought about it in that way. We take religion as the most orthodox thing — the traditional, the conventional. It is not. Religion is the most revolutionary thing in human consciousness, because it can lead you toward the unity which is higher than animal, higher than man. These techniques are concerned with that revolution.

So when Shiva says be authentic, he means do not be phony, do not continue to be phony. Be aware about your false persona, about your clothings, dressings, masks — and then be authentic. Whatsoever you are, realize it.

The real problem is that one becomes deceived by one's own deceptions. You talk about compassion. In India we talk too much about compassion, non-violence. Everyone thinks that he is non-violent, but if you look at a person's acts, at his relationships, at his gestures, he is violent. But he is not aware that he is violent. He may be violent even in his non-violence. If he is trying to force others to be non-violent, that is violence. If he is forcing himself to be non-violent, that is violence. To be authentic means he must understand and realize what is his real state of mind — not ideas, not principles, but the state of mind: what is his state of mind ? Is he violent ? Is he angry ?

This is what is meant by Shiva when he says be authentic. Know what is your real "fact" because only a fact can be changed. A fiction cannot be changed. If you want to transform yourself, you must know your "facticity". You cannot change a fiction. You are violent and you think that you are non-violent. Then there is no possibility of any transformation. That non-violence is nowhere, so you cannot change. And the violence is there — but you are not aware of it, so how can you change it ?

First know the facts as they are. How to know the facts ? Encounter them without your interpretations. That is what yesterday's sutra said: "consider". Your servant has come: consider how you look at your servant. Your boss has come in the room: consider how you look at your boss. Is the look the same when you look at your servant as when you look at your boss ? Are your eyes the same, or is there any difference ? If there is any difference you are a violent man.

You do not look personally at the man, at the human being. Your look is an interpretation. If he is rich you look in a different way; if he is poor you look in a different way. Your look becomes economical. You are not looking at the man right before you. You are looking at some bank balance. And if the man is poor, your look has a subtle violence in it, a degrading, insulting look. If the man is rich you have a subtle appreciation, a welcome. A deep concern is there always, whatsoever you are doing.

Look at your concern. You are angry at your son or at your daughter, and you say you are angry for his or her sake, for his or her good. Go deep down; consider whether it is true. Your son has been disobedient. You are angry; you say you want to change him because it is for his good. Look within and consider the fact. Is the fact that you are thinking about his good, or do you simply feel insulted because he has disobeyed you ? You feel hurt because he has disobeyed you. Your ego is hurt because he has disobeyed you.

If your ego is hurt this is the fact, and you go on pretending that that is not the thing — that you are just thinking about his good, and that is why you are angry. You are angry just for him: you are not really angry. How can you be angry? You are a loving father, so you are not angry at all. How can you be angry? You love him so much, but "because he is going on a wrong path", because of your "love", you want to change him, and that is why you are angry. You are just pretending to help him.

But is this the fact? Are you just pretending or do you feel hurt because he has disobeyed you? And are you so sure that whatsoever you say is right for him? Go down within yourself, look at the fact, consider it — and be authentic. If you are really offended by his disobedience, then know it well that you are offended and you feel hurt, and that is why you are angry. This is being authentic.

Then you can do much for your change because facts can be changed. Fictions cannot be changed. With everything that you are doing or you are thinking, go deep down. Dig out the facts, and do not allow interpretations and words to colour it.

If this consideration is there, by and by you will become authentic. And this authenticity will not be like that of an animal. This authenticity will be like that of a saint, because the more you know how ugly you are, the more you know how violent you are, the more you penetrate inside your facts and become aware of the nonsense that you are doing, then the more this awareness will help you. And by and by your ugliness will drop away, will wither away, because if you are aware of your ugliness it cannot continue.

If you want it to continue, do not be aware of it and create a façade of beauty around it. Then you will see the beauty, and the ugliness will remain behind, never to be seen directly. Everyone else will see it; that is the problem. The son will see that the father is not angry for his good: he will see that the father is angry because he has been disobeyed and he feels hurt. He will know it. You cannot hide your ugliness from others. You can hide it from only yourself. Your look will reveal to everyone that there is violence.

You can only deceive yourself that there was compassion. That is why everyone thinks of himself as a very superior being, and no one else agrees with him. Your wife doesn't agree with you that you are a superior being. Your children are not in agreement with you that you are a superior being. Your friends do not agree, no one agrees with you, that you are a superior being.

They have a popular saying in Russia that if everyone says their mind totally, exactly as it is, there will not be four friends in the whole world. Impossible! Whatsoever your friend thinks about you, he never says to you. That is why friendship continues. But he is always saying things behind you, and you are saying what you think about your friend behind him. No one says honestly what he thinks because then there will be no possibility of any friendship. Why? No one agrees with you and the reason is only this: you can only deceive yourself; you cannot deceive anyone else. Only self-deception is possible.

And when you think you are deceiving others you are simply deceiving yourself. It may be that others may deceive you, that they have been deceived by you, because there are moments when it is convenient to play the role of being deceived. It may be beneficial for the person. You talk to someone about your greatness. Everyone is talking directly or indirectly about his greatness, his superiority. Someone may agree with you. If it is beneficial to him he will deceive you that he is being deceived by you, but he knows inside who you are.

You cannot deceive anyone unless someone is ready to be deceived; that is another thing. By authenticity I mean remember your facticity. Always discover it from your interpretations. Throw your interpretations and look at the fact of what you are. And do not be afraid. Much ugliness is there. If you are afraid, then you will never be able to change it. If it is there, accept that it is there; consider it.

This is what consideration means: consider it; look at it in its total nakedness. Move around it; go to its roots; analyze it. See why it is there, how you help it to be there, how you feed it, how you protect it, how it has grown to be such a big tree. See your ugliness, your violence, your hatred, your anger, how you have protected it, how you have helped it to grow up to now. Look at the roots; look at the whole phenomenon.

And Shiva says if you consider it totally you can drop it immediately, this very moment, because it is you who have been protecting it. It is you who have been helping it to become rooted in you. It is your creation. You can drop it immediately — just now. You can leave it, and there is no need to look again toward it. But before you can do this, you will have to know it — what it is, the whole mechanism, the whole complexity of it, how you help it every moment.

If someone says something insulting to you, how do you react ? Have you ever thought about it — that he may be right ? Then look ! He may be right. There is every possibility of him being more right than you about yourself, because he is aloof, far away; he can observe.

So do not react. Wait ! Tell him, "I will consider what you have said. You have insulted me, and I will consider the fact. You may be right. If you are right, then I will give you my thanks. Let me consider it. And if I find that you are wrong. I will inform you." But do not react. Reaction is different.

If you insult me, I say to you, instead of reacting, "Wait. Come back after seven days. I will consider whatsoever you have said. You may be right. I will put myself in your place and will observe myself; I will create a distance. You may be right, so let me look at the fact. It is very kind of you to have pointed it out, so I will look at it. If I feel that you are right, I will thank you; if I feel that you were wrong, I will inform you that you were wrong." But what is the need of reaction ?

You insult me. Then what do I do ? I insult you immediately then and there. I escape consideration. I have reacted. You insulted me, so I have insulted you.

And remember, reaction can never be right. It can NEVER be right! If you insult me, you create the possibility of my being angry. And when I am angry I am not conscious. I say something which I have never thought about you. This very moment, because of your insult, I react in a violent way. A moment later I may repent.

Do not react. Consider about facts. And if your consideration is total, you can drop anything. It is in your hands. Because you are clinging to it, it is there. But you can drop it immediately, and there will be no suppression — remember. When you have considered a fact, there will never be any suppression. Either you like it and you continue it, or you do not like it and you drop it.

The second question: "*According to last night's technique, when anger, violence, sex, etc., arises, one should consider it and then suddenly quit it. But when one does it, one sometimes feels like being sick and uneasy. What are the reasons for these negative feelings?*"

Only one reason: your consideration is not total. Everyone wants to quit anger without understanding it; everyone wants to quit sex without understanding it. And there is no revolution without understanding. You will create more problems and you will create more misery for yourself. Do not think of renouncing anything. Just think of how to understand it: understanding — not renunciation. There is no need of thinking to quit anything. The only need is to understand it in its totality. If you have understood it in its totality, the transformation will follow. If it is good for you, if it is good for your being, it will grow. If it is bad for you, it will drop. So the real thing is not quitting: it is understanding.

Why do you think about renouncing anger? Why? Because you have been taught that anger is bad. But have YOU understood it as bad? Have YOU come to a personal conclusion through your own deepening insight that anger is bad? If you have come to this conclusion through your own inner search, there will be no need to quit it: it will have already disappeared.

The very fact of knowing that this is poisonous is enough. Then you are a different man.

But you go on thinking of leaving, quitting, renouncing. Why? Because people say that anger is bad, and you are simply influenced by whatsoever they say. Then you go on thinking that anger is bad, and when the moment comes you go on being angry.

This is how a double mind is created: you remain with anger, and yet you always think anger is bad. This is inauthenticity. If you think that anger is good, then do it and do not say that anger is bad. Or if you say anger is bad, then try to understand whether this is your realization or whether someone else has said it to you.

Everyone is creating misery around himself because of others. Someone says this is bad and someone says that it is good, and they go on forcing the idea in your mind. The parents are doing this, the society is doing this, and then one day you are just following others' ideas. And your nature and others' ideas cause a split; you will become a schizophrenic. You will do something and you will believe in the very contrary. That will create guilt.

Everyone feels guilty. Not that everyone is guilty: everyone feels guilty because of this mechanism. They say anger is bad. Everyone has said to you anger is bad, but no one has told you how to know what anger is.

Everyone says sex is bad. They have been teaching, teaching, that sex is bad, and no one says what sex is, and how to know it. Ask your father, and he will become uneasy. He will say, "Do not talk about such bad things!" But these bad things are facts. Even your father could not escape; otherwise you would not have been. You are a naked fact. And no matter what your father says about sex, he couldn't escape it. But he will feel uneasy if you ask because no one has told him. His parents never told him why sex is bad.

Why? And how to know it? And how to go deep in it? No one will tell this to you. They will just go on labelling things:

this is bad and that is good. That labelling creates misery and hell.

So one thing to remember — for any seeker, a real seeker, this is a basic thing to be understood: remain with your facts. Try to know them; do not allow the society to force its ideology on you. Do not look at yourself through others' eyes. You have eyes; you are not blind. And you have facts of inner life. Use your eyes! That is what consideration means. And if YOU consider, then this will not be a problem.

But when one does it, one sometimes feels like being sick and uneasy. You will feel (if you have not understood the facts), you will feel uneasy, because it is subtle repression. You know already anger is bad. If I say consider it, you consider only so that it can be renounced. That renouncing is there, always present in your mind.

Someone was here, a very old man, sixty years of age. He is a very religious man — and not only a religious man, but a type of religious leader. He has been teaching many people and he has written many books. He is a moralizer, and now, at the age of sixty, he comes to me and he says, "You are the only person to whom I can tell my real problems. How can I get rid of sex?"

And I have heard him speak about the misery of sex. He has written books, and he has tortured his sons and daughters. If you want to torture someone, morality is the best trick — the easiest. Immediately you create guilt in the other person. That is the subtlest torture. Talk about *brahmacharya* and you create guilt, because it is so difficult to be a *brahmachari,* to be a pure celibate. It is so difficult, that when you talk about *brahmacharya* and the other cannot be, he feels guilty.

You have created guilt; now you can torture. You have made the other man degraded, inferior. Now he will never be at ease. He will have to live in sex and he will feel guilty. And he will always think about *brahmacharya,* and he won't know what to do. His mind will think of *brahmacharya,* and his body will live with sex. Then he will go against his body. Then he will think that "I am not my body. This body is an evil thing." And once you create guilt in someone, you have destroyed a mind, poisoned it.

The old man came and asked how to get rid of sex. So I told him first to be aware of the fact — and he has missed much opportunity. Now the sex will be weak, and the awareness will need more effort. When sex is violent and the energy is there and sex is young, you can be aware of it very easily. It is so forceful, it is not difficult to see and know and feel it. This man, at the age of sixty, now feebled, weak, ill, will have difficulty in being aware of sex. When he was young he was thinking about *brahmacharya*. He couldn't have lived that; he has five children. Then he was thinking about *brahmacharya* and missing the opportunity. And now he is thinking of what to do about sex. So I told him to be aware of it — to forget his teachings and burn his books, and not to say anything about sex to anyone without knowing it himself. I told him to be aware of it.

So he said, "If I try to be aware, in how many days will I get rid of it?" This is how the mind works. He is ready even to be aware, but just to get rid of it. So I told him, "If YOU are not aware of it, who decides to get rid of it? How do you conclude that this is bad? Is this taken for granted? Is there no need to discover it within yourself?"

Do not think of renouncing anything. Renunciation means you are just being forced by others. Be individual. Do not allow society too much domination over you. Do not be a slave. You have eyes, you have consciousness, you have sex, anger and other facts. Use your consciousness; use your eyes. Be aware.

Think of yourself as if you are alone. No one is there to teach you. What will you do? Start from the very beginning, from ABC, and go inside. Be totally aware. Do not decide; do not be in haste; do not conclude so soon. If you can reach a conclusion through your own awareness, that very conclusion will become a transformation. Then you will not feel any unease. There will be no repression. Only then can you quit anything. I am not saying be aware to quit. Remember, I am saying if you are aware, you can quit anything.

Do not make awareness a technique to quit. Quitting is just a consequence. If you are aware you can quit anything, but you may not decide to quit; there is no necessity. You may never decide to quit. Sex is there. If you will become fully aware of it, you may not decide to quit it. If with full awareness you decide not to quit it, then sex has its own beauty. If with full awareness you decide to quit it, then your renunciation is also beautiful.

Try to understand me. Whatsoever comes, whatsoever happens through awareness, is beautiful, and whatsoever happens without awareness is ugly. That is why your so-called *brahmacharis*, celibate monks, are basically ugly. Their whole way of life is ugly. That celibacy has not come as a consequence. It is not their own search. Now look at a person like D. H. Lawrence. His sex is beautiful — more beautiful than the renunciation of your celibate monks, because his sex is with full awareness. Through inner search he has come to conclude that he is going to live with sex. He has accepted the fact. Now there is no hitch, no guilt. Rather, sex has become glorious. So a D. H. Lawrence, fully aware of his sex, accepting it, living it, has a beauty of his own.

A Mahavir, fully aware of the fact and then coming to leave it, to quit it, has a beauty of his own. They both are beautiful — D. H. Lawrence and Mahavir. They BOTH are beautiful! But the beauty is not of sex and not of quitting sex. The beauty is of awareness.

This must also be constantly remembered — that you may not come to the same conclusion as Buddha; there is no necessity. You may not come to the same conclusion as Mahavir; there is no inevitability. If there is any inevitability there is only one, and that is of awareness. When you are fully aware, whatsoever happens to you is beautiful, is Divine.

Look at the sages of the past: Shiva sitting with Parvati. Parvati is sitting in his lap in a deep love gesture. You cannot conceive of Mahavir in such a pose. Impossible! You cannot conceive of Buddha in such a pose. Just because Ram is pictured with Sita, Jains cannot accept him as an Avatar, as a Divine incarnation, because he is still with women. It is impossible for Jains to conceive of him as an incarnation of God, so they say he is a great man — *mahamanava,* but not an Avatar. He is a great man, but still a man because the woman is there. When the woman is there, you cannot go beyond man. The counterpart is there, so you are still a man — of course, Ram was a great man, but not beyond man, Jains say.

If you ask Hindus, they have not talked about Mahavir at all — not even talked about him, not even mentioned him in their books — because for the Hindu mind, man alone without woman is half, a fragment, not the whole. Ram alone is not the whole, so Hindus say "Sitaram". They put the woman first. They will never say "Ramsita". They will say "Sitaram". They will say "Radhakrishna". They will put woman first for a basic reason — because man is born out of woman and man alone is half. With woman he becomes whole.

So no Hindu god is alone. The other part, the other half, is there. Sitaram is really the whole; Radhakrishna is the whole. Krishna alone is half. There is no need for Ram to quit Sita and there is no need for Krishna to quit Radha. Why? They are fully aware.

You cannot find a more aware man, a more conscious man, than Shiva, but he is sitting with Parvati in his lap. It creates problems. Then who is right? Is a Buddha right or is a Shiva right? Problems are created because we do not know that everyone flowers individually. Buddha and Shiva both are fully conscious, but it happens to Buddha that he leaves something in this full consciousness. That is his choice. It happens to Shiva in his full consciousness that he accepts everything. They are both at the same point of Realization, of awareness, but their expression will be different.

So do not fall into any pattern. No one knows what will happen when you become aware. Do not decide before becoming aware that you are going to quit this and that. Do not decide. No one knows. Wait! Be aware, and let your being flower. No one knows what will happen. With everyone there is an unknown possibility of flowering, and you need not follow anyone — because every following is dangerous, destructive; every imitation is suicide. Wait !

These techniques are only to make you aware. And when you are aware, you can quit anything or you can accept anything. When you are not aware, remember what is happening: neither can you accept, nor can you quit. You have sex: neither can you accept it totally and forget about it, nor can you quit it. I say either accept it and forget, or quit it and forget.

But you cannot do any of the two. You will always be doing both. You will accept, and then you will think of quitting it. And this is a vicious circle. When you have had sex, then for few hours or a few days you will think of quitting it. Really, you are doing nothing else but regaining energy. When you have regained energy, you will again think of having it. And this will go on for your whole life. It has been so for so many lives. When you become fully aware, you can decide. Either you accept it: then that acceptance gives a beauty; or, you quit it: then that quitting is also beautiful.

One thing is certain: when you are aware you can forget it — either way. It is not a problem then. Your decision is total and the problem drops. But if you feel any uneasiness, it means you have not considered, you have not been aware.

So be more aware. Consider any fact more — more deeply, more individually — without the conclusions of others.

The third question: *"When impulse is authentic, I am unaware. How can I exercise 'stop'?"*

This is a very significant question. It is easy to stop anything when you are false, and it is difficult to stop anything when you are authentic. When the anger is real, you will forget about the technique of stop. When the anger is false, you will remember; you can do it. But when the anger is false there is no meaning. There is no energy. You can stop it, but it is useless. When the anger is real, only then is the energy there, and if you stop it the energy will take an inner turn.

So what to do? Try to be aware — not of anger directly, but of easier things. You are walking: be aware of it. Do not start with anger. Start with easier things. You are walking: be aware of it; there is no problem. Then suddenly stop your walk. Start with easy things, and then go on to a deep complex thing. Do not start with complex things. Do not jump to sex immediately. It is more subtle, and you will need a more deep awareness for it.

So first create awareness with easier things. You are walking, you are taking a bath, you feel thirsty, you feel hungry: start with these things, all very ordinary things. You were just going to speak something to someone: stop — even in the middle of a sentence. You were going to relate a story you have been relating a thousand times, and you have bored everyone with it. You were again starting, "Once there was a king..." Stop! Start with easy things — more easy things.

There is a fly on your head: you were just going to send it away by your hand. Stop! Let the fly be there. Let your hand remain stopped. Do it with easy things so that you have the feeling, the feel, of stopping with awareness. Then move to complex things.

Anger is a very complex thing. Take a mechanical thing: every day in the morning you step out of your bed. Have you observed? You step out every day in the same way. If your right foot comes first, it comes first always. Tomorrow morning when the right foot is coming out, stop and let the left foot come.

Do it with easier things; then there is nothing to sacrifice but a habit. Always you start your walk with the right foot first. Stop! Anything — anything can be used. Find something. The easier, the better. And when you become a master of easier things and you can stop suddenly, and you can have the feel of awareness, a sudden calmness comes to you. For a second, an inner silence explodes.

Gurdjieff used to train his disciples in very easy things. For example, you say something and you nod your head. Then he would say to you, "Say the same thing, but do not nod your head." It is a mechanical habit. I am saying something; I make a gesture with my hand. Gurdjieff would say, "Do not make this gesture when you say this thing; remember this. Make any other gesture, but remember only this: when you are saying this, do not make this gesture. Be aware of it."

Use anything — anything! You always start your conversation with a particular sentence. Do not start with it. Someone says something. You have a mechanical response. Do not respond that way; say something else. Or, if you have started saying the old thing, stop in the middle. Stop with a jerk, suddenly. Try this— and only when you feel a mastery, move to complex things.

This is one of the basic tricks of the mind — that it will always say to you jump to a complex thing. Then you are a failure. Then you will never try again. You know that it cannot be done. This is a trick of the mind. The mind will say, "Okay, now you know that the exercise of stopping will be a failure when you are angry, hot angry. Then you will not try again.

Try with cold things; do not move to the hot. And when you can do it with cold things, then move to the hot. With gradual steps feel the path, and do not be hasty. Otherwise nothing will be accomplished.

The last question: *"After hearing about so many meditation techniques in 'Vigyana Bhairava Tantra', I am beginning to feel that the inner door cannot really open by techniques, but that it really depends on things like initiation, grace of the guru, etc. Is that not really the case? And when and how can one become capable of receiving initiation?"*

Really, grace of guru is again a technique. Just by changing the words nothing changes. It means surrender. You can receive the grace of the guru only when you surrender, and surrender is a technique. If you do not know how to surrender, you will not receive any grace. So, really, grace is not given: it is received. No one can give grace; you can receive it. With an Enlightened person the grace is flowing always. It is there; it is just his nature.

Just as a lamp is burning and the light is radiating, the Enlightened person is always radiating grace. It is not any effort.

It is flowing effortlessly. It is there. If you can receive, you can receive. If you cannot receive, you cannot receive.

So it may look paradoxical if I say this, but it is the truth: the grace is not given by the guru. It is received by the disciple. But how to be a disciple ? Again, it is a technique. How to surrender ? How to become receptive ? Surrendering is the most difficult of things. You cannot surrender your anger, you cannot surrender your sadness, so how can you surrender your total being ? You cannot surrender nonsensical things, you cannot surrender your diseases, so how can you surrender yourself ?

Surrendering means surrendering totally. You leave everything totally to your teacher, to your Master. You say, "Now I am no more. Now you are; do whatsoever you like." And when you wait, and when you do not again go and ask him when he is going to do this or that, you have surrendered; you are finished. There is nothing to be asked any more. In the right moment the thing will happen. But how to do it ?

This also will need a very great awareness. Ordinarily, stupid people think that surrender is very easy. That is stupidity. They think that if you go and touch the feet of a Teacher you have surrendered. Just touching the feet can be a surrender, but do not think that because you have touched the feet you have surrendered. Surrendering is an inner attitude. It is putting yourself off, forgetting yourself completely. Only the Master remains; you are no more. Only the Master is.

This can be done only with a very deep awareness. What is that awareness ? That awareness will come if you go on doing these techniques and you feel continuously that you are helpless. But do not decide your helplessness before doing them. It will be false. First do them, and do them authentically. If the techniques happen to help you, there will be no need of surrender; you will be transformed. If you do them authentically, really, fully, if you are not deceiving yourself and still nothing happens, then you will feel a helplessness. You will feel, "I cannot do anything." If this goes deep in you, this feeling of helplessness, only then will you be capable of surrendering — not before.

Do you feel helpless ? No one feels helpless. NO ONE feels helpless ! Everyone knows "I can do: if I want I can do. It is because I do not want to that I am not doing." Everyone thinks that if they wish, if they will, they will do. They think, "The moment I will 'will' it, I will do. The only reason I am not doing is because I am not willing just now."

But no one feels helpless. If someone says that through the grace of the guru it can happen, you think you are ready just this very moment. If it is a question of doing something, you say you can do it whenever you want. But if it is the question of grace, you say, "Okay ! If it can be received from someone, I can receive it this very moment."

You are not helpless. You are just lazy. And there is a great difference. In laziness no grace can be received — only in help-lessness. And helplessness is not part of laziness. Helplessness comes only to those who first make every effort to reach, to penetrate, to do. When you have done everything and nothing happens, you feel helpless. Only then can you surrender to some-one. Then your surrendering will become a technique.

That is the last of techniques, but people try it first. That is the last, the ultimate. When nohing happens by doing, if there is only helplessness and helplessness and helplessness, if you lose all hope and your ego is shattered, then you know that nothing can be done alone. Then your hand reaches to the feet of a Master. It is a different type of reach. You are helplessly search-ing for him. Your whole being moves to his feet. You become just a womb to receive.

Then the grace is available. It has never been unavailable: it is always available. In every age, in every period, there are Enlightened persons. But unless you are ready to lose yourself, you will not be in contact with him. You may be just sitting behind him or just sitting by the side of him, but there will be no contact.

There are three types of distances. One distance is of space. You are sitting there, I am sitting here, and there is space between the two points. This is a distance in space. You can come near; the distance will be less. You can just touch me, and the distance is lost — but only in space.

There is a second type of distance — in time. Your beloved has died, your friend has died. In space one point has disappeared completely. There is infinite distance. But in time, you will feel your friend just nearby. You close your eyes, and the friend is there. In time it may be that the person who is sitting by your side is more distant than your beloved who is no more in the world.

But there is a third type of distance, and that is of love. The beloved is dead. Then by and by, by and by, there will be a greater distance of time. People say time heals. When time is very, very, very distant, the memory becomes more and more faint, and it disappears.

A third distance exists — a third dimension — which is love. If you are in love with someone, then he may be on another star, but in your love he is just near you. He may have died; there may be centuries of distance between you and him. But in love there is no distance.

Someone can be near Buddha just now. Twenty-five centuries means nothing because the distance is of love. In space there is no Buddha now; the body has disappeared. In time there is 2,500 years distance, but in love there is no distance. If someone is in love with Buddha, time and space distances disappear. He is just here, and you can receive his grace.

You may be just sitting by the side of a Buddha. There is no gap as far as space is concerned; there is no distance as far as time is concerned. But if there is no love, then there is infinite distance. So someone may have lived with Buddha without being in contact, and someone may be just here now who is in contact with Buddha.

Grace happens in the dimension of love. For love everything is always eternally present. So if you are in love, grace can happen. But love is surrendering. Love means now the other has become more important than yourself. Now, for the other's life, you are ready to die. For the other to live, you will sacrifice yourself. The other has become the center; you are just the periphery. By and by you disappear completely, and the other remains. In that right moment, grace is received.

So do not think of a Master as one who can give you grace. Think of becoming a helpless disciple — totally surrendered, in love.

The Master will come to you. When the disciple is ready, the Master always comes. It is not a question of physical presence. When you are ready, from an unknown dimension of love grace happens. But do not think about grace as an escape.

Because I am talking about so many techniques, I know there are two possibilities: you may try some or you may just become confused, and the latter is more possible. With 112 techniques, listening to one and then another and another continuously, you will become confused. You will think it is beyond you. So many techniques, so what to do and what not to do ?

It may come to your mind that it is better to receive grace — *"Gurukripa"* than to go into this jungle-like world of techniques. This is very complex, so it is easier to receive grace.

But that will not happen to you if this is the way of your thinking. Try these techniques and try honestly. If you are a failure, then that very failure will become your surrender. That is the ultimate technique.

Okay ?

3

A Technique For The Intellectual And A Technique For The Feeling Type

December 12, 1972, Bombay, India

SUTRAS:

4. *Suppose you are gradually being deprived of strength or of knowledge. At the instant of deprivation, transcend.*

5. *Devotion frees.*

For tantra, man himself is the disease. It is not that your mind is disturbed: rather, your mind is the disturbance. It is not that you are tense within, but, rather, you are the tension. Understand the distinction clearly. If the mind is ill then the illness can be treated, but if the mind itself is the illness then this illness cannot be treated. It can be transcended, but it cannot be treated. That makes the basic difference between Western psychology, and Eastern tantric and yogic psychology; that is the difference between Eastern tantra and yoga, and Western psychology.

Western psychology thinks that the mind can be healthy, the mind as it is can be treated and helped, because for Western thinking there is no transcendence as there is nothing beyond mind. Transcendence is possible only if there is something beyond, so that you can live in your present state and move further. But if there is no beyond and the mind is the end, then transcendence is impossible.

If you think you are just a body, then you cannot transcend your body — because who will transcend and to where will you transcend? If you are simply the body, then you cannot go beyond the body. If you can go beyond the body, that means you are not simply the body, but something plus. That "plus" becomes the dimension to move into.

Similarly, if you are just the mind and nothing else, then no transcendence is possible. Then we can treat individual diseases.

Someone is mentally ill: we can treat the illness. We will not touch the mind, but we will treat the illness and make the mind normal. And no one will think about whether the normal mind itself is healthy or not.

The normal mind is just a sceptical mind. Freud says that as everyone is, we can only bring a diseased mind to normality. But whether everyone is healthy or not, that question cannot be raised. We take it for granted that the collective mind, the average mind, is okay. So whenever someone goes beyond that average mind, moves somewhere else, he has to be brought back and readjusted. Thus, the whole of Western psychology has been an effort toward readjustment — readjustment to the ordinary mind, the average mind.

In this sense, there are thinkers, particularly one very intelligent thinker — Geoffrey, who says that genius is a disease because genius is abnormal. If normality is health, then genius is disease. A genius is not normal: he is in a certain way mad. His madness may be useful, so we allow him to live.

An Einstein or a Van Gogh or an Ezra Pound — poets, painters, scientists, mystics — they are mad, but their madness is allowed for two reasons: either their madness is harmless or their madness is utilitarian. Through their madness they contribute something which normal minds cannot contribute. Because they are mad they have moved to one extreme, and they can see certain things that the normal mind cannot see. So we can allow these madmen — and we even make them nobel laureates. But they are "ill".

If normality is the criterion and the standard of health, then everyone who is not normal is ill. Geoffrey says that a day will come when we will treat scientists and poets in the same way we treat madmen: we will make them readjust to the average mind. This attitude is because of a particular hypothesis that mind is the end and there is no beyond.

Just opposite to this attitude is the Eastern approach. We say here that mind itself is the disease. So whether normal or abnormal, we will make only the distinction of "normally ill" and "abnormally ill". A normal man is normally ill. He is not so much ill that you can detect it. He is just average. Because everyone else is like him, he cannot be detected. Even the person, the psychoanalyst who treats him is himself a "normally ill" person. Mind itself is the disease for us.

Why? Why call mind itself the disease? We will have to approach it from a different dimension; then it will be easy. For us, body is death; for the Eastern approach body is the death. So you cannot create a perfectly healthy body; otherwise it will not die. You can create a certain balance, but body as such, because it is going to die, is prone to be ill. So health can only be a relative thing. The body cannot be perfectly healthy; it cannot be.

That is why medical science has no standard and no definition of what health is. They can define diseases; they can define a particular disease. But they cannot define what health is — or at the most they can only define negatively that when a person is not ill, not particularly ill, he is healthy.

But to define health in a negative way looks absurd, because then disease becomes the primary thing by which you define health. But health cannot be defined, because, really, the body can never be really healthy. Every moment the body is only in a relative balance because death is progressing with life: you are dying also. You are not simply alive. You are dying simultaneously.

Death and life are not two ends far away from each other. They are like two legs simultaneously walking — and they both belong to you. This very moment you are alive and dying both. Something is dying within you every moment. Within a span of seventy years death will reach the goal. Every moment you will go on dying and dying and dying, and then you will die.

The day you were born you have started dying. The birthday is also the death day. If you are dying continuously — and death is not something which will come from without, but something which will grow within — then the body can never be really healthy. How can it be? When it is dying every moment, how can it be really healthy? It can only be relatively healthy. So if you are normally healthy, it is enough.

The same is with the mind. The mind cannot be really healthy, whole, because the very existence of the mind is such that it is bound to remain diseased, ill at ease, tense, anxious — in anxiety. The very nature of the mind is such, so we will have to understand what is this nature.

Three things: One, mind is a link between the body and the "no-body" which is within you. It is a link between the material and the non-material within you. It is one of the most mysterious bridges. It bridges two quite contradictory things — matter and spirit.

If you can, conceive of the paradox: usually you make a bridge over a river where both the banks are material. In this case, mind is the bridge between one bank which is material, and the other which is non-material — between the visible and the invisible, between the dying and the non-dying, between life and death, between body and spirit — or whatsoever you name these two banks. Because mind bridges such contradictions, it is bound to remain tense. It cannot be at ease.

It is always moving from the visible to the invisible, from the invisible to the visible. Every moment the mind is in deep tension. It has to bridge two things which cannot be bridged. That is the tension; that is the anxiety. You are every moment in anxiety.

I am not talking about your financial anxiety or other such anxieties: they are boundary anxieties, frame anxieties. The real anxiety is not that: the real anxiety is that of the Buddha. You are also in that anxiety, but you are so much burdened by your day-to-day anxieties, you cannot discover your basic anxiety. Once you find your basic anxiety, you will become religious.

Religion is a concern for the basic anxiety. Buddha became anxious in a different way. He was not worried about finance, he was not worried about a beautiful wife, he was not worried about anything. There was no worry; ordinary worries were not there. He was secure, safe, the son of a great king, the husband of a very beautiful wife, and everything was available. The moment he desired anything he would get it. All that was possible was possible for him.

But suddenly he became anxiety-ridden — and that anxiety was a basic anxiety, a primary anxiety. He saw a dead man being carried away, and he asked his chariot driver what had happened to this man. The driver said, "This man is dead now. He has died." This was Buddha's first encounter with death, so he asked immediately, "Is everyone prone to death? Am I also going to die?"

Look at the question. You may not have asked it. You may have asked who has died, why he has died, or you might have said he looks too young and this is not the age to die. Those anxieties are not basic; they are not concerned with you. You may have felt sympathetic, you may have felt sad, but still that is just on the circumference — and you will have forgotten within a few moments.

Buddha turned the whole question toward himself and he asked, "Am I going to die?" The chariot driver said, "I cannot lie to you. Everyone is prone to death, everyone is to die." Buddha said, "Then turn back the chariot. If I am going to die, then what is the use of life? You have created a deep anxiety in me. Unless this anxiety is resolved, I cannot be at ease."

What is this anxiety? It is a basic anxiety. So if you become basically aware of the very situation of life — of body, of mind, a subtle anxiety will creep in, and then that anxiety will continue to tremble within you. Whatsoever you are doing or not doing, the anxiety will be there — a deep anguish. The mind is bridging an abyss — an impossible abyss. The body is to die, and you have something — X — within you which is deathless.

These are two contradictions. It is as if you are standing in two boats which are moving in opposite directions. Then you will be in a deep conflict. That conflict is the conflict of the mind. The mind is between two opposites: that is one thing.

Secondly, mind is a process, not a thing. Mind is not a thing: it is a process. The word "mind" is a false notion. When we say "mind", it appears as if there is something like a mind within you. There is nothing ! Mind is not a thing: mind is a process. So it is better to call it "minding", not mind. We have a word in Sanskrit, *chitta*, which means minding: not mind, but minding — a process.

A process can never be silent. A process will always be tense; a process means a turmoil. And mind is always moving from the past to the future. The past goes on being a burden on it, so it has to move into the future. This constant movement creates another tension within you. If you become too much conscious about it, you may go mad.

So that is why we are always engaged in something or other; we do not want to be unoccupied. If you are unoccupied, then you will become conscious of the inner process, of the minding, and that will give you very strange and peculiar tensions. So everyone wants to be occupied in some way or other. If there is nothing else to do, one goes on reading the same newspaper again and again. Why ? Can you not sit silent ? It is difficult because if you sit silent you become aware of the totally tense process within.

So everyone is in search of escapes. Alcohol can give that: you become unconscious. Sex can give that: for a moment you forget yourself completely. Television can give that; music can give that: anything where you can forget yourself and become occupied so much that for the time being you are as if you are not. This constant escaping from oneself is really because of this process of minding. If you are unoccupied (and unoccupiedness means meditation), if you are totally unoccupied, you will become aware of your inner processes. And mind is the basic process within.

That is why so many people come to me and say they have come to meditate, but when they start meditating they become more tense. They say, "We were not so tense before and we were not so worried before. Ordinarily the whole day we are not so much worried. But when we sit down quietly and start meditating, thoughts rush upon us; they crowd in. That is something new." So they think it is because of meditation that thoughts are crowding them.

It is not because of meditation. Thoughts are crowding you every moment of your existence, but you are so occupied outwardly you cannot be conscious of it. Whenever you sit down you become conscious: you become conscious of something you have been escaping constantly. Mind, minding, is a process, and a process is an effort. Energy is wasted in it, dissipated in it. It is necessary: it is needed for life, it is part of the struggle for survival. It is a weapon — and one of the most violent weapons.

That is why man could survive other animals. The animals are more strong physically, but they lack a subtle weapon — minding. They have dangerous teeth, dangerous nails; they are more powerful than man. They can instantly kill a man completely. But they lack one weapon — minding. Because of that weapon, man could kill, survive.

So the mind is a survival measure. It is needed. It is necessary, and it is violent. The mind is violent. It is part of the long violence man had to pass through. It has been built through violence. So whenever you sit down, you will feel inner violence — thoughts rushing, violent thoughts, a turmoil, as if you are going to explode. That is why no one wants to sit silently.

Everyone comes and says, "Give me some support, some inner support. I cannot just sit silently. Give me a name that I can repeat like "Ram-Ram-Ram": give me a name that I can repeat; then I can be silent." Really, what are you doing? You are creating a new occupation. Then you can be silent because the mind is still occupied. Now you are focused on "Ram-Ram-Ram", on chanting: the mind is still not unoccupied. The mind as a process is bound to be always ill. It cannot be so balanced as silence needs.

Thirdly, mind is created from without. When you are born you have just the capacity for mind, but no mind — just a possibility, a potentiality. So if a child is brought up without society, without a society, the child will grow. He will have a body, but not a mind. He will not be able to speak any language; he will not be able to think in concepts; he will be like any animal.

Society trains your capacity into an actuality: it gives you a mind. That is why a Hindu has a different mind and a Mohammedan has a different mind. Both are men, but their minds are different. A Christian has a different mind. These minds are different because different societies have cultivated them with different purposes, different goals.

A child, a boy, is born, or a girl is born. They do not have minds. They have only the possibility that the mind can sprout. It can be there, but it is not there. It is just a seed. Then you train them. Then a boy becomes a different mind and a girl becomes a different mind because you teach them differently. Then a Hindu becomes different and a Mohammedan becomes different. Then a theist is different and an atheist is different. These minds are brought up in you. They are conditioned, forced upon you.

Because of this, mind as such is always old and orthodox. There can be no progressive mind. This statement may look strange: "There can be no progressive mind." Mind is orthodox because it is a conditioning. So these so-called progressives are as much orthodox about their progressiveness as any other orthodox person. Look at a communist. He thinks he is very progressive, but Marx's "Das Capital" is just as authoritative upon him as any Koran on any Mohammedan or any Gita on any Hindu. And if you start criticizing Marx, he feels as much hurt as any Jain will feel if you start criticizing Mahavir. Mind is orthodox because it is conditioned by the past, by the society, by others, for certain purposes.

Why am I making you aware of this fact? Because life changes every moment and mind belongs to the past. Mind is always old and life is always new. There is bound to be tension and conflict.

A new situation arises. You fall in love with a woman, and you have a Hindu mind and the woman is Mohammedan. Now there will be conflict. Now there is going to be much anguish unnecessarily. The woman is Mohammedan, and life has brought you to a situation where you fell in love with her. Now life gives you a new phenomenon, and mind does not know how to deal with it. There is no know-how, so there will be conflict.

That is why, in a very changing world, people become uprooted; their lives become anxious. This was not so in past ages. Man was more silent — not so really, but he appeared more silent because the state of affairs around him was so static and the mind was not in much conflict. Now everything is changing so fast, and the mind cannot change so fast. Mind clings to the past, and everything changes every moment.

That is why there is, so much anxiety in the West. In the East there is less anxiety. This is strange because the East has to face more basic problems. Food is not there, clothes are not there, houses are not there. Everyone is just starved. But they are in less anxiety, and the West is in more anxiety. The West is affluent, scientifically developed, technologically on a higher state of living, so why so much anxiety? Because technology gives life such a rapid change that the mind cannot cope with it. Before you are adjusted to a new thing, the new has become old and has changed.

Again the gap! Life is forcing new situations, and the mind always tries to react with the old conditioning. That gap goes on growing. The more the gap will be there, the more will be the anxiety. Mind is orthodox and life is not orthodox.

These are three reasons why mind itself is the disease. So what to do? If you are to treat the mind, there are easy ways. Psychoanalysis is easy. It may take a long time, it may not succeed, but still it is not difficult. But this transcendence of the mind is difficult, arduous, because you have to leave the mind completely. You have to take wing and go beyond, and leave the mind as it is; do not touch it.

For example, I am here and the room is hot. I can do two things. I can air-condition the room, but I live in the room. I can go on making arrangements so that the room is not hot, but then every arrangement has to be looked after and then every arrangement creates its own anxieties and problems. There is another possibility: I can leave the room and go out.

This is the difference. The West goes on living in the same room of the mind, trying to adjust, to make arrangements, so that living in the mind becomes at least normal. It may not be very blissful, but it becomes less and less unhappy. It may not reach a point, a peak of happiness, but one is saved from much suffering: there is less and less suffering.

Freud has said that there is no possibility for man to be happy. At the most, if you can arrange your mind in such a way that you are normal, you will be less unhappy than others; that is all. This is very hopeless. But Freud is a very genuine authentic thinker, and his insight is right in a way because he cannot see beyond the mind.

That is why the East has not really developed any psychology comparable to Freud, Jung or Adler. And that is strange because the East has been talking about the mind at least for five thousand years.

With five thousand years of talking about mind, meditation, going beyond, why couldn't the East create psychology? Psychology is a very recent development in the West. Why couldn't the East create a psychology? Buddha was here who talked about the deepest layers of the mind. He talked about the conscious, he talked about the subconscious, he talked about the unconscious. He must have known. But why couldn't he develop psychologies about the conscious, subconscious and unconscious?

The reason is this: the East has not been interested in the room. It talks about the room a little in order to go beyond, to go out. We have been interested in the room just to find the door; that is all. We are not interested in details about the room; we are not going to live in it. So the only interest has been in knowing where the door is and how to go out. We have talked about the room only so that the door can be located — so that we can know how to open it and go out.

This has been our whole interest. That is why psychology could not be developed in India. If you are not interested in this room, you will not make maps of the room; you will not measure every wall and every inch of space. You are not bothered about these things. You are only interested in where the door is, where the window is, so that you can jump out. And the moment you are out you will forget the room completely, because then you are under the great infinite sky. You will not even remember that there was a room and you lived in a cave, while all the time the infinite sky was beyond and you could have moved any moment. You will forget the room completely. If you can go beyond the mind, what happens ? The mind remains the same. You do not make any change in the mind, but you go beyond it and everything changes.

Then you can come back to the room again if you need to, but you will be a different person. This going out and coming in will have made you qualitatively different. A man who has been living in a room and who has not known what it is like on the outside is a different man. He is not really a man: he lives like a beetle, he lives like an insect. When he moves out to the sky — the open sky — and to the sun and the clouds and the infinite expanse, he becomes different immediately. This impact of the infinite makes him for the first time, a man, a consciousness.

Now he can move into the room again, but he will be a different man. Now the room can only be something which is used. It is not now a prison. He can move out any moment. Then the room becomes just something to be used, something utilitarian. Previously he was imprisoned in it, now he is not imprisoned. He is now a master, and he knows the sky is outside and the infinite is awaiting him. And even this room is part of that infinite now and even this small limited sky and space within the room is the space, the same space, which is outside. The man comes in again and lives in the room, uses the room, but now he is not imprisoned in it. This is a qualitative change.

The East is concerned with how to go beyond the mind and then use it. Do not be identified with the mind: that is the message. And all the techniques of meditation are concerned only about how to find the door, how to use the key, how to unlock it and go out.

We will discuss two methods today. The first is concerned with stopping in the middle of an activity. We discussed three "stop" methods before; now this one remains.

The fourth method: *"Suppose you are gradually being deprived of strength or of knowledge. At the instant of deprivation, transcend."*

You can do it in an actual situation or you can imagine a situation. For example: lie down, relax and feel as if your body is going to die. Close your eyes; start feeling that you are dying. Soon you will feel that your body is becoming heavy. Imagine: "I am dying, I am dying, I am dying." If the feeling is authentic, the body will start becoming heavy; you will feel as if your body has become like lead. You want to move your hand, but you cannot move; it has become so heavy and dead. Go on feeling that you are dying, dying, dying, dying, dying, and when you feel that now the moment has come, just a jump and you will be dead, then suddenly forget your body and transcend.

"Suppose you are gradually being deprived of strength or of knowledge. At the instant of deprivation, transcend": When you feel that the body is dead, what is meant now by transcending? Look at the body. Up to now you were feeling that you are dying. Now the body has become a dead weight. Look at the body. Forget that you are dying and now be the observer. The body is lying dead and you are looking at it. There will be a transcendence. You will be out of your mind because a dead body needs no mind. A dead body relaxes so much that the very process of the mind stops. You are there and the body is there, but the mind is absent. Remember, mind is needed for life, not for death.

If suddenly you come to know that within an hour you will die, what will you do in that hour? One hour left, and it is certain that you are going to die after one hour — exactly after one hour. What will you do? Your thinking will drop completely because the whole of thinking is concerned with either the past or the future.

You were planning to purchase a house or to purchase a car, or you were planning to marry someone or divorce someone. You were thinking many things, and they were constantly on your mind. Now, with only one hour more, there is no meaning in marriage and no meaning in divorce. Now you can leave all the planning to others who are going to live. With death planning ceases, with death worrying ceases, because every worry is life oriented.

You have to live tomorrow; that is why there is worry. So all those who have been teaching meditation to the world have always been saying do not think of tomorrow. Jesus says to his disciples, "Do not think of the tomorrow," because if you think of the tomorrow you cannot go into meditation. Then you move into worries. But we are so fond of worries that not only do we think of the tomorrow: we think of the other life. So we plan not only for this life: we plan for the other life beyond death also.

One day I was passing through a street and someone gave me a pamphlet. A very beautiful house was painted on the cover and a very beautiful garden. It was lovely — divinely lovely. And in very big capital letters was the question: "Do you want such a beautiful house and such a beautiful garden? And without any price, without any cost? For free?" I turned it over. It was not of this earth. It was a Christian pamphlet. It read, "If you want such a beautiful house and such a beautiful garden, believe in Jesus." Those who believe in him will get such houses free of cost in the Kingdom of God.

The mind goes on not only thinking of tomorrow, but thinking beyond death, arranging and making reservations for the after-life. Such a mind cannot be a religious mind. A religious mind cannot think of tomorrow. So those who think of the after-life are constantly worried about whether God will behave rightly with them or not.

Churchill was dying and someone asked him, "Are you ready to meet the Father there in heaven?" Churchill said, "That is not my worry. I am constantly worried whether the Divine Father is ready to meet me."

But either way one goes on worrying about the future. Buddha said, "There is no heaven and no afterlife." And he said, "There is no soul, and your death will be total and complete; nothing will survive." People thought he was an atheist. He was not. He was just trying to create a situation in which you can forget the tomorrow and can remain in this very moment here and now. Then meditation follows very easily.

So if you are thinking of death (not death which will come or is to come later), fall down on the ground and lie dead. Relax and feel, "I am dying, I am dying, I am dying." And not only think: feel it in every limb of the body, in every fibre of the body. Let death creep in. It is one of the most beautiful meditations. When you feel that the body is a dead weight and you cannot move your hand, you cannot move your head and everything has become dead, suddenly look at your own body.

Mind will not be there. You can look! You will be there; consciousness will be there. Look at your body. It will not look like yours. It will be just a body. The gap between you and the body will be clear — crystal clear. There will be no bridge. The body is lying dead and you are there standing as a witness, not in it: NOT in it!

Remember, the feeling that you are in the body is because of the mind. This feeling that you are in the body is because of the MIND! If the mind is not there, if it is absent, you will not say you are in the body or out of the body: you will simply be there, no in and out. "In" and "out" are both relative terms associated with the mind. Simply, you will be there witnessing. This is transcendence. You can do it in many ways.

Sometimes it is possible in actual situations. You are ill and you are feeling that there is no hope: you are going to die. This is a very useful situation. Use it for meditation. You can try it in other ways also. Suppose you are gradually being deprived of strength. Lie down and feel as if the whole Existence is sucking your strength out. You are being sucked from everywhere: your strength is being sucked. Soon you will be impotent, completely devoid of strength. Your energy is flowing out, being taken out. Soon nothing will be left inside. That is how life is. You are being sucked out. Everything that is around you is sucking you out. One day you will be just a dead cell; everything will have been sucked out. The life will have flown out of you, and the dead body remains there.

Even this very moment you can do it. Imagine this: lie down and feel that the energy is being sucked out. Within a few days you will have the knack of how energy goes out. And when you feel that everything has moved out, nothing is now left within you, TRANSCEND: "At the instant of deprivation, transcend." When the last quantum of energy is leaving you, transcend. Be an onlooker; just become a witness. Then this universe and this body both are not you. You are looking at the phenomenon.

This transcendence will bring you out of the mind. This is the key. And whatsoever is your liking, you can do it in many ways. For example, we were talking about a run-around. Exhaust yourself. Go on running and running and running. Do not stop by yourself; let the body fall. When every fibre is exhausted, you will fall down. When you are falling down, become aware. Just look and see that the body is falling down. Sometimes a very miraculous happening happens. You remain standing, and the body has fallen down and you can look at it. You can look, as only the body has fallen down and you are still standing. Do not fall with the body. Roam around, run, dance, exhaust the body. But, remember, you are not to lie down. Then the inner consciousness also moves with the body and lies down.

You are not to lie down. You just go on doing it until the body falls by itself. Then it falls like a dead weight. Immediately, you feel the body is falling and you cannot do anything. Open your eyes, be alert, do not miss the point. Be alert and see what is happening. You may be still standing, and the body has fallen down. And once you know it, you can never forget that you are different from the body.

This "standing out" is the real meaning of the English word "ecstasy". "Ecstasy" means to stand out. And once you can feel you are out of the body there is no mind in that moment, because mind is the bridge that gives you the feeling that you are in the body. If you are out of the body for a single moment, there will be no mind in that moment. This is transcendence. Then move in the body, then move in the mind. But you cannot forget the experience now. That experience has become part and parcel of your being. It will be there always. Go on doing it every day, and many things happen through such a simple process.

The West is always worried how to tackle mind, and it tries to find many ways. But, still, nothing works or seems to work. Everything becomes a fashion and then dies. Now psychoanalysis is a dead movement. New movements are there — encounter groups, group psychology, action psychology and many things — but just like a fashion they come and go. Why? Because within mind at the most you can only make arrangements. They will be disturbed again and again. Making arrangements with the mind is making a house on sand or making a house of playing cards. It is always wavering and the fear is always there that now it is going. At any moment it may not be there.

Going beyond the mind is the only way to be inwardly happy and healthy, to be whole. Then move in the mind and use this mind, but the mind becomes the instrument and you are not identified with it. So two things: either you are identified with the mind: this is illness for tantra; or you are not identified with the mind: then you use it is an instrument, and then you are healthy and whole.

The fifth technique (very simple in one sense and the most difficult in another, and only of two words): the fifth technique says, *"Devotion frees."*

Just two words: "Devotion frees." It is simply one word really, because "frees" is the consequence of devotion. What is meant by devotion? In "Vigyana Bhairava Tantra," there are two types of techniques. One is for those who are intellectually oriented, scientifically oriented, and another is for those who are heart oriented, emotion oriented, poetically oriented. And there are only two types of minds: the scientific mind and the poetic mind — and these are poles apart. They meet nowhere and they cannot meet. Sometimes they run parallel, but, still, no meeting.

Sometimes it happens in a single individual that he is a poet and a scientist. Rarely, but sometimes it happens that he is both a poet and a scientist. Then he has a split personality. He is really two persons, not one. And when he is a poet, he forgets the scientist completely; otherwise the scientist will be disturbing. And when he is a scientist, he has to forget the poet completely and move into another world with another arrangement of concepts — ideas, logic, reason, mathematics.

When he moves to the world of poetry, the mathematics is no more there: music is there. Concepts are no more there: words are there — but liquid, not solid. And one word flows into another, and one word can mean many things or it may not mean anything. The grammar is lost; only the rhythm remains. It is a different world.

Thinking and feeling — these are the two types, basic types. The first technique I taught was for a scientific mind. The second technique, "devotion frees," is for a feeling type. And remember to find out your type, and no type is higher or lower. Do not think that the intellectual type is higher or the feeling type is higher — no! They are simply types. No one is higher or lower. So just think factually what is your type.

This second technique is for the feeling type. Why? Because devotion is toward something else and devotion is a blind thing. In devotion the other becomes more important than you. It is a trust. The intellectual cannot trust anybody; he can only criticize. He cannot trust. He can doubt, but he cannot have faith. And if sometimes some intellectual comes to faith, it is never authentic. First he tries to convince himself about his faith; it is never authentic. He finds proofs, arguments, and when he is satisfied that the arguments help, the proofs help, then he believes. But he has missed the point because faith is not argumentative and faith is not based on proofs. If proofs are there, then there is no need of faith.

You do not believe in the sun, you do not believe in the sky: you know. How can you "believe" in the sun rising! If someone asks what is your belief about the sun rising, you do not have to say, "I believe in it. I am a great believer." You say, "The sun is rising and I know it." No question of belief or disbelief. Is there someone who disbelieves in the sun? There is no one. Faith means a jump into the unknown without any proofs.

It is difficult — difficult for the intellectual type because the whole thing becomes absurd, foolish. First proofs must be there. If you say there is a God and surrender yourself to God, first God has to be proven. But then God becomes a theorem — of course, proven, but useless. God must remain unproven; otherwise He is of no use because then faith is meaningless. If you believe in a proven God, then your God is just a theorem of geometry. No one believes in the theorems of Euclid. There is no need; they can be proven. That which can be proven cannot be made a base of faith.

One of the most mysterious Christian saints, Tertullian, said, "I believe in God because He is absurd." That is right. That is the attitude of the feeling type. He says, "Because he cannot be proven: that is why I believe in Him." This statement is illogical, irrational, because a logical statement must be like this: "These are the proofs of God; therefore, I believe in Him." And he says, "Because there are no proofs and no argument can prove that God is, therefore, I believe in Him." And he is right in a way because faith means a jump into the unknown without any reasons. Only a feeling type can do that.

Forget devotion. First understand love; then you will be able to understand devotion. You fall in love. Why do we say "falling in love" ? Nothing falls — just your head. What falls in love but your head ? You fall down from the head. That is why we say "falling in love" — because the language is created by intelllectual types. For them love is a lunacy, love is madness. One has "fallen" in love: it means now you can expect anything from him. Now he is mad; now no reasoning will help: you cannot reason with him. Can you reason with someone who is in love ? People try. People try, but nothing can be proven.

You have fallen in love with someone. Everyone says that one is not worthwhile or you are entering a dangerous terrain or you are proving yourself foolish and you can find a better partner. But nothing will help; no reasoning will help. You are in love: now reason is useless. Love has its own reasoning. We say "falling in love". It means now your behaviour will be irrational.

Look at two lovers, at their behaviour, their communication. It becomes irrational. They start using baby talk. Why ? Even a great scientist, when he falls in love, will use baby language. Why not use a highly developed technological language ? Why use this baby talk ? Because highly technological language is of no use.

One of my friends married a girl. The girl was Czechoslovakian. She did know a little English, however, and this man knew a little Czechoslovakian. They got married. He was a highly educated man, a professor in a university, and the girl was also a professor. But the man said to me (I was staying with him), "It is very difficult because I know only technological Czech, technological terminology, and she also only knows technological English, so we cannot have baby talk. So it is strange. Our love is just that somewhere on the surface, we feel. It cannot move deep. The language becomes the barrier. I can talk as a professor. As far as my subject is concerned I can talk about it, and she can talk about her subject. And love has been no one's subject."

So why do you fall into baby talk ? Because that was your first love experience with your mother. Those words that you uttered first were love words. They were not head oriented: they came from the heart; they belonged to the feeling. They had a different quality.

So even when you have a very developed language, when you love you again fall back: you fall back into baby talk. Those words are different. They do not belong to this category of the mind; they belong to the heart. They may not be so expressive, so meaningful. Still, they are more expressive and more meaningful, but their meaning is of a different dimension altogether. Only if you are very deeply in love will you fall silent. Then you cannot talk with your beloved. Or, you can talk just by the way, but, really, there is no talk.

If the love goes deep, words become useless; you remain silent. If you cannot remain silent with your beloved, know well there is no love — because it is very difficult to live in silence with someone you are not in love with. With a stranger you immediately start talking. When you are riding in a train or in a bus you immediately start talking, because to sit by the side of a stranger silently is very difficult, awkward. There is no other bridge, so unless you create a language bridge there is no bridge.

No inner bridge is possible with that stranger. You are closed in yourself and he is closed in himself, and two enclosures are just side by side. There is every fear of colliding and of danger, so you create a bridge. You start talking about the weather or about anything, any nonsense that gives a feeling that you are bridged and you are communicating. Two lovers will fall silent, and when two lovers start talking again you can know well that the love has disappeared: they have become strangers.

So go and look: wives and husbands, whenever they are alone, they will talk about anything. And they both know. They both are aware that there is no need to talk, but it is so difficult to remain silent. So anything, any trivia, will do, but talk so that you can have the feeling that communication is there. But two lovers will fall silent. Language will disappear because language belongs to reason. First it will become a baby talk, and then this will disappear. Then they will be silently in communication.

What is their communication? It is irrational. They feel attuned to a different dimension of existence, and they feel happy in that attunement. And if you ask them to prove what is their happiness, they cannot prove it.

No lover has been able to prove up to now why he is happy in love. Why? Because love implies much suffering. Still, lovers are happy. Love has a deep suffering, because when you become one with someone it is always difficult. Two minds become one: it is not only of two bodies becoming one. That is the difference between sex and love. If only two bodies become one, it is not very difficult and there is no suffering. It is one of the easiest things; any animal can do it. It is easy.

But when two people are in love, it is very difficult because two minds have to dissolve. Two minds have to be absent. Only then is the space created, and love can flower. No one reasons about love; no one can prove that love gives happiness. No one can even prove that love exists. And there are scientists, Behaviourists, followers of Watson and Skinner, who say love is just an illusion. There is no love; you are just in illusion. You feel that you are in love, but there is no love. You just dream.

And no one can prove they are wrong. They say that love is just a hallucination, a psychedelic experience. Nothing real: just body chemistry influencing you, just body hormones, chemicals, influencing your behaviour and giving a false well-being to you. No one can prove them wrong.

But the miracle is this, that even a Watson will fall in love. Even a Watson will fall in love, knowing well that this is just a chemical affair. And even a Watson will be happy. But love cannot be proven. It is so inner and subjective. What happens in love? The other becomes important — more important than you. You become the periphery and he becomes the center.

Logic always remains self-centered; mind always remains ego-centered. "I" am the center and everything just encircles around "me", for "me", but "I" am the center. This is how reason works. If you move with reason too much, you will come to the conclusion to which Berkeley came. He said, "Only I exist and everything else is just an idea on the mind. How can I prove that you are there, sitting there just before me? How can I prove reasonably, rationally, that you are really there? You may be just a dream. I may be just dreaming and talking; you may not be there at all. How can I prove to myself that really you are there? I can, of course, touch you, but I can touch you even in a dream. And even in a dream I feel it when I touch someone. I can hit you and you will scream, but even in a dream, if I hit someone, the dream figure screams. So how can I make a distinction that my audience here just now is not a dream but a reality? It may be just a fiction."

Go to a madhouse, and you will find people sitting alone talking. To whom are they talking? I may be talking to no one. How can I prove rationally that you are there really? So if reason goes to the extreme, to the very logical extreme, then only I remain and everything becomes a dream. This is how reason works.

Quite the contrary is the path of heart. I become the mystery and you, thou, the other, the beloved, become the real. If you move to the very extreme, then it becomes devotion. If your love comes to such an extreme point that you forget completely that you are, you have no notion of yourself and only the other remains, that is devotion.

Love can become devotion. Love is the first step. Only then can devotion flower. But for us even love is a far-away reality. Only sex is the real. Love has two possibilities: either it falls into sex and becomes a bodily thing or it rises into devotion and becomes a thing of the spirit. Love is just in between. Just below it is the abyss of sex, and beyond it is the open sky — the infinite sky of devotion.

If your love grows deeper, the other becomes more and more significant — so significant that you begin to call the other your God. That is why Meera goes on calling Krishna "God". No one can see Krishna, and Meera cannot prove that Krishna is there, but she is not interested in proving it at all. She has made that point, Krishna, her love object. And remember, whether you make a real person your love object or whether it is just your imagination, it makes no difference, because the whole transformation comes through devotion, not through the beloved — remember this. Krishna may not be there at all; it is irrelevant. For the lover, it is irrelevant.

For Radha, Krishna was there in reality. For Meera, Krishna was not there in reality. That is why Meera is a greater devotee than Radha. And even Radha would become jealous of Meera because for Radha the real person was there. It is not so difficult to feel Krishna's reality when he is present. But when Krishna is no more there, Meera alone is living in a room and talking to Krishna and living for him who is nowhere. For her, he is everything and all. She cannot prove; it is irrational. But she took a jump and she became transformed. Devotion freed her.

I want to emphasize the fact that it is not a question whether Krishna is there or not. It is not! This feeling that Krishna is there, this total feeling of love, this total surrender, this losing oneself into one who may be or may not be, this losing itself, is the transformation. Suddenly one is purified — totally purified — because when the ego is not there you cannot be impure in any way: because ego is the seed of all impurity.

The feeling of ego is the root of all madness. For the feeling world, for the world of the devotee, ego is the disease. Ego dissolves, and it dissolves in only one way and there is no other way. There is only one way: the other becomes so important, so significant, that by and by you fade out and disappear. One day you are no more; just a consciousness of the other remains.

And when you are no more, the other is also not the other, because he is the other only when you are there. When the "I" disappears, the "thou" also disappears. In love you take the first step: the other becomes important. You remain, but for certain moments there may be a peak when you are not. Those are rare peaks of love, but ordinarily you remain and the lover is there. When the lover becomes more important than you, you can die for him or her. If you can die for someone, there is love. The other has become the meaning of your life.

And only if you can die for someone can you live for someone. If you cannot die for someone, you cannot live for someone. Life acquires a meaning only through death. In love, the other has become important, but you are still there. In some higher peaks of communication you may disappear, but you will come again. However, this will be only for moments. So lovers have glimpses of devotion. That is why, in India, the beloved used to call her lover her God. Only in peaks does the other become Divine, and the other becomes Divine only when you are not. This can grow. And if you make it a *sadhana* (a spiritual practice), if you make it an inner search, if you are not just enjoying love but transforming yourself through love, then it becomes devotion.

In devotion you surrender yourself completely, and this surrender can be to a God who may not be in the sky or who may be, or to a Teacher who may not be Awakened or who may be, or to a beloved who may not be worthwhile or who may be; that is irrelevant. If you can allow yourself to dissolve for the other, you will be transformed.

"Devotion frees": that is why we have glimpses of freedom only in love. When you are in love, you have a subtle freedom. This is paradoxical because everyone else will see that you have become a slave. If you are in love with someone, those around you will think that you both have become slaves of each other. But you will have glimpses of freedom. Love is freedom.

Why? Because ego is the bondage: there is no other bondage. You may be in a prison and you cannot escape. If your beloved comes into the prison, the prison disappears that very moment. The walls are there still, but they do not imprison you. Now you can forget them completely. You can dissolve into each other and you can become for each other a sky in which to fly. The prison has disappeared; it is no more there. And you may be under the open sky, totally free, untethered, without love, but you are in a prison because you have nowhere to fly. This sky will not do.

Birds fly in that sky, but you cannot. You need a different sky — the sky of consciousness. Only the other can give you that sky, the first taste of it. When the other opens for you and you move into the other, you can fly.

Love is freedom, but not total. If love becomes devotion, then it becomes total freedom. It means surrendering yourself completely. So those who are of the feeling type, for them is this sutra: "Devotion frees."

Take Ramakrishna: if you look at Ramakrishna you will think that he is just a slave to the goddess Kali — to Mother Kali. He cannot do anything without her permission; he is just like a slave. But no one was more free than him. When he was appointed for the first time as priest in Dakshineshwar, at the temple, he started behaving strangely. The committee, the trustees, gathered, and they said, "Throw this man out. He is behaving undevotionally." This happened because first he would smell a flower and then the flower would be put at the feet of the goddess. That is against ritual. A smelled flower cannot be offered to the Divine: it has become impure.

First he would taste the food which was made for the offering, and then he would offer it. And he was the priest, so the trustees asked him, "What are you doing? This cannot be allowed." He said, "Then I will leave this post. I will move out of the temple, but I cannot offer food to my Mother without tasting it. My mother used to taste. Whenever she would prepare something, she would taste first and then only would she give it to me. And I cannot offer a flower without smelling it first. So I can go out, and you cannot check me, you cannot prevent me. I will go on offering anywhere because my Mother is everywhere. She is not confined in your temple. So wherever I will be, I will be doing the same."

It happened that someone, some Mohammedan, told him, "If your Mother is everywhere, then why not come to the mosque?"

He said, "Okay, I am coming." He remained for six months. He forgot Dakshineshwar completely; he was in a mosque. Then his friend said, "Now you can go back." He said, "Everywhere she is." So one may think that he is a slave, but his devotion is such that now the beloved is everywhere.

If you are nowhere, the beloved will be everywhere. If you are somewhere, then the beloved will be nowhere.

4
Ordinary Love And The Love
Of A Buddha

December 13, 1972, Bombay, India

QUESTIONS:

1. *Should love be continuous, and when does it become devotion?*
2. *Why does tantra give the body so much importance?*
3. *Tell us something about attachment and freedom.*

The first question: *"It seems very difficult to love someone for twenty-four hours a day. Why does it happen so? Should love be a continuous process? And at which stage does love become devotion?"*

Love is not an act; it is not something that you do. If you do it, it is not love. No doing is involved in love. It is a state of being, not an act. No one can do anything continuously for twenty-four hours. If you are "doing" love, then, of course, you cannot do it for twenty-four hours. With any act you will get tired; with any act you get bored. And then, after any act, you have to relax. So if you are "doing" love, you will have to relax into hate, because you can relax only into the opposite.

That is why our love goes on always mixed with hatred. You love this moment, and the next moment you hate the same person. The same person becomes the object of both love and hate; that is the conflict of lovers. Because your love is an act, that is why there is this misery.

So the first thing to be understood is that love is not an act; you cannot do it. You can be in love, but you cannot "do" love. Doing is absurd. But other things are also implied. It is not an effort because if it were an effort you would get tired. It is a state of mind.

And do not think in terms of relationship. Think in terms of states of mind. If you are in love, this is a state of mind. This

state of mind may be focused on one person or it may be unfocused – on the whole. When it is focused on one person, it is
known as love. When it becomes unfocused, it becomes prayer.
Then you are just in love – not with someone, but just in love,
as you are breathing.

If breathing were an effort you would get tired of it, and you
would have to relax and then you would die. If it were an effort,
then at some time you might forget to do it and then you would
die. Love is just like breathing: it is a higher plane of breathing.
If you do not breathe, your body will die. If you are not in love,
your spirit cannot be born.

So take love as a breathing of the soul. When you are in love
your soul becomes vital, alive, just like breathing. But think in
this way. If I say to you, "Only breathe when you are near me
and do not breathe anywhere else," then you will die. And the
next time you will be near me you will be just dead and you
will not even be able to breathe near me.

That has happened with love. We possess: the love object is
possessed and the lover says, "Don't love anybody else. Only
love me." Then the love is atrophied and then the lover cannot
love. It becomes impossible. It doesn't mean that you have to
love everyone, but you have to be in a loving state of mind. It is
just like breathing: even if your enemy is there you will breathe.

That is the meaning of Jesus' saying, "Love your enemy."
It has been a problem for Christianity: how to understand this
saying, "Love your enemy." It seems contradictory. But if loving is not an act, if it is just a state of mind, then there is no
question of enemy or friend. You are in love.

Look at it from the other side. There are persons who are
continuously in hate, and whenever they try to show love they
have to make much effort. Their love is an effort because their
continuous state of mind is hate. That is why effort is needed.
There are persons who are continuously sad; then their laughter
is an effort. They have to fight against themselves; then their
laughter becomes a painted laughter – just false, imposed, put

together, not coming from deep within but just arranged, no spontaneity in it but just artificial.

There are persons who are continuously in anger — not angry at something or someone: just angry. Then love becomes an effort. On the other hand, if love is your state of mind anger will be an effort. You can do it, but you cannot be angry. Then you will have to create it artificially. It will be false.

If a Buddha tries to be angry, much effort will be needed and then too it will be false. And only those who do not know him can be deceived. Those who know him, they know that that anger is false, just painted, created. It is not coming from within; that is impossible.

A Buddha, a Jesus, cannot hate. Then effort is needed. If they tried to show hatred, then they will have to do it.

But you do not need any effort to be hateful; you need effort to be loving. Change the state of mind. How to change the state of mind ? How to be loving ? And it is not a question of time, of how to be loving twenty-four hours a day. This is absurd: this question is absurd.

It is not a question of time. If you can be loving in a single moment that is enough, because you never have two moments together. Only one moment is given. When one is lost, a second is given. You have only one moment always with you. If you know how to be loving in one single moment, you know the secret. You need not think about twenty-four hours or of the whole life.

Only a single moment of love and you know how to fill a moment with love. Then the second moment will be given to you, and you can fill that second moment also with love. So, remember, it is not a question of time. There is a question only of a single moment, and a single moment is not part of time. A single moment is not a process: a single moment is just now.

Once you know how to enter a single moment with love, you have entered eternity: time is no more. A Buddha lives in the now; you live in time. Time means thinking of the past, thinking of the future. And while you are thinking of the past and of the future, the present is lost.

You are engaged with the future and the past, and the present is being lost — and the present is the only existence. The past is no more and the future has yet to be: they both are not; they are non-existential. This very moment, this single atomic moment, is the only existence — here and now. If you know to be loving, you know the secret. And you will never be given two moments together, so you need not bother about time.

A single moment is always — and it is always in the shape of now. Remember, there are not really two types of "nows". This single moment is the same; it doesn't differ in any way from the moment that has gone before it and it doesn't differ in any way from the moment that is going to follow it.

This atomic "now" is always the some. That is why Eckhart says, "It is not that time passes. Time remains the same. Rather, we go on passing." Pure time remains the same; we go on passing. So do not think about "twenty-four hours" and then you need not think of the present moment.

One thing more: thinking needs time; living doesn't need time. You cannot think in this very moment. In this very moment, if you want to be, you will have to cease thinking because thinking is basically concerned with either the past or the future. Of what can you think in the present? The moment you think, it has become the past.

A flower is there: you say this is a beautiful flower. This saying is now no more in the present. It has become the past. When you come to grasp something in thinking, it has become the past. In the present you can be, but you cannot think. You can be with the flower, but you cannot think about it. Thinking needs time.

So in another way, thinking is time. If you do not think, there is no time. That is why, in meditation, you feel a timelessness. That is why, in love, you feel a timelessness. Love is not thinking. It is a cessation of thought. You are! When you are with your beloved, you are not thinking about love, you are not thinking about the beloved. You are not thinking at all. And if you are thinking, then you are not with your beloved. You are somewhere else. Thinking means absence from the now. You are not there.

That is why those who are too much obsessed with thinking cannot love, because even when they are there, even if they reach to the original Divine Source, even if they meet God, they will go on thinking about Him and they will miss Him completely. You can go on thinking about and about and about, but it is never the fact.

A moment of love is a timeless moment. Then there is no question of thinking how to love twenty-four hours. You never think about how to live twenty-four hours, how to be alive twenty-four hours. Either you are alive or you are not. So the basic thing to be understood is not time, but "now" — how to be here and now in a state of love.

Why is there hate? When you feel hatred go to the cause of it. Only then can love flower. When do you feel hatred? When you feel that your existence, your life, is in danger, when you feel that your existence can be annihilated, suddenly hate surges in you. When you feel that you can be destroyed, you start destroying others. That is a safety measure. It is just a part of you that is struggling for survival. Whenever you feel that your existence is in danger, you are filled with hatred.

So unless you come to feel that your existence cannot be in danger, that it is impossible to culminate you, you cannot be filled with love. A Jesus can be in love because he knows something which is deathless. You cannot be in love because you know only that which belongs to death. And every moment death is there; every moment you are afraid. How can you love when you are afraid? Love cannot exist with fear. And fear is there, so you can only create a "make-believe" that you love.

And, again, your love is really nothing but a safety measure. You love so that you will not fear. Whenever you believe that you are in love, you are less afraid. For the moment you can forget death. An illusion is created in which you can feel that you are accepted by the Existence. You are not denied, rejected. That is why there is so much need of love and of being loved.

Whenever you are being loved by someone, you create around you an illusion that you are needed by the Existence — at least by someone. You are needed by someone, so you are not just futile. You are not just accidental: you are needed somewhere. Without you the Existence will miss something. That gives you a feeling of well-being. You feel a purpose, a destiny, a meaning, a worthiness.

When you are not loved by anyone you feel rejected, you feel denied, you feel meaningless. Then you feel there is no purpose, no destiny. If no one loves you and you die, there will be no feeling of your absence. It will not be felt that you are no more. No one will feel that you were, and now you will be no more.

Love gives you the feeling of being needed. That is why, in love, one becomes or feels less afraid. Whenever love is not there you become more fearful, and in fear, as a protection, you become hateful. Hate is a protection. You are afraid of being destroyed; you become destructive.

In love, you feel that you are accepted, welcome, not an uninvited guest but rather that you are invited, welcome, waited for, received, that the Existence is happy that you are. The one who loves you becomes the representative of the whole Existence, but this love is basically fear based. You are protecting against fear, against death, against the inhuman indifference of Existence.

Really, Existence is indifferent — at least on the surface. The sun, the sea, the stars, the earth, they are totally indifferent to you; no one is worried about you. And it is apparently clear that you are not needed. Without you everything will be as good as it is with you; nothing will be lost. Look at the Existence superficially: no one, nothing, cares about you. They may not even be aware of you. The stars are not aware of you, even the earth which you call mother is not aware of you. And when you die, the earth will not be sad. Nothing will have changed; things will be as they are and as they always have been. With you or without you, there is no difference.

You feel you are just an accident. You were not needed; un-invited you have come — just a chance product. This gives fear. This is what Kierkegaard calls anguish. There is a subtle continuous fear. You are not needed.

When someone loves you, you feel that a different dimension has come into existence. Now at least one person will be there who will weep, who will feel sorry, who will be sad. There will be tears: you will be needed. At least there will be one person who will always feel your absence if you are not. At least for one you have gained a destiny, a purpose.

That is why there is so much need of love. And if you are not loved, you are uprooted. But this love is not the love I am talking about. This is a relationship and a mutual creation of illusion — a mutual illusion: "I need you, you need me. I give you this illusion that without you my purpose, my meaning, my life will be lost; you give me this illusion that without you everything will be lost. So we both are mutually helping each other to be in illusion. We are creating one separate, private existence in which we become meaningful, in which the whole indifference of this vast space is forgotten."

Two lovers live in each other: they have created a private world. That is why love needs so much privacy. If you are not in privacy, the world goes on impinging upon you. It goes on telling you that whatsoever you are doing is just a dream and this is a mutual illusion. Love needs privacy because then the whole world is forgotten. Only two lovers exist, and the indifference, the total indifference of Existence, is forgotten. You feel loved, welcomed. Without you nothing will be the same. At least in this private world nothing will be the same without you.

Life is meaningful. I am not talking about this love. This is really illusory: it is a cultivated illusion. And man is so weak that he cannot live without this illusion. Those who can, they live without this illusion. A Buddha can live without this illusion, and then he will not create it.

When it becomes possible to live "illusionlessly" — to live without illusion, a second, a different dimension of love, comes into being. It is not that one person needs you. It is coming to understand, to realize, that you are not different from this Existence which looks so indifferent. You are part of it, organically one with it. And if a tree is flowering, it is not separate from you. You have flowered in the tree and the tree has become conscious in you.

The sea and the sand and the stars, they are one with you. You are not an island: you are organically one with this universe. The whole universe is within you and the whole of you is in this universe. Unless you come to know it and feel it and realize it, you will not get that love which is a state of mind.

If you come to realize this, you will not need to create a private illusion that someone loves you. Then there is meaning, and if no one loves you no meaning is lost. Then you are not afraid at all because even death will not annihilate you. It may annihilate the form, it may annihilate the body, but it cannot annihilate you because you are the Existence.

This is what happens in meditation. This is for what meditation is meant. In it you become a part, an opening. You come to feel, "Existence and I are one." Then you are welcomed, and there is no fear and there is no death. Then love flows from you. Then love is not an effort. You cannot do anything except love. Then it is like breathing. Deep inside you breathe love; in and out you breathe love.

This love grows into devotion. Then ultimately you will even forget it just as you forget your breathing. When do you remember your breathing? Have you observed? You remember only when something is wrong. When you feel any difficulty, then you know that you have been breathing; otherwise there is no need even to be aware of it. And if you are aware of your breathing, that shows that something is wrong with your breathing process. There is no need of being aware of the breathing process. Silently it goes on.

So when you are aware of your love, the love that is a state of mind, it means that something is still wrong. By and by even that awareness is lost. You simply breathe love in and out. You have forgotten everything, even that you love. Then it has become devotion. That is the ultimate peak – the ultimate possibility: you may call it anything.

Love can become devotion only when this awareness is lost, forgotten. It doesn't mean that you have become unconscious. It only means that the process has become so silent that there is no noise around it. You are not unconscious of it, but you are not conscious of it either. It has become so natural. It is there, but it does not create any disturbance inside: it has become so harmonious.

So, remember, when I am talking about love, I am not talking about your love. But if you try to understand your love, it will become a step toward growing into a different kind of love. So I am not against your love. I am simply stating the fact that if your love is fear-based, it is just ordinary animal love. And no derogation, no condemnation, is implied: simply a fact.

Man is afraid. He needs someone who gives him the feeling that he is welcomed. Do not be afraid. At least with one person you need not be filled with fear. This is good as far as it goes, but this is not what Buddha or Jesus called love. They called love a state of mind, not a relationship. So go beyond relationship, and by and by just be loving. First you will not be capable of it unless you move into meditation. Unless you come to know the deathless within, unless you come to know a deep unity between the inner and the outer, unless you feel that you are Existence, it will be difficult.

So these techniques of meditation are just to help you grow from relationship into a state of mind. And do not think of time at all: time is irrelevant for love.

The second question: *"Most of the techniques which you have discussed have used the body as an instrument. What are the reasons for the body to be given so much importance by tantra?"*

Many basic points are to be understood. One, you are your body. Right now you are just your body and nothing else. You may have notions about the soul, the *Atman*, etc. Those are simply notions — just ideas.

As you are right now you are just a body. And do not go on deceiving yourself that you are the deathless soul, the immortal Atman. Do not go on deceiving yourself. That is just an idea, and that idea too is fear based.

You do not know whether the soul exists or not; you have never penetrated to the innermost core where one Realizes the deathless. You have only heard about it, and you cling to the idea because you are afraid of death. You know death is real, so you go on wishing and believing that something in you must be there which is deathless. This is a wish fulfillment.

I am not saying that there is no soul, I am not saying that there is nothing which is deathless. No, I am not saying that. But as far as you are concerned, you are just the body with an idea that there is a soul which is deathless. This is just in the mind, and this too you have collected because of the fear. That is why the weaker you will become, the older, the more you will become a believer in the immortal soul and God. Then you will go to the church or temple or the mosque. If you go to the mosque or the church or the temple, you will find that old men, just on the verge of death, are gathered there.

Youth is basically atheistic; always this has been so. The younger you are, the less theistic. The younger you are, the more you are an unbeliever. Why? Because you are still strong and you feel less fear, and you are still ignorant of death. Death is far away somewhere. It happens only to others. It happens only to others, not to you. But the older you grow, you will by and by begin to feel that now it is going to happen to you also.

Death comes near, and one begins to believe. So all beliefs are fear based. All beliefs are fear based! And one who believes because of fear is really deceiving himself. You are the body right now: this is a fact. You do not know anything about the deathless. You know only about the "deathful". But the deathless is there; you can know it. Believing won't do. Only knowing can help. You can realize it, but just ideas are of no use unless they become a concrete experience.

So do not be deceived by ideas and do not take ideas and beliefs for experiences. That is why tantra always starts with the body: because that is a fact. You have to travel from the body because you are in the body. And that too is not good: when I say you are in the body, that too is not good. As far as you are concerned you are the body, not in the body. You do not know anything about what is in the body. You know only the body. That experience of something beyond body is still far away.

If you go to metaphysicians, to theologians, they are going to start with soul. But tantra is absolutely scientific. It starts from where you are, not from where you can be. Starting from where you can be is absurd: you cannot start from where you can be. You can start only from where you are.

Tantra has no condemnation against the body. Tantra is a total acceptance of things as they are. Christian theologians and those of other religions also are condemnatory, against the body. They create a dualism, a dichotomy, that you are two. And the body is the enemy, the evil for them, so fight with it. This duality is basically wrong, and this duality will divide your mind into two and will create a split personality.

Religions have helped the human mind to be schizophrenic. Any division will divide you deeply, and you will become two or you will become many. And everyone is a crowd of many divisions, with no organic unity and with no center. You are not an "individual" as far as the meaning of the word is concerned. The word means indivisible: "individual" means indivisible. But you are just divided into many things.

Not only are your mind and your body divided: your soul and body are divided also. The nonsense has gone so deep that even the body is divided: the lower body is evil and the upper body is good. It is stupid, but it is there. Even you yourself cannot feel at ease with your lower body. Some uneasiness creeps in. There is division and division and division.

Tantra accepts everything. Whatsoever is, is accepted whole-heartedly. That is why tantra could accept sex totally. For five thousand years tantra has been the only tradition which has accepted sex totally, the only one all over the world. Why? Because sex is the point where you are and any movement is going to be from the point where you are.

You are at the sex center: your energy is at the sex center. And from that point it has to move up, far beyond. If you reject the center itself, then you can go on deceiving yourself that you are moving, but you cannot move. Then you are rejecting the only point from where movement is possible. So tantra accepts the body, accepts sex, accepts everything. And tantra says wisdom accepts everything and transforms it; only ignorance rejects. Only ignorance rejects: wisdom accepts everything. Even a poison can become a medicine, but through wisdom.

The body can become a vehicle to that which is beyond body, and sex energy can become a spiritual force. And, remember, when you ask what are the reasons that the body is given so much importance in tantra, why do you ask? Why?

You are born as a body; you live as a body; you become ill as a body; you are treated, given medicine, helped, made whole and healthy, as a body. You become young as a body, you will become old as a body; you will die as a body. Your whole life is body centered — centered around the body. You will love someone. You will make love to someone and you will create other bodies: you will reproduce other bodies.

What are you doing the whole life? Preserving yourself. What are you preserving with food, with water, with shelter? The body is preserved. What are you doing by reproducing children? The body is being reproduced. The whole life, 99.9%, is body oriented. You can go beyond, but that journey has to be through the body, by the body, and you have to use the body. But why do you ask? Because the body is just the outer thing. Deep down the body is a symbol of sex.

So those traditions which are against sex will be against the body. Those traditions which are not against sex can only be friendly toward the body. Tantra is absolutely friendly, and tantra says that the body is sacred, holy. For tantra, to condemn the body is a sacrilege. To say that the body is impure or to say that the body is sin is nonsense for tantra — a very poisonous teaching. Tantra accepts body — not only accepts it, but says that the body is holy, pure, innocent. You can use it and you can make it a vehicle, a medium, to go beyond! It helps even in going beyond.

But if you start fighting with body, you are lost. If you start fighting with it, you will become more and more diseased. And if you go on fighting with it, you will miss an opportunity. Fighting is negative; tantra is a positive transformation. Do not fight with it: there is no need. It is as if you are sitting in a car and you start fighting with the car. Then you cannot move because you are fighting with the vehicle which has to be used — not fought against. And you will destroy the vehicle by your fighting, and then it will be more and more difficult to move.

The body is a beautiful vehicle — very mysterious, very complex. Use it; do not fight with it. Help it. The moment you go against it you are going against yourself. It is as if a man wants to reach somewhere, but he fights with his own legs and cuts them. Tantra says know the body and know the secrets of it. Know the energies of it and know how those energies can be transformed — how they can be moved and turned into different dimensions.

For example, take sex which is the basic energy in the body. Ordinarily, sex energy is just used for reproduction. One body creates another body and it goes on. The biological utility of sex energy is only reproduction. But that is only one of the uses, and the lowest. No condemnation is implied, but it is the lowest. The same energy can do other creative acts also. Reproduction is a basic creative act: you create something. That is why a woman feels a subtle well-being when she becomes a mother: she has created something.

Psychologists say that because man cannot reproduce like woman, because man cannot become a mother, he feels a certain unease, and to destroy that unease or to overcome it he goes on creating other things. He will paint, he will do something in which he becomes a creator, in which he becomes a mother. That is one of the reasons why women are less creative and men are more creative — because they have a natural dimension in which to be creative: they can become mothers and they can have a fulfillment, an easy fulfillment. A deep biological creativity is felt.

But man lacks that and feels somewhere an imbalance. He wants to create, so he will substitute something. He will paint, he will sing, he will dance. He will do somehing in which he also becomes a mother. Sex energy, psychologists say now (and tantra has always been saying that), is always the source of all creation. So it happens that if a painter is really deep in his creation, he may forget sex completely. When a poet is very involved with his poetry, he will forget sex completely. He need not force any "brahmacharya" (any celibacy) upon it.

Only monks, non-creative monks living in a monastery, need to force brahmacharya — because if you are creative, the same energy which moves through sex moves into creation. You can forget it completely, and there is no need to make any effort to forget it because that is impossible. You cannot make any effort to forget anything, because the very effort will make you remember it again and again.That is futile — in fact, suicidal. You cannot try to forget anything.

That is why those who force themselves to be "brahmacharies" (celibates) become simply cerebral sex perverts. Then sex revolves in the mind: the whole thing goes in the mind — not in the body, but in the mind. And that is worse, because then the mind becomes totally mad. Any creativity will help sex to disappear.

Tantra says if you move in meditation sex will disappear completely: it can disappear completely. The whole energy is being absorbed at higher centers, and your body has many centers.

Sex is the lowest center and man exists at the lowest center. The more energy moves higher, the more the higher centers begin to flower. When the same energy comes to the heart, then it becomes love. When the same energy comes higher still, new dimensions and new experiences begin to flower. And when the same energy is at the highest, at the last peak in your body, it has reached that which tantra calls "sahasrar"—the last chakra in the head.

Sex is the lowest chakra and sahasrar is the highest, and between these two the sex energy moves. It can be released from the sex center. When it is released from the sex center you become a cause to reproduce someone else. When the same energy is released from the sahasrar, from the head into the Cosmos, you give a new birth to yourself. It is also reproduction, but not biologically. Then it is spiritually a re-production. Then you are reborn. In India we used to call such a person twice-born — *dwij*. Now he has given himself a new birth. The same energy has moved.

Tantra has no condemnations, only secret techniques for how to transform. That is why tantra talks so much about body: it is needed. The body has to be understood and you can start only from where you are.

The third question: *"You said that love can make you free. But ordinarily we see that love becomes attachment, and instead of freeing us it makes us more bound. So tell us something about attachment and freedom."*

Love becomes attachment because there is no love. You were just playing, deceiving yourself. The attachment is the reality; the love was just a foreplay. So whenever you fall in love, sooner or later you discover you have become an instrument — and then the whole misery begins. What is the mechanism? Why does it happen?

Just a few days ago a man came to me and he was feeling very guilty. He said, "I loved a woman. I loved her very much. The day she died I was weeping and crying, but suddenly I became aware of a certain freedom within me as if some burden had left me. I felt a deep breath, as if I had become free."

That moment he became aware of a second layer of his feeling. Outwardly he was weeping and crying and saying, "I cannot live without her. Now it will be impossible, or the life will be just like death." But "Deep down," he said, "I became aware that I am feeling very good, that now I am free."

A third layer began to feel guilt. It said to him, "What are you doing?" And the dead body was lying there just before him, he said to me, and he began to feel a great deal of guilt. He said to me, "Help me. What has happened to my mind? Have I betrayed her so soon?"

Nothing has happened; no one has betrayed. When love becomes attachment, it becomes a burden, a bondage. But why does love become an attachment? The first thing to be understood is that if love becomes an attachment, you were just in an illusion that it was love. You were just playing with yourself and thinking that this was love. Really, you were in need of attachment. And if you go still deeper, you will find that you were also in need of becoming a slave.

There is a subtle fear of freedom, and everyone wants to be a slave. Everyone, of course, talks about freedom, but no one has the courage to be really free, because when you are really free you are alone. If you have the courage to be alone, then only can you be free.

But no one is courageous enough to be alone. You need someone. Why do you need someone? You are afraid of your own loneliness. You become bored with yourself. And, really, when you are lonely, nothing seems meaningful. With someone you are occupied and you create artificial meanings around you.

You cannot live for yourself, so you start to live for someone else. And the same is the case with the "someone else" also: he (or she) cannot live alone, so he is in search to find someone. Two persons who are afraid of their own loneliness come together and they start a play — a play of love. But deep down they are searching for attachment, commitment, bondage.

So sooner or later, whatsoever you desire happens. This is one of the most unfortunate things in this world. Whatsoever you desire comes to happen. You will get it sooner or later and the foreplay will disappear. When its function is done, it will disappear. When you have become a wife and husband, slaves to each other, when marriage has happened, love will disappear because love was just an illusion in which two persons could become slaves to each other.

Directly you cannot ask for slavery; it is too humiliating. And directly you cannot say to someone, "Become my slave": he will revolt. Nor can you say, "I want to become a slave to you," so you say, "I cannot live without you." But the meaning is there; it is the same. And when this — the real desire — is fulfilled, love disappears. Then you feel bondage, slavery, and then you start struggling to become free.

Remember this. It is one of the paradoxes of the mind: whatsoever you get you will get bored with, and whatsoever you do not get you will long for. When you are alone, you will long for some slavery, some bondage. When you are in bondage, you will begin longing for freedom. Really, only slaves long for freedom, and free people try again to be slaves. The mind goes on like a pendulum moving from one extreme to the other.

Love doesn't become attachment. Attachment was the need; love was just a bait. You were in search of a fish named "attachment": love was just a bait to catch the fish. When the fish is caught, the bait is thrown. Remember this, and whenever you are doing something go deep within yourself to find out the basic cause.

If there is real love, it will never become attachment. What is the mechanism for love to become attachment ? The moment you say to your lover or beloved, "Love only me," you have started possessing. And the moment you possess someone you have insulted him deeply because you have made him into a thing.

When I possess you, you are not a person then, but just one more item among my furniture — a thing. Then I use you, and you are my thing, my possession, so I won't allow anyone else to use you. It is a bargain in which I am possessed by you and you make me a thing. It is the bargain that now no one else can use you. Both partners feel bound and enslaved. I make a slave of you, then you in return make a slave of me.

Then the struggle starts. I want to be a free person, and still I want you to be possessed by me; you want to retain your freedom and still possess me: this is the struggle. If I possess you, I will be possessed by you. If I do not want to be possessed by you, I should not possess you.

Possession should not come in between. We must remain individuals and we must move as independent, free consciousnesses. We can come together, we can merge into each other, but no one possesses. Then there is no bondage and then there is no attachment.

Attachment is one of the ugliest things. And when I say "ugliest", I do not mean only religiously: I mean aesthetically also. When you are attached, you have lost your loneliness, your aloneness: you have lost everything. Just to feel good that someone needs you and someone is with you, you have lost everything, you have lost yourself.

But the trick is that you try to be independent, and you make the other the possession — and the other is doing the same. So do not possess if you do not want to be possessed.

Jesus said somewhere, "Judge ye not so that ye should not be judged." It is the same: "Possess not so that ye should not be possessed." Do not make anyone a slave; otherwise you will become a slave.

Masters, so-called masters, are always slaves of their own slaves. You cannot become a master without becoming a slave; that is impossible. You can only be a master when no one is a slave to you. This seems paradoxical because when I say you can only be a master when no one is a slave to you, you will say, "Then what is the mastery? How am I a master when no one is a slave to me ?" But I say only then are you a master. Then no one is a slave to you and no one will try to make a slave out of you.

To love freedom, to try to be free, means basically that you have come to a deep understanding of yourself. And now you know that you are enough unto yourself. You can share with someone, but you are not dependent. I can share myself with someone. I can share my love, I can share my happiness, I can share my bliss, my silence, with someone. But that is a sharing, not a dependence. If no one is there, I will be just as happy, just as blissful. If someone is there, that is also good and I can share.

When you Realize your inner consciousness, your center, only then will love not become an attachment. If you do not know your inner center, love will become an attachment. If you know your inner center, love will become devotion. You must first be there to love, but you are not.

Buddha was passing from a village. One young man came to him and said, "Teach me something: how can I serve others ?" Buddha laughed at him and said, "First be. Forget others. First be yourself and then everything will follow."

Right now you are not. When you say, "When I love someone it becomes an attachment," you are saying you are not. So whatsoever you do goes wrong because the doer is absent. The inner point of awareness is not there, so whatsoever you do goes wrong. First BE, and then you can share your being. And that sharing will be love. Before that, whatsoever you do will become an attachment.

And lastly: if you are struggling against attachment, you have taken a wrong turn. You can struggle. So many monks, recluses, sannyasins are doing that. They feel that they are attached to their house, to their property, to their wives, to their children, and they feel caged, imprisoned. They escape. They leave their homes, they leave their wives, they leave their children and possessions, and they become beggars and escape to a forest, to a loneliness. But go and observe them. They will become attached to their new surroundings.

I was visiting a friend who was a recluse living under a tree in a deep forest, but there were other ascetics also. One day it happened that I was staying with this recluse under his tree, and a new seeker came while my friend was absent. He had gone to the river to take a bath. Under his tree the new sannyasin started meditating.

The man came back from the river, and he pushed that new man away from the tree and said, "This is my tree. You go and find another somewhere else. No one can sit under my tree." And this man had left his house, his wife, his children. Now the tree had become a possession. You cannot meditate under his tree.

You cannot escape so easily from attachment. It will take new forms, new shapes. You will be deceived, but this will be there. So do not fight with attachment: just try to understand why it is there. And then know the deep cause. Because you are not, so this attachment is there.

Inside you your own Self is so much absent that you try to cling to anything in order to feel safe. You are not rooted, so you try to make anything your roots. When you are rooted in your Self, when you will know who you are, what this being is which is in you and what this consciousness is which is in you, then you will not cling to anyone.

That doesn't mean you will not love. Really, only then can you love because then sharing is possible — and with no conditions, with no expectations. You simply share because you have an abundance — because you have so much it is overflowing.

This overflowing of yourself is love. And when this overflowing becomes a flood, when by your own overflowing the whole universe is filled and your love touches the stars, in your love the earth feels good and in your love the whole universe is bathed, then it is devotion.

5
Three "Looking" Techniques

December 14, 1972, Bombay, India

SUTRAS:

6. *Eyes closed, see your inner being in detail. Thus see your true nature.*

7. *Look upon a bowl without seeing the sides or the material. In a few moments become aware.*

8. *See as if for the first time a beauteous person or an ordinary object.*

Tonight's techniques are concerned with the practice of looking. Before we enter these techniques, something has to be understood about the eyes, because all these seven techniques depend on that. The first thing: eyes are the most non-bodily part in the human body, the least bodily. If matter can become non-matter, then such is the case with eyes. Eyes are material, but simultaneously they are also non-material. Eyes are a meeting point of you and your body. Nowhere else in the body is the meeting so deep.

The human body and you are much separated. A great distance is there, but at the point of the eyes you are nearest to your body and the body is nearest to you. That is why eyes can be used for the inner journey. A single jump from the eyes can lead you to the source. That is not possible from the hand, not possible from the heart, not possible from anywhere else in the body. From elsewhere you will have to travel long; the distance is great. But from the eyes a single step is enough to enter into yourself. That is why eyes have been used continuously in religious yogic and tantric practices.

The first reason is because you are "nearest" from there. That is why, if you know how to look into someone's eyes, you can look into his depths. He is there. He is not so present anywhere else in the body, but if you can look into the eyes you will find him there. It is a difficult art to look into someone else's eyes, and it comes to you only when you have taken a jump from your own eyes within. Otherwise you cannot look. If you have not looked within beyond your own eyes, you cannot have a look into someone else's eyes. But if you know how to look into the eyes, you can touch the depth of the person.

That is why only in love can you look straight and stare into another's eyes. Otherwise, if you stare into someone's eyes he will feel offended. You are trespassing; this is a trespass. You can look at the body; there is no trespass. But the moment you stare into somebody's eyes, you are trespassing his individuality, you are trespassing his individual freedom, you are entering him without any invitation. That is why there is a limit, and now the limit can be measured. At the most, you can be allowed to look for three seconds. You can be allowed just a casual look and then you have to move your eyes. Otherwise the other will feel offended. This is violent because you can have a glimpse of his inner secrets, and that cannot be allowed.

Only in deep love can you look into another's eyes, because love means that now you do not want to maintain any secrets. You are now open to the other and the other is always welcome and invited to enter you. And when lovers look into each other's eyes, there is a meeting which is non-bodily, there is a meeting which is not of the body. So the second thing to be remembered: your mind, your consciousness, your soul, whatsoever is within you, can be glimpsed through the eyes.

That is why a blind man has a dead face. It is not only that the eyes are lacking, but that the face is dead — not alive. Eyes are the light of the face: they enlighten your face; they give it an inner aliveness. When the eyes are not there, your face lacks aliveness. And a blind man is really closed. You cannot enter him so easily. That is why blind men are very secretive and you can rely upon a blind man. If you give him a secret, you can rely upon him. He will maintain it, and it will be difficult to judge whether he has a secret. But with a man who has alive eyes, it can be judged immediately that he has a secret.

For example, you are travelling without a ticket on a railway train. Your eyes will go on betraying you that you are without a ticket. It is a secret. No one knows; only you know. But your eyes will have a different look, and you will look at anyone who enters the train with a different quality. If the other could understand the quality, he would know immediately that you are without a ticket. The look will be different when you have a ticket; the look will be different!

So if you are hiding a secret, your eyes will reveal it. And to control the eyes is very difficult. The most difficult thing in the body is to control the eyes. So everyone cannot become a great detective because the basic training of the detective is the training of the eyes. His eyes should not reveal anything, or on the contrary they should reveal the contrary. When he is travelling without a ticket, his eyes should reveal that he has a ticket. It is very difficult because eyes are not voluntary: they are non-voluntary.

Now many experiments are being done on the eyes. Someone is a *brahmachari* — a celibate, and he says he has no attraction toward women. But his eyes will reveal everything; he may be hiding his attraction. A beautiful woman enters the room. He may not look at her, but even his not looking at her will be revealing. There will be an effort, a subtle suppression, and the eyes will show it. Not only that: the surface of the eyes will expand. When a beautiful woman enters, the pupils of the eyes will expand immediately to allow the beautiful woman more space to go in. And you cannot do anything about it because those pupils and their expansion is non-voluntary. You cannot do anything! It is absolutely impossible to control them. So the second thing to remember is that your eyes are the keys to your secrets. If anyone wants to enter into your secret world, your privacy, your eyes are the doors.

If you know how to unlock them, you will become vulnerable, open. And if you want to enter into your own secret life, your inner life, then again you will have to use the same lock and the unlocking system. You will have to work on your eyes: only then can you enter.

Thirdly, eyes are very liquid, moving, in constant movement, and that movement has its own rhythm, its own system, its own mechanism. Your eyes are not moving at random anarchically. They have a rhythm of their own and that rhythm shows many things. If you have a sexual thought in the mind, your eyes move differently — with a different rhythm. Just by looking at your eyes and the movement, one can say what type of thought is moving inside. When you feel hungry and a thought of food is inside, eyes have a different movement.

So now even your dreams can be penetrated. Your eye movements can be recorded while you are asleep. And, remember, even in dreams your eyes behave similarly. If you are seeing a naked woman in your dream, this can be judged from your eye movements. Now they have mechanical devices to know what are the movements of the eyes.

These movements are now called "REM" — Rapid Eye Movements. They can be recorded just on a graph, just like an electro-cardiogram. If you have been sleeping for the whole life, your eye movements can be recorded continuously. And then the graph can show when you were dreaming and when you were not, because when you are not dreaming the eyes stop and become static. When you are dreaming they move, and the movement is like when you are seeing something on the screen. If you are seeing a film, the eyes have to move. In the same way, in your dream your eyes move: they are seeing something. They follow the movements of the film. For your eyes there is no difference between an actual film being shown on the screen or just a dream film.

So these REM recorders tell how much you dreamt in the night and for how many moments you were not dreaming, because the eyes stop their movement when you are not dreaming. There are many persons who say they never dream. They just have a very absentminded memory — nothing else. They cannot remember: that is the only thing. They are actually dreaming. For the whole night they are dreaming, but they cannot remember. Their memory is not good, that is all. So in the morning when they say there was no dream, do not believe them.

Why do the eyes move when there is a dream and why do the eyes stop when there is no dream? Each eye movement is joined to the thought process. If thinking is there, the eyes will move. If there is no thinking, the eyes will not move: there is no need.

So remember this third point also, that eye movements and thinking are joined together. That is why, if you stop your eyes and their movements, your thought process will stop immediately. Or if your thought process stops your eyes will stop automatically. And one point more — the fourth: the eyes move continuously from one object to another. From A to B, from B to C, they go on moving. Movement is their nature. It is just like a river flowing: movement is their nature! And because of that movement, they are so alive! Movement is also life.

You can try to stop your eyes at a particular point, at a particular object, and not allow them to move, but movement is their nature. You cannot stop movement, but you can stop your eyes: understand the distinction. You can stop your eyes at a particular fixed point — on a dot on the wall. You can stare at the dot; you can stop your eyes. But movement is their nature. So they may not move from object A to object B because you have forced them to remain at A, but then a very strange phenomenon happens.

Movement is bound to be there; that is their nature. If you do not allow them movement from A to B, they will move from outwards to inwards. Either they can move from A to B, or if you do not allow this outward movement they will move inwards. Movement is their nature; they need movement. If you suddenly stop and do not allow them to move outwards, they will start moving inwards.

So there are two possibilities of movement. One is from object A to object B: this is an outward movement. This is how it is happening naturally. But there is another possibility which is of tantra and yoga — not allowing movement from one outside object to another and stopping this movement. Then the eyes jump from an outside object to the inner consciousness. They begin to move inwards. Remember these four points; then it will be easy to understand the techniques.

The first technique: *"Eyes closed, see your inner being in detail. Thus see your true nature."*

"Eyes closed": Close your eyes. But this closing is not enough. Total closing means to close your eyes and stop their movements. Otherwise the eyes will continue to see something which is of the outside. Even with closed eyes you will see things — images of things. Actual things are not there, but images, ideas, collected memories — they will start flowing. They are also from outside, so your eyes are still not totally closed. "Totally" closed eyes means nothing to see.

Understand the difference. You can close your eyes; that is easy. Everyone closes them every moment. In the night you close your eyes, but that will not reveal the inner nature to you. Close your eyes so that nothing remains to be seen — no outside object, no inside image of any outside object, just a blank darkness as if you have suddenly gone blind — not blind only to reality, but to the dream reality also.

One has to practise it. A long period will be needed; it cannot be done suddenly. You will need a long training. Close your eyes. Anytime you feel that it is easy and you have time, close your eyes and then inwardly stop all movements of the eyes. Do not allow any movement. Feel! Do not allow any movement. Stop all movements of the eyes. Feel as if they have become stones, and then remain in that "stoney" state of the eyes. Do not do anything; just remain there. Suddenly someday, you will become aware that you are looking inside yourself.

You can go just outside this building, move around the building and have a look, but that is looking at the building from the outside. Then you can enter into the room and you can stand in this room and have a look. That is looking at the building from the inside. When you are taking a round outside, you see the same walls, but not the same side. The walls are the same, but then you are seeing the outside of the walls. When you come in the walls are the same, but now you will see the inside of the walls.

You have seen your body only from the outside. You have seen your body in a mirror or you have seen your hands from the outside. You do not know what the inside of your body is. You have never entered into your own self; you have never been at the center of your body and being to look around at what is there from the inside.

This technique is very helpful for having a look from the inside, and that transforms your total consciousness, your total existence — because if you can have a look from the inside, you immediately become different from the world. This false identity that "I am the body" is only because we have been looking at our bodies from the outside. If you can have a look from the inside, the looker becomes different. And then you can move your consciousness into your body from your toe to your head; you can now have a round inside the body. And once you become capable of having a look from the inside and moving there, then it is not difficult to go outside at all.

Once you know how to move, once you know that you are separate from the body, you are freed from a great bondage. Now you have no gravitational pull; now you have no limitation. Now you are absolute freedom. You can go out of the body; you can go and come. And then your body becomes just an abode.

Close your eyes, see your inner being in detail and move from limb to limb inside. Just go to your toe. Forget the whole body: move to the toe. Stay there and have a look. Then move through the legs, come on upwards, go to every limb. Then many things happen. MANY things happen!

Then your body becomes such a sensitive vehicle, you cannot even imagine it. Then if you touch someone, you can move into your hand totally and that touch will become transforming. That is what is meant by a Teacher's touch, a Master's touch: he can move to any limb totally, and then he is concentrated there. If you can move to any part of your body totally, that part becomes alive — so much alive that you cannot imagine what happens to that part. Then you can move to the eyes totally. If you can move to your eyes totally and then look in someone's eyes, you will penetrate him; you will go to his very depths.

Now psychoanalysts are trying to go to the depths through psychoanalysis. Then they take one year, two years, three years. This is a sheer wastage of time. And life is so short that if three years are taken to analyze a person's mind, it is nonsense. And then too you cannot rely on whether the analysis is complete or not. You are groping in the dark. The Eastern approach has been through the eyes. No need of analyzing the person for such a long time. The work can be done by just entering through his eyes totally, touching his depths, knowing many things about him of which even he is not aware.

The Guru has many things to do. One of the basic things is this: to analyze you, to go deep in you, to move into your darker realms which are unknown to you. And if he says to you that something is hidden in you, you will not believe it. How can you believe it? You are not aware of it. You know only one part of the mind — a very small fragment which is just the upper part, just the first layer. Behind it there are nine layers hidden which are not known to you, but through your eyes a penetration is possible.

Close your eyes; see your inner being in detail. The first, outer part of it is to look at your body from inwardly — from your inner center. Stand there and have a look. You will be separated from the body because the looker is never the looked at. The observer is different from the object.

If you can see your body totally from the inside, then you can never fall into the illusion that you are the body. Then you will remain different — totally different: inside it but not it, in the body but not the body. This is the first part. Then you can move. Then you are free to move. Once freed from the body, freed from the identity, you are free to move. Now you can move into your mind — deep down. Those nine layers which are within and unconscious can now be entered into.

This is the inner cave of the mind. If you enter this cave of the mind, you will become separate from the mind also. Then you will see that the mind is also an object which you can look at, and that which is entering the mind is, again, separate and different. This entering into the mind is what is meant by "inner being in detail". Body and mind both should be entered and looked at from within. Then you are simply a witness, and this witness cannot be penetrated.

That is why it is your innermost core: that is you. That which can be penetrated, that which can be seen, is not you. When you have come to that which cannot be penetrated, that in which you cannot move, which cannot be observed, then only have you come to the real Self. You cannot witness the witnessing source, remember; that is absurd.

If someone says that "I have witnessed my witness", that is absurd. Why is it absurd? Because if you have witnessed your witnessing Self, then the witnessing Self is not the witnessing Self. That who has witnessed it is the witness. That which you can see, you are not; that which you can observe, you are not; that which you can become aware of, you are not.

But a point comes beyond the mind where simply you are. Now you cannot divide your single existence into two, object and subject. Simple subjectivity is there, just witnessing. This is very, very difficult to comprehend through intellect because all the categories of the intellect are broken there.

Because of this logical difficulty, Charwak — the expounder of one of the most logical philosophical systems in the world — says that you cannot know the Self; there is no Self-knowledge. And because there is no Self-knowledge, how can you say that there is a Self? Whatsoever you know is not the Self. The knower is the Self, not the known, so you cannot say logically that "I have known my Self". That is absurd, illogical. How can you know your Self? Then who will be the knower and who will be the known? Knowledge means a dichotomy, a division between object and subject, the knower and the known.

So Charwak says that all those who say they have known the Self are talking nonsense. Self-knowledge is impossible because the Self is irreducibly the knower. It cannot be converted into the known.

Then Charwak says that if you cannot know the Self, how can you say that there is Self? Those like Charwak who do not believe in the presence of a Self are called *anatmavadin*: they say no Self is; they say there is no self. That which cannot be known is not. And they are right logically. If logic is all, they are right.

But this is the mystery of life, that logic is only the beginning — not the end. A moment comes when logic ends, but you do not end. A moment comes when logic is finished, but you are still there. Life is illogical. That is why it is difficult to comprehend, to conceive of what is meant, when it is said that only the witness remains. For example, if there is a lamp in this room, you see many objects around you. When the lamp is turned off, there is darkness and nothing can be seen. When the lamp is put on, there is light and you can see everything in the room.

But have you ever oberved what is happening? If there are no objects, will you be able to see the lamp and its light? You will not be able to see its light, because to be seen the light must reflect something. It must strike an object. The rays must go to an object and then be reflected. Then they will reach to your eyes. So first you see objects, then you infer that light is there. When you burn a lamp or a candle, you never see the light first. First you see the objects, and because of the objects you come to know about the light.

Scientists say that if there are no objects then light cannot be seen. Look at the sky: it looks blue but it is not blue. It is filled with cosmic rays. It looks blue because there are no objects. Those rays cannot reflect and come to your eyes. If you go into space and there are no objects, then there will be darkness. Of course, rays will be passing just by your side, but there will be darkness. To know the light some objects have to be there.

Charwak says that if you enter within and come to the point where only the witness has remained and there is nothing to be witnessed, how can you know about it? Some object must be there to be witnessed; only then can you know the witnessing. Logically, scientifically, it is right. But existentially it is not right.

Those who really move inside come to a point where there is no object left but just the consciousness of being. You are, but nothing is there to be seen — only the seer: ONLY the seer! There is simple subjectivity without any object around it. The moment you come to this point, you have entered your ultimate goal of being. You can call it the alpha — the beginning, or you can call it the omega — the end. It is both, alpha and omega. This is called Self-knowledge.

Linguistically the word is wrong because linguistically nothing can be said about it. Language becomes meaningless, when you enter the world of the One. Language is meaningful only when you are in the world of two. In the world of duality, language is meaningful because language is created, is part, of the dualistic world. It becomes meaningless when you enter the One, the non-dual. That is why those who know have remained silent — or even if they say something they hurriedly add that whatsoever they are saying is just symbolic and whatsoever they are saying is not exactly true: it is false.

Lao Tse said that that which can be said cannot be true, and that which is true cannot be said. He remained silent; for most of his life he would not write anything. He said, "If I say something, it will be untrue because nothing can be said about the realm where only the One remains."

"Eyes closed, see your inner being in detail" — body and mind both. "Thus see your true nature." See your body and mind, your structure. And, remember, body and mind are not two things. Rather, you are both — body-mind: psychosomatic. Mind is the finer part of the body and body is the grosser part of the mind.

So if you can become aware of the structure of body-mind, if you can become conscious of the structure, you are freed from the structure, you are freed from the vehicle, you have become different. And this KNOWING that you are separate from the structure is your true nature. That is what you really are. This body will die, but that true nature never dies. This mind will die and change and die again and again, but that true nature never dies. That true nature is eternal. That is why that true nature is neither your name nor your form. It is beyond both.

So how to do this technique? Total closing of the eyes is needed. If you try it, close your eyes and then stop the movements. Let your eyes become just like stones. No movements allowed. Suddenly, any day while practising this, suddenly it will happen that you will become able to look within. The eyes which were always looking outside will turn in and you will have a glimpse inside.

Then there is no difficulty. Once you have the glimpse inside, you know what to do and how to move. Only the first glimpse is difficult. After that you have the knack. Then it becomes just like a trick. Any moment you can close your eyes, make your eyes static, and you can enter the realm.

Buddha was dying. It was the last day of his life, and he asked his disciples if they wanted to ask any questions. They were weeping, crying, and they said, "You have told us so much. Now nothing is left to ask." Buddha had a habit of asking thrice. He would never stop by asking once. He would ask again, and then he would ask still again whether you had to ask any question. Many times Buddha was asked, "Why do you ask a single thing three times?" He said, "Because man is so unaware, so unconscious, he may not have heard the first time and he may have missed the second time."

Thrice he asked, and thrice his *bhikkhus* (monks), his disciples, said, "Now we do not want to ask anything. You have said so much." Then he closed his eyes and said, "If you do not have to ask anything, before death occurs to the body I will move from it. Before death enters the body I will move from it."

He closed his eyes. His eyes became static and he started moving. It is said that there were four parts to his movement inwards. First he closed his eyes; secondly, his eyes became static: there were no movements. If you had then the instrument of recording REM, the graph would not come. The eyes became static; that was the second thing. And thirdly, he looked at his body; then fourthly, he looked at his mind.

This was the whole journey. Before death occurred he was back at his center, in his original Source. That is why this death is not called death. We call it "Nirvana", and this is the difference: we call it "Nirvana — cessation", not death. Ordinarily, we die because death occurs to us. It never occurred to Buddha. Before death came, he had already returned to the Source.

Death occurred only to the dead body. He was not there to be found. So in Buddhist tradition it is said that he never died. Death could not catch him. It followed as it follows everyone, but he could not be trapped. He tricked death out of it. He must have been laughing, standing beyond, and death was there only with a dead body.

This technique is the same. Make four parts of it and move. And when you know one glimpse, the whole thing will become very easy and simple. Then any moment you can move in and come out and go in and come out, just like coming out of your house and going in, coming out and going in.

The second technique: *"Look upon a bowl without seeing the sides or the material. In a few moments become aware."*

Look at anything. A bowl or any object will do, but look with a different quality. "Look upon a bowl without seeing the sides or the material." Look upon any object, but with these two conditions. Do not look at the sides: look at the object as a whole. Ordinarily, we look at parts. It may not be done so consciously, but we look at parts. If I look at you, first I see your face, then your torso and then your whole body. Look at an object as a whole; do not divide it in parts. Why? Because when you divide in parts, the eyes have an opportunity to move from one part to another. Look at a thing as a whole. You can do it.

I can look at all of you in two ways. I can look from this side and then move. I can look at A, then at B, then I look at C and go on moving. When I look at A, B and C, I am not present — or just present on the fringe, but not focused. When I look at B, I am leaving A. When I look at C, A has been completely lost; he has gone out of my focus. I can look at this group in this manner, but I can look at the whole group without dividing it into individuals, into units, taking it as a whole.

Try it. First look at a thing from one fragment to another. Then suddenly look at this thing as a whole; do not divide it. When you look at a thing as a whole, the eyes have no need to move. In order not to give any opportunity for movement, this has been made a condition: look at an object totally, taken as a whole; secondly, without seeing the material. If the bowl is of wood, do not see the wood: just see the bowl, the form. Do not see the substance.

It may be of gold, it may be of silver. Observe it. Do not look at the material of which it is made. Just look at the form. The first thing is to look at it as a whole. Secondly, look at it as a form, not as a substance. Why? Because substance is the material part, form is the spiritual part, and you are to move from the material to the non-material. It will be helpful.

Try it. You can try it with anyone. Some man or some woman is standing: look and take the man or woman wholely into your look, totally into it. It will be a weird feeling in the beginning because you are not habituated, but it is very beautiful in the end. And then, do not think about whether the body is beautiful or not, white or black, man or woman. Do not think; just look at the form. Forget the substance and just look at the form.

In a few moments become aware. Go on looking at the form as a whole. Do not allow the eyes any movement. Do not start thinking about "the material". What will happen? You will suddenly become aware of your Self. Looking at something, you will become aware of your Self. Why? Because for the eyes there is no possibility to move outwards. The form has been taken as a whole, so you cannot move to the parts. The material has been dropped; pure form has been taken. Now you cannot think about gold, wood, silver, etc.

A form is pure form. No thinking about it is possible. A form is just a form; you cannot think about it. If it is of gold, you can think many things. You would like, you may like, to steal it, or to do something with it, or to sell it, or you can think about the price: many things are possible. But of pure form, no thinking is possible. Pure form stops thinking. And there is no possibility of changing from one part to another. You have taken it as a whole.

Remain with the whole and the form. Suddenly you will become aware of yourself because now the eyes cannot move. And they need movement; that is their nature: so your look will move toward you. It will come back, it will return home, and suddenly you will become aware of your Self. This becoming aware of one's Self is one of the most ecstatic moments possible. When for the first time you become aware of your Self, it has such beauty and such bliss that you cannot compare it with anything else you have known.

Really, for the first time you become your Self; for the first time you know you are. Your Being is revealed in a flash. But why does it happen ? You might have seen, in children's books particularly, a picture, or in some psychological treatises, but I hope everyone must have seen somewhere or other, a picture of an old woman — and in the same lines a beautiful young woman is also hidden. There is one picture, the same lines, but two figures in it: one old woman, one one young woman.

Look at the picture: you cannot become aware of both simultaneously. You will become aware either of one or the other. If you have become aware of the old woman, you cannot see where the young woman is hiding. But if you try to find her, it will be difficult, and the very effort will become a barrier. Because you have become aware of the old woman, she will have become a fixed thing in your eyes. With this fixed thing, you are trying to find the young woman. It is impossible. You will not be able to find her. You have to do a technique.

Just stare at the old woman; forget the young completely. Stare at the old woman — at the old-woman figure. Stare! Go on staring. Suddenly the old woman will disappear, and you will become aware of the young woman hiding there. Why? If you try to find her out you will miss. And this type of picture is given to children like a puzzle, and it is said to them, "Find the other." Then they start trying to find her, and because of that they miss.

The trick is not to try to find her: just stare at the figure and you will become aware. Forget the other. No need to think about it. Your eyes cannot remain at one point, so if you stare at the old woman figure the eyes will be tired. Then suddenly they will move from the figure, and in that movement, you will become aware of the other figure which is hidden just by the old woman's side, in the same line. But the miracle is that when you become aware of the young woman, you cannot see the old woman. But you know that both are there now.

In the beginning you may not have believed that the young woman is hiding, but now you know because you have seen the old woman first. Now you know that the old woman is there, but while looking at the young one you cannot simultaneously become aware of the old one. And if you become aware of the old one, you will miss the young again. Both cannot be seen simultaneously; you can see only one at a time.

The same happens with the outside and the inside look. You cannot have both looks simultaneously. When you are looking at a bowl or at any object, you are looking out: the consciousness is moving out; the river is flowing out. You are focused at the bowl. Go on staring at it. That very staring will create the opportunity to move in. Your eyes will be tired; they would like to move. Finding nothing to move out toward, suddenly the river will turn back. That remains the only possibility. You will have forced your consciousness to fall back. And when you will become aware of YOU, you will miss the bowl; it will not be there.

That is why a Shankara or a Nagarjuna says the whole world is illusory. They have known it so. When we come to know ourselves, the world is not. Really, the world is not illusory; it is there. But you cannot see both worlds simultaneously: that is the problem. So when a Shankara enters into himself, when he comes to know his Self, when he becomes a witness, the world is not there. So he is right. He says it is "maya" — illusion. It simply appears to be; it is not there.

Be aware of the fact. When you know the world, you are not. You ARE there — hidden, and you cannot believe that you are hidden there. The world is too much present for you. And if you start to look for yourself directly, it will be difficult. The very effort may become a barrier. So tantra says fix your stare somewhere in the world, on any object, and do not move from there: remain there. This very effort to remain there will create the possibility for the consciousness to begin to flow upwards — backwards. Then you will become aware of your Self.

But when you become aware of your Self, the bowl will not be there. It is there, but FOR YOU it will not be there. So Shankara says the world is illusory because when you come to know your Self it is not there. It disappears like a dream.

But Charwak and Epicurus and Marx, they are also right. They say the world is true, and your Self is just false. It is nowhere to be found. They say science is real. Science says only matter is, only objects are: there is no subject. They are right because the eyes are focused on the object.

A scientist is constantly focusing on objects. He forgets the Self completely. Both Shankara and Marx are right in one sense and wrong in another. If you are fixed upon the world, if your look is fixed on the world, the Self will look illusory — like it is just a dream. If you are looking inwards, the world will become a dream. Both are real, but you cannot be aware of both simultaneously: that is the problem. And nothing can be done. You will meet the old woman or you will meet the young woman.

One will become maya — illusory. But this technique can be used easily. It will take a little time, but it is not difficult.

Once you know the turning of consciousness, you can do it anywhere. Just riding in a bus or sitting in a train you can do it — anywhere. No need of a bowl or any particular object: you can do it with anything. With anything, stare, stare, stare, and suddenly turn inwards, and the train disappears. Of course, when you come back from your inner journey you will have travelled, but the train will have disappeared. From one station you will reach to another. In between there will be no train — just a gap. Of course, the train was there; otherwise how can you come to the other station ? But it was not there for you. For you it was not.

Those who can practise this technique, they can live in the world very easily. Any moment they can make anything disappear — remember this. You are bothered with your wife or with your husband: you can have her or him disappear. The wife is there sitting just by your side and she is not there. She is maya: she has disappeared. Just by staring and then turning your consciousness inwards, she has ceased to be there. And it has happened many times.

I remember Socrates. His wife Xanthippe was very much worried about him, and any wife would have been in the same dilemma. To find a Socrates as a husband is one of the most difficult things to tolerate. Socrates is good as a teacher, but not as a husband.

One day it happened (and because of it his wife has been condemned for 2,000 years continuously, but that is not just: I do not think she has done anything wrong). Socrates was sitting there. He must have done something like this (it is not recorded; I am just assuming): His wife came with a tray, a teapot, to give him tea. She must have found that he was not there, so it is reported that she poured the tea upon Socrates, over his face.

Then suddenly he came back. The face remained burned for his whole life. And because of this his wife has been condemned very much, but no one knows what Socrates was doing there — because no wife would do this suddenly; there is no need. He must have done something; something must have been happening there. That is why Xanthippe had to throw tea over him. He must have been in an inner trance, and the burning sensation of the tea must have brought him back. The consciousness must have returned.

I assume that this was the case because there are many other cases reported about Socrates which are similar. For 48 hours he was not found. He was sought all over; the whole Athens went in search of Socrates. But he was not to be found anywhere. Then he was found outside the city, miles away, standing under a tree. Half of his body was just under snow. Snow was falling, and he was just frozen, standing there with open eyes. But he was not looking at anyone.

When the crowd gathered around, they looked into his eyes and they thought he is dead. His eyes were just like stones — looking, but not looking at anyone: just static, unmoving. They felt his heart. It was beating slowly; he was alive. Then they had to give him shocks. Only then did he come back to look at them. Immediately he was asked, "What is the time now?" He missed 48 hours completely. They never existed for him. He was not in this world of time and space.

So they asked, "What were you doing? We thought you are dead already. Forty-eight hours!" He said, "I was staring at the stars, and just suddenly it happened that the stars disappeared. And then, I don't know: then the whole world disappeared. But I remained in such a cool, calm, blissful state, that if it is death it is worth thousands of lives. If it is death, then I would like to enter it again and again."

It may have happened without his knowledge, because Socrates was not a yogi, not a tantric. He was not in any way concerned consciously with any spiritual practice. But he was a great thinker, and it may have happened as an accident that he was staring at the stars in the night, and suddenly his look returned back inwards. You can do it. And stars are really rare good objects.

Lie down on the ground, look at the black sky, and then fix yourself on one star. Concentrate on it; stare at it. Narrow down your consciousness to one star; forget other stars. By and by, concentrate, narrow down your gaze. Other stars will be there just on the fringe, on the boundary. But by and by they will disappear, and only one star will remain. Then go on staring, go on staring. A moment will come when that star will disappear. And when that star disappears, YOU will appear to yourself.

The third technique: *"See as if for the first time a beauteous person or an ordinary object."* Some basic things first; then you can do this technique. We look at things always with old eyes. You come to your home; you look at it without looking at it. You know it. There is no need to look at it. You have entered it again and again for years together. You go to the door. You enter the door; you may unlock the door. But there is no need to look.

This whole process goes on robot-like, mechanically, unconsciously. If something goes wrong, only if your key is not fitting into the lock, then you look at the lock. If the key fits, you never lock at the lock. Because of mechanical habits, repeatedly doing the same thing again and again, you lose the capacity to look; you lose the freshness to look. Really, you lose the function of your eyes — remember this. You become basically blind, because eyes are not needed.

Remember the last time you looked at your wife. The last time you looked at your wife or at your husband may have been years ago. For how many years have you not looked? You just pass giving a casual glimpse, but not a look. Go again and look at your wife or at your husband as if you were looking for the first time. Why? Because if you are looking for the first time, your eyes will be filled with a freshness. They will become alive.

You are passing through a street. A beautiful woman passes. Your eyes become alive — lighted. A sudden flame comes to them. This woman may be a wife to someone. He will not look at her; he may become as blind as you have become seeing your wife. Why? For the first time eyes are needed, the second time not so much, and the third time they are not needed. After a few repetitions you become blind. We live blindly.

Be aware. When you meet your children, are you looking at them? You are not looking at them. This habit kills the eyes; the eyes become bored. Repeatedly there is the old again and again, and nothing is old really. It is just that your habit makes you feel that it is so. Your wife is not the same as she was yesterday; she cannot be. Otherwise she is a miracle. Nothing can be the same the next moment. Life is flux; everything is flowing; nothing is the same.

The same sunrise will not happen. In a very typical sense also, the sun is not the same. Every day it is new; basic changes have occurred. And the sky will not be the same again; this morning is not going to come again. And every morning has its own individuality, and the sky and the colours, they will not gather in the same pattern again. But you go on moving as if everything is just the same.

They say nothing is new under the sky. Really, nothing is old under the sky. Only the eyes become old, accustomed to things; then nothing is new. For children everything is new: that is why everything gives them excitement. Even a coloured stone on a beach, and they become so excited. You will not be excited even seeing God himself coming to your house. You will not be so excited! You will say, "I know Him; I have read about Him." Children are so excited because their eyes are new and fresh. And everything is a new world, a new dimension.

Look at children's eyes — at the freshness, the radiant aliveness, the vitality. They look mirror-like, silent, but penetrating. Only such eyes can reach within.

So this technique says, "See as if for the first time a beauteous person or an ordinary object." Anything will do. Look at your shoes. You have been using them for years, but look as if for the first time and see the difference: the quality of your consciousness suddenly changes.

I wonder whether you have seen Van Gogh's painting of his shoe. It is one of the rarest things. There is just an old shoe — tired, sad, as if just on the verge of death. It is just an old shoe, but look at it, feel it, and you will feel what a long, boring life this shoe must have passed through. It is so sad, just praying to be taken away from life, tired completely, every nerve broken, just an old man, an old shoe. It is one of the most original paintings. But how could Van Gogh see it ?

You have even more old shoes with you — more tired, more dead, more sad, depressed, but you have never looked at them — at what you have done to them, how you have behaved with them. They tell a life story about you because they are YOUR shoes. They can say everything about you. If they could write, they would write a most authentic biography of the person they had to live with — every mood, every face. When their owner was in love, he behaved differently with the shoes; when he was angry he behaved differently. And the shoes were not concerned at all, and everything has left a mark.

Look at Van Gogh's painting, and then you will see what he could see in the shoes. Everything is there — a whole biography of the person who was using them. But how could he see ? To be a painter, one has to regain the child's look — the freshness. He can look at everything — at most ordinary things even. He can look !

Cézanne has painted a chair, just an ordinary chair, and you may even wonder why to paint a chair. There is no need. But he worked on that painting for months together. You may have stopped for a single moment to look at it, and he worked for months because he could look at a chair. A chair has its own spirit, its own story, its own miseries and happinesses. It has lived ! It has passed through life ! It has its own experiences, memories. They are all revealed in Cézanne's painting. But do you look at your chair ? No one looks at it, no one feels it.

Any object will do. This technique is just to make your eyes fresh, so fresh, alive, radiantly vital, that they can move within and you can have a look at your inner self. See as if for the first time. Make it a point to see everything as if for the first time, and sometime, suddenly, you will be surprised at what a beautiful world you have been missing. Suddenly become aware and look at your wife as if for the first time. And it is no wonder if you may feel again the same love you felt the first time, the same surge of energy, the same attraction in its fullest. But look as if for the first time — at a beauteous person or an ordinary object. What will happen ? You will regain your eyesight. You are blind. Just now, as you are, you are blind. And this blindness is more fatal than physical blindness, because you have eyes and still you cannot look.

Jesus says many times, "Those who have eyes, let them see. Those who have ears, let them hear." It seems that he was talking to blind men or to deaf men. But he goes on repeating. What was he — a superintendent in some institute for the blind ? He goes on repeating, "If you have eyes look." He must be talking with ordinary men who have eyes. But why insistence on "If you have eyes, look" ? He is talking about the eyes which this technique can give you.

Look at everything you pass as if for the first time. Make it a continuous attitude. Touch everything as if for the first time. What will happen ? If you can do this, you will be freed from your past. The burden, the depth, the dirtiness, the accumulated experiences — you will be freed from them.

Every moment move from the past. Do not allow it to enter with you; do not allow it to be carried. Leave it. Look at everything as if for the first time. This is a great technique to help you to be freed from the past. Then you are constantly in the present. And by and by, you will have an affinity with the present. Then everything will be new. Then you will be able to understand Heraclitus' saying that you cannot step twice in the same river.

You cannot see a person twice — the same person — because nothing is static. Everything is river-like, flowing and flowing and flowing. If you are freed from the past and you have the look which can see the present, you will enter the Existence.

And this entry will be double: you will enter into everything — in its spirit, and you will enter into yourself also because the present is the door. All meditations in one way or the other try to get you to live in the present. So this technique is one of the most beautiful techniques — and easy. And you can try it, and without any danger.

If you are looking afresh even when passing through the same street again, it is a new street. Meeting the same friend as if he is a stranger, looking at your wife as you looked for the first time when she was a stranger, can you really say that he or she is not still a stranger ? You may have lived for twenty years or thirty years or forty years with your wife, but can you say that you are acquainted with her ? She is still a stranger: you are two strangers living together. You know the outer habits of each other, the outer reactions, but the inner core of the being is unknown, untouched.

Look freshly again, as if for the first time, and you will see the same stranger. Nothing, NOTHING, has become old; everything is new. This will give you a freshness to your look. Your eyes will become innocent. Those innocent eyes can see. Those innocent eyes can enter into the inner world.

6
The Third Eye And Psychic Eye Power

December 15, 1972, Bombay, India

QUESTIONS:

1. *How do the looking techniques affect the third eye?*

2. *Why do persons involved in psychic sciences have tense and fearful eyes?*

3. *Why does the stopping of eye movements create psychic tensions?*

The first question: *"Explain the relationship of the two eyes with the third eye. In which way do the techniques concerned with looking affect the third eye?"*

Firstly, two points are to be understood: one, the energy of the third eye is really the same as that which moves in the two ordinary eyes — the same energy. It begins to move in a new center. The third eye is already there, but non-functioning — and it cannot see unless these ordinary eyes become unseeing.

The same energy has to move in it. When the energy is not moving in the two eyes it can move in the third, and when it moves in the third the two eyes will become unseeing. They will be there, but you won't be able to see through them. That energy that looks through them will be absent. It will move through a new center. That center is between these two eyes. It is already there complete; any moment it can function. But it needs energy to function, and the same energy has to be diverted.

Secondly, when you are seeing through the two eyes, you are seeing through the physical body. The third eye is not really a part of the physical body. It is part of the second body which is hidden — the subtle body, the *sukshma sharir*. It has a corresponding spot in the physical body, but it is not part of it. That is why physiology cannot believe that there exists a third eye or anything like it — because your skull can be analyzed, penetrated, x-rayed, and there is no point, no physical entity, which can be said to be the third eye. The third eye is part of the subtle body, the *sukshma sharir*.

When you die your physical body dies, but your *sukshma sharir*, your subtle body, moves with you; it takes another birth. Unless the subtle body dies, you can never be freed from the circle of birth-death, rebirth-"re-death". The circle moves on.

The third eye belongs to the subtle body. When the energy is moving through the physical body, you are looking through the physical. That is why through the physical eyes you cannot look at anything other than the physical, than the material. The two eyes are physical. Through these eyes you cannot look at anything, cannot see anything, which is not physical.

Only with the third eye functioning can you enter a different dimension. Now you can see things which are invisible to the physical eyes, but they become visible to the subtle eyes. Then, with the third eye functioning, if you look at a person you look at his soul, at his spirit, not at his body, just like you look at the physical body through the physical eyes, but you cannot see the soul. The same happens when you look through the third eye: you look, and the body is not there — just the one who resides in the body.

Remember these two points. Firstly, the same energy has to move. It has to be taken away from the ordinary physical eyes and allowed to move through the third eye. Secondly, the third eye is not part of the physical body. It is part of the subtle body, the second body that is within. Because it is part of the subtle body, the moment you can look through it you look at the subtle world. You are sitting here. If a ghost is sitting here you cannot see it, but if your third eye is functioning you will see the ghost, because subtle existence can be seen only through the subtle eye.

How is the third eye related with this technique of looking? It is deeply related. Really, this technique is to open the third eye. If your two eyes stop completely, if they become non-moving, static like stones with no movement in these eyes, the energy stops flowing through them. If you stop them, the energy stops flowing through them. The energy flows; that is why they move. The vibration, the movement, is because of the energy. If the energy is not moving, your eyes will become just like a dead man's eyes — stoney, dead.

Looking at a spot, staring at it without allowing your eyes to move anywhere else, will give a staticness. Suddenly the energy which was moving through the two eyes will not be moving through these eyes. And energy has to move; energy cannot be static. Eyes can be static, but energy cannot be static. When these eyes are closed to the energy, if suddenly the doors are closed and the energy cannot move through these eyes, it tries to find a new path. And the third eye is just near, just between the two eyebrows, half an inch deep. It is just near, the nearest point.

If your energy is released from these eyes, the first thing that can happen is that it will move through the third eye. It is just as if water is flowing and you close one hole: it will find another — the nearest which can be found with the least resistance. It will find it automatically; you do not have to do anything specifically. With these physical eyes, you just have to stop energy from moving through them, and then energy will find its own path and it will move through the third eye.

This movement through the third eye transforms you into a different world. You start seeing things you have never seen, you start feeling things you have never felt, you start smelling things you have never smelled. A new world, a subtle world, starts functioning. It is already there. The eye is there; the world, the subtle world, is already there. Both are there, but not revealed.

Once you function in that dimension, many things become apparent to you. For example, if a person is going to die, if your third eye is functioning you will become immediately aware that he is going to die. No physical analysis, no physical diagnosis, can say that certainly he is going to die. At the most, we can talk about probabilities. We can say perhaps he will die, and this statement will be conditional: "If such and such remains the case, he may die; if something can be done he may not die."

Medical diagnosis cannot yet be certain about death. Why? So much development and yet so much uncertainty about death! Really, medical science is trying to deduce death, to infer death, through physical symptoms, and death is a subtle phenomenon, not physical. It is an invisible phenomenon of a different dimension. But with the third eye functioning, you suddenly feel that a man is going to die. How do you feel it? Death has an impact. If you are going to die, then death has already cast its shadow there, and that shadow can be felt with the third eye at anytime.

When a child is born, those who have had much deep practice using the third eye can see the time of his death that very moment. But then the shadow is very subtle. When a person is going to die in six months, then anyone whose third eye functions a little can see the death six months before it comes. The shadow darkens. Really, around you a dark shadow settles down and that can be felt, but not with these two eyes.

With the third eye, you begin to see auras. A person comes to you: he cannot deceive you, because whatever he says is meaningless unless it corresponds to his aura. He may say he is a person who never gets angry, but the red aura will show that he is filled with anger. He cannot deceive as far as his aura is concerned because he is completely unaware about the aura. Whatsoever he says can be judged through his aura — whether it is right or wrong. With the third eye you start seeing radiations, auras.

In the old days that was how someone was initiated. Unless the aura was right, the Master would wait, because your wish fulfillment was not the question. You may have wanted to be initiated, but that was not enough unless your aura said that you are ready. So for years the disciple had to wait until the aura was ready, not his desire to the initiated. That is futile. Sometimes even for lives, one had to wait.

For example, Buddha resisted the temptation to initiate women for many years. So much pressure was put upon him; still he would reject this. Ultimately he agreed to initiate women, but then he said, "Now my religion will not be alive after five hundred years; I have compromised. And because you force me, I initiate women."

What was the reason why he would not initiate women? One basic reason was this: with man, sexual energy can be regulated very easily. A man can become a celibate very easily. With a woman's body it is difficult because menses is a regular phenomenon — unconscious, uncontrollable, non-voluntary. Semen ejaculation can be controlled, but menses cannot be controlled. Or, if one tries to control it, then it will have very bad effects on the body.

The moment a woman enters her period of menses, her aura changes completely. It becomes sexual, aggressive, depressed. All that is negative surrounds the woman every month. Only because of this Buddha was not ready to initiate women. He said that it was difficult because every month the menses moves in a circle periodically, and nothing can be done voluntarily. Something can be done, but it was difficult to do that in Buddha's time. Now it can be done.

Mahavir completely denied any possibility of a woman being liberated from a woman's body. He said that a woman has to be born again to be a man, and only then can she be Liberated. So all the effort should be channelized for a woman to enter a new birth as a man. Why? It was a problem of the aura.

If you initiate a woman, every month she will fall down and the whole effort will be lost. There was no discrimination, no evaluation about whether or not woman and man are equal; that was not the question. But for Mahavir the question was this: how to help? So he found an easier way: to help a woman to be reborn as a man. That was easier. It meant that a woman had to wait for another life, and the whole effort had to be directed toward the goal that she should be born in a male body.

This appeared easier to Mahavir than to initiate a woman, because every month she comes back down to the original state and all effort is lost. But these two thousand years have done much. Particularly, tantra has done much.

Tantra has found different doors, and tantra is the only system in the world which makes no differentiation between man and woman. Rather, on the contrary, it says that a woman can become easily Liberated, and the reason is the same — only looked at from a different angle. Tantra says that because a woman's body is periodically regulated, she can detach herself from her body more easily than man. Because man's mind is more involved in the body, that is why he can regulate it. Man's mind is more involved in the body. That is why he can control his sex.

Woman's mind is not so involved in the body. The body functions as an automata — different, on a different layer, and the woman cannot do anything about it. It is like an automatic mechanism; it goes on. Tantra says that because of this woman can detach herself from her body very easily. And if this becomes possible — this detachment, this gap — then there is no problem. Then there is NO problem !

So it is a very paradoxical thing: if a woman decides to be celibate and to detach herself from her body, she can maintain her purity more easily than a man. Once the detachment is there, then she can forget the body completely. Man can detach himself very easily, can control very easily, but his mind is more involved in the body. That is why he can control, but then he will have to control every day, continuously. And because feminine sex is passive, it is very easy for a woman to be relaxed about sex. Man's sex is active. It is easy for him to control it, but difficult for him to relax about it.

So tantra has been trying to find many, many ways, and tantra is the only system which says there is no difference, that even a feminine structure can be used. So tantra is the only path which gives women similar, equal status. Otherwise, every religion, whatsoever it may say, deep down feels that women are inferior. It may be Christianity, it may be Islam, it may be Jainism, it may be Buddhism, but deep down it feels this, and the reason is the diagnosis through the third eye, the aura — the forming of the aura every month at the time of menses.

With the third eye you become capable of seeing things which are there, but which cannot be seen with ordinary eyes. All the methods about looking affect the third eye, because looking means a certain energy moving from you outwardly — toward the world. If blocked, if suddenly blocked, the energy will find another path where to move, and the third eye is just near.

In Tibet there were even surgical operations for the third eye. Sometimes it happens that your third eye is blocked because you have not used it for millennia. It may be blocked! If the third eye is blocked and you stop your eyes, you will feel a certain uneasiness because the energy is there and there is no path where to move. In Tibet they devised certain operations to have the passage clear. This can be done. And if it is not done, then many things can happen.

Just two or three days before, one sannyasin (she is here) came to me. She said there is a very hot sensation at the third eye. And not only was there the sensation: the skin had become burnt as if really someone had burned it from the outside. The sensation, the burning, was inside, but the skin was affected. It became completely burnt. She was afraid. What had happened? The feeling was pleasant. The warmth was very pleasant as if something were melting. Something was happening. But even the physical body had become affected as if actual fire had touched it.

The reason? The third eye had started functioning. The energy began to move in it. It had been cold for lives together; energy never moved through it. When for the first time energy moves there is the warmth. When for the first time energy moves there is the burning sensation. And because the passage has to be created and forced, it may become like fire. It is concentrated energy hammering on the third eye.

In India we have been using sandalwood powder and other things, ghee and other things, just on the third-eye spot. We call this mark a *"tilak"*. It is put just on the third-eye spot in order to give a certain coolness from the outside. So if warmth comes within and fire moves within, it should not affect the skin outside. Not only can the skin be burnt by it: sometimes even holes have appeared on the skull.

I was reading one of the most penetrating books about one of the very deep mysteries of human existence on the earth. There have always been proposals that man came from some other star, because there seems to be no possibility that man suddenly had evolved on earth. There seems to be no possibility really that man could have evolved from a baboon or a chimpanzee. And there has been no link, because if man evolved from the chimpanzee to be man, there must be links — something that is between man and chimpanzee — but there is no such thing. With all the available data and discoveries, we have not yet found a single body structure, a skull or anything, by which we can say that this is a link between the chimpanzee and man.

Evolution means steps. Suddenly a chimpanzee cannot become a man. Stages must have followed, but there is no proof. So Darwin's theory remains a hypothesis. There are no in-between links.

So there have always been fantastic proposals that man must have appeared on the earth suddenly. A man's skull dating very far back, a hundred thousand years back, has been found. But in comparison with other skulls there is nothing lacking in it. It is the same type of skull, with the same brain, with the same structure. We have not evolved really as far as mind structure is concerned.

So it seems man suddenly appeared on earth. He must have come from some other planet. For example, now we are travelling into space, and if we find some planet worth living upon, we will populate it; then suddenly man will appear there. I was reading a book about such a proposal, and the author has been finding many things to prove, to help, his hypothesis.

There is one thing that I wanted to tell you about in connection with this matter of looking: he has found one skull in Mexico and one in Tibet. Both of these skulls have holes at the third-eye spot, and the holes are such that they could only have been made by a gun bullet. The skulls are at least one-half million to one million (5 to 10 lakh) years old. If the holes were made by an arrow, they could not be round. They are so round that they could not have been made by an arrow. Only a bullet could make such holes, so that author tries to prove by this that bullets existed one million years before. Otherwise how were these two men killed ?

But, really, that doesn't prove anything about bullets. Whenever the third eye is blocked completely and the energy moves suddenly, this hole can appear. The energy is just like a bullet coming from within — just like a bullet. It is concentrated fire; it will create a hole. Those two skulls with holes show not that those men were killed by bullets, but simply that there was a third-eye phenomenon: the third eye was blocked completely. Energy became concentrated. The eyes were stopped completely. Energy could not move, and it became fire. Then it exploded. Just so that there would not be such an accident, in Tibet they discovered and devised methods to make a hole so that the energy could move easily.

So whenever you are trying this "looking", remember this: if you feel a burning sensation, do not be afraid. But if you feel that the energy has become a great fire — as if a live bullet is there and wants to penetrate the skull — stop the method and come immediately to me. Do not do it further. If you feel as if a bullet is there and it wants to penetrate the skull, stop. Open your eyes and move them as much as you can. Immediately, the sensation will drop. The energy will have moved through the eyes. And unless I say something to you do not proceed, because sometimes it has happened that the skull is broken.

Nothing is wrong even if it happens. Even if one dies in it nothing is wrong, because one has achieved something which is beyond death. But just to be safe, stop whenever you feel that something wrong can happen — with any method, not only with this. With any method, if you feel something wrong is possible, stop.

In India now, many methods are being taught and many, many seekers suffer unnecessarily because those who teach are not even aware of the dangers. And those who follow, they follow in a blind maze. They do not know where they are moving or what they are doing.

I am talking about these 112 methods specifically because of this — so that you become aware of all the methods, all the possibilities, the dangers, and so that you can then find out which will suit you best. Then if you proceed in any method, you will be fully aware of what can happen, what you have to be aware of and when something happens, how you have to tackle it.

The second question: *"It is observed that the practitioners of psychic sciences possess tense and fearful eyes. Explain what this indicates and how to overcome this phenomenon."*

Those who practise hynotism, mesmerism, magnetism, or things like this will have very tense eyes — obviously, because they are trying to move their energy through the eyes forcibly. They are bringing their total energy near the eyes just to influence, impress or dominate someone. Their eyes will become tense because then eyes are flooded with energy, more than they can tolerate. Their eyes will be red, tense, and if you look at them you will feel a sudden shivering: they are using their eyes in a very political way. If they look at you, they are sending their energy to dominate. And through eyes, domination is very easy.

This was the case with Rasputin, who dominated Russia before Lenin just through his eyes. He was an ordinary peasant, uneducated, but with very magnetic eyes. And he came to know how to use this. The moment he would look at you, you would forget yourself, and in that moment he could send any suggestion to you telepathetically and you would follow it. That is how he dominated the Czar and the Czarina, the royal family, and through them, the whole Russia. Nothing could be done without his will.

You can have those eyes also; it is not difficult. You have just to learn how to bring your total body energy to the eyes. They become flooded, and then, whenever you look at someone, your energy starts flowing toward him. It envelopes the person, penetrates his mind, and in this flooded shock his thinking stops. And this is not a very rare thing that happens just with man. It happens all over the animal kingdom. There are many animals who will just look at their prey, and if the prey looks at them he is done for. Then the prey's eyes become fixed. He cannot move; he cannot escape.

Hunters know this well, and hunters develop very powerful eyes because they are always in search in the darkness for animals. Their eyes become powerful. Thieves and hunters by and by gather more energy in their eyes automatically because of their work.

Suddenly a lion comes before a hunter, and he is without weapons and he cannot do anything. Then this is what has been done always: the hunter can stare into the eyes of the lion, and now it will depend on whether he has more magnetic eyes or the lion. If the lion is less magnetic and the hunter can bring his total energy to his eyes (and it is easy: he can bring it because when death is there one can do anything, when death is there the hunter can put his total energy at stake), if the hunter can look directly into the eyes of the lion and forget everything and just look, if he can just become the look, then the whole energy will move from his eyes and the lion will escape. He will be trembling with fear.

Through eyes you can cause your whole energy to overflood, but when you do that your eyes will be tense: you will not be able to sleep, you will not be able to relax. So all those who are trying to dominate others will be restless. If you look at their faces their eyes will be alive, but their faces will be dead. Look at any hypnotist: his eyes will be very much alive, but his face will be dead because his eyes are sucking the whole energy and nothing is left anywhere.

Do not do this because it is useless to dominate anyone. The only useful thing is to dominate yourself. It is useless, a wasting of your energy. Nothing is achieved through it — just an egotistic feeling that you can dominate. So this is evil — a black art. That is the difference between black magic and white magic. Black magic means using your energy, wasting it in dominating others. White magic means the same methods, but using your energy in dominating your own life, becoming a master of yourself.

And, remember, sometimes similarities happen. If a Buddha moves amidst you, you will be dominated by him, although he is not dominating you. He is not trying to dominate you, but you will be dominated because he is the master of himself. And he is such a master, that all around him whosoever moves will become a slave. But there is no conscious effort on his part. Rather, on the contrary, he will continuously insist, "Be your own Master" — remember this. And this insistence is because of this knowledge.

Buddha knows that whosoever comes around him will become a slave. He is not doing anything; he is not trying to dominate anyone. But he knows this will happen. His last dying words were, "Be a lamp unto yourself." He was dying, and Ananda asked him (just a day before his actual death), "When you will be no more, what shall we do ?" He said, "It is good that I shall be no more. Then you can be your own master. Be a lamp unto yourself; forget me. It is good, because when I am no more you will be freed from my domination."

Those who try to dominate others will try in every way to make a slave of you. That is evil, satanic. Those who become their own masters will help you to become masters, and they will try in every way to cut their influence. That can be done in many ways.

For example, I will tell a very recent incident. Ouspensky, the chief disciple of Gurdjieff, was working under Gurdjieff for ten years. It was very difficult to work under Gurdjieff. He was a man of infinite magnetism. Whosoever would come around him would be pulled.

With such people, either you are pulled or you become afraid and go against them, but you cannot remain indifferent. You are either for or against; you cannot be indifferent to such people. And that going against is just a safety measure. If you come around a person who is magnetic, either you will become a slave to him or, just to protect yourself, you will become an enemy, because that is a protection.

Ouspensky came to him, stayed with him, worked with him, and there was no theoretical knowledge to be imparted. He was a man of action. He would give techniques, and one had to work. Then Ouspensky achieved a certain crystallization. He became an integrated man; he was transformed. He was not fully Enlightened yet, but he was not fast asleep as we are. He was in between, just on the verge.

When you feel that the morning is near, when you start listening to the noises which indicate morning is near, you are asleep, but not totally asleep. The sleep is just on the verge of going. You are not yet awake, but you may again fall into a sleep. You are just on the surface, just near awakening.

And when Ouspensky was just near awakening, he was thinking that now Gurdjieff will help him more because this was the moment. But suddenly Gurdjieff started behaving in such a strange way that Ouspensky had to leave. He started up in such strange ways with him, did such absurd things, contradictory, nonsensical on the surface, that Ouspensky had to leave him — on his own account.

Gurdjieff never told him to leave. On his own account he left him, went against him, said that he had gone mad. He started teaching, and he always said, "I am teaching according to Gurdjieff, my teacher, but now he is mad." He would say, "according to the early Gurdjieff." He would not talk about the later Gurdjieff.

But the basic reason why Gurdjieff did it is deep compassion. That was the moment when Ouspensky had to be left alone;

otherwise he would have become a constant dependent. The moment came when he had to be thrown out, and in such a way that he would never become aware that he has been thrown consciously.

Such persons like Buddha or Gurdjieff will affect you without their conscious effort and you will be pulled toward them. But they will try in every way that you are not pulled in that way: that you are not attracted hypnotically, that you are not dominated by them. And they will help to make you masters on your feet.

Those who are trying to dominate others, their eyes will be tense, evilish. You will not feel any innocence in their eyes, you will not feel purity in their eyes. You will feel attraction, but the attraction will be like alcohol. You will feel a magnetic pull, but the pull will be not to free you but to enslave you.

Remember, never use any energy to dominate anyone. Because of this, Buddha, Mahavir, Jesus — they made it a point, and they went on hammering, that the moment you enter the spiritual search be filled with love for everyone, even for your enemy, because if you are filled with love you will not be attracted to the inner violence which wants to dominate.

Only love can become an antidote. Otherwise when the energy comes to you and you are overfilled with it, you will start dominating. This happens every day. I have come across many, many people. I start helping them, they will grow a little, and the moment they feel that a certain energy is coming to them they will start dominating others. They will try now to use it.

Remember, never use spiritual energy to dominate. You are wasting your efforts. Sooner or later you will be empty again, and you will fall down suddenly. And this is pure wastage, but it is very difficult to control it because you become aware that now you can do certain things. If you touch someone who was ill and he becomes okay, how can you resist touching others now ? How can you resist ?

If you cannot resist, you will waste your energy. Something has happened to you, but soon you will throw it unnecessarily.

And, really, the mind is so cunning that you may be thinking that you are helping others by healing. That may be just a cunning trick of the mind, because if you have no love, how can you be so concerned with others' diseases, their illnesses, their health ? You are not concerned. Really, now this is a power. If you can heal, you can dominate them.

You may say that "I am just helping them", but even in your help you are simply trying to dominate them. Your ego will be fulfilled. This will become a food for your ego. So all the old treatises say beware. They say beware because when the energy comes to you, you are at a dangerous point. You can waste it, you can throw it. When you feel any energy, make it a secret. Do not allow anyone to know about it.

Jesus said, "If your right hand is doing something, do not allow the left hand to know about it." In the Sufi mystic tradition, they say when energy starts coming, do not even pray before others, do not go to a mosque before others. Why ? When the energy comes and someone is praying, and there are many persons present, they will feel immediately that something is happening. So the Sufis say that then you should do your prayers deep in the night — at midnight — when everyone is asleep and no one can be aware of what is happening to you. Do not tell anyone what is happening to you.

But the mind is just a chattering box. If something happens, immediately you will go and spread the good news that something has happened to you. Then you have wasted it. And if people are impressed, then all you have gained is their good opinion and nothing else. This is not a good bargain. Wait ! A moment will come when your energy becomes accumulated until it reaches a point where it becomes integrated, transformed. Then things will happen around you without your doing anything. And only then can you help others to be their own masters — when you are your own master.

I remember one Sufi mystic Junnaid. One day a man came to him and he said, "Junnaid, Master, Great Master, I have come to know your inner seret. People say you have a golden secret and that you have not told it to anyone until now. I will do anything you say, but tell me the secret." Junnaid said, "I have been keeping it, hiding it, for thirty years, so how much time can you wait? You will have to go through a preparation. It is a thirty-year secret but I will tell it to you. But how much time will you keep patient?"

The man became afraid, scared. He said, "How long do you suggest?" Junnaid said, "At least thirty years. It is not too much. I am not asking too much." The man said, "Thirty years? I will think it over." Junnaid said, "Then if you come back again, I will not be ready to give it to you in thirty years. Remember, if you decide just now, then okay. Otherwise I will also have to think." So the man agreed.

It is said that he remained for thirty years with Junnaid. Then the last day came, and he went to Junnaid and said to him, "Now communicate your secret." Junnaid said, "I will give it to you on one condition, that you will keep it a secret. You are not to tell it to anyone. This secret must die with you unknown." The man said, "Why have you wasted my whole life? Thirty years I was waiting for the secret just to tell others, and now there is a condition! Then what is the use of knowing it if I cannot tell it to others? If you make this condition, then please do not tell it to me; otherwise it will become a haunting: I will know something which I cannot tell to others. So be kind enough and do not tell it to me. You have wasted my thirty years. A little life is left, so let me live it relaxedly. This will be too much, knowing something without telling it to others."

Whatsoever you gain through any spiritual method, let it remain secret. Do not go on spreading it, do not try to use it in any way. Let it remain unused, pure. Only then will it be used for inner transformation. If you use it outwardly, it is a wastage.

The third question: *"You mentioned that rapid eye movements indicate mental processes and that if eye movements are stopped the mental processes will also stop. But this physiological control on the mental processes, this stopping of eye movements, seems to create psychic tensions such as happens when we keep our eyes closed under a blindfold for a long time."*

Firstly, your mind and your body are not two things as far as tantra is concerned. Remember that always. Do not say, "physiological process" and "mental process". They are not two — just two parts of one whole. Whatsoever you do physiologically affects the mind. Whatsoever you do psychologically affects the body. They are not two: they are one.

You can say that body is a solid state of the same energy and mind is a liquid state of the same energy — of the same energy! So no matter what you are doing physiologically, do not think that this is just physiological. Do not wonder how it is going to help any transformation in the mind. If you take alcohol, what happens to your mind? Alcohol is taken into the body, not into the mind, but what happens to the mind? If you take LSD, it goes into the body, not into the mind, but what happens to the mind?

Or, if you go on a fast, fasting is done by the body, but what happens to the mind? Or, from the other end, if you think sexual thoughts, what happens to your body? The body is affected immediately. You think in the mind of a sex object and your body starts getting ready.

There was a theory by William James. In the first part of this century it apparently looked very absurd, but in a sense it is right. He and another scientist named Lange proposed this theory which is known as the James-Lange theory. Ordinarily, we say you are afraid and that is why you escape and run away, or you are angry and that is why your eyes get red and you start beating your enemy.

But James and Lange proposed quite the contrary. They said because you run away, that is why you feel fear; and because your eyes get red and you start beating your enemy, you feel anger. It is just the opposite. They said that if this is not so, then we want to see even one instance of anger when the eyes are not red and the body is not affected and one is simply angry. Do not allow your body to be affected and try to be angry. Then you will know that you cannot be angry.

In Japan they teach their children a very simple method of controlling anger. They say whenever you feel angry, do not do anything with the anger. Just start taking deep breaths. Try it, and you will not be able to get angry. Why? Just because you take deep breaths, why can you not get angry? It becomes impossible to get angry. Two reasons: You start taking deep breaths, but anger needs a particular rhythm of breathing. Without that rhythm anger is not possible. A particular rhythm in breathing or chaotic breathing is needed for anger to be.

If you start taking deep breaths it is impossible for the anger to come out. If you are consciously taking deep breaths, then the anger cannot express itself. It needs a different breathing which should be allowed. You need not do it; the anger will do it itself. With deep breathing you cannot be angry.

And secondly, your mind shifts. When you feel angry and you start to take deep breaths; your mind is shifted from anger to breathing. The body is not in a state to be angry, and the mind has shifted its concentration toward something else. Then it is difficult to be angry. That is why the Japanese are the most controlled people on earth — the most controlled! It is just a training from childhood.

It is difficult anywhere else to find such an incident, but in Japan it happens even today. It is becoming less and less because Japan is becoming less and less Japan. It is becoming more and more Westernized, and the traditional methods and ways are becoming lost. But it was happening, and it still happens today.

One of my friends was there in Kyoto, and he wrote me a letter saying, "I have seen such a beautiful phenomenon today that I want to write it to you. And when I come back, I will want to understand how it is possible. One man was struck by a car. He fell down, stood up, thanked the driver, and went away. Thanked the driver!"

In Japan it is not difficult. He must have taken a few deep breaths, and then it was possible. You are transformed into a different attitude, and you can thank even a person who was just going to kill you or who has "already killed you".

Physiological processes and psychological processes are not two things. They are one, and you can start from either pole to affect and change the other. And any science will do that. For example, tantra believes deeply in body. Only philosophy is vague, airy, verbal; it may start from something else. Otherwise, any scientific approach is bound to start from the body because that is within your reach. If I talk of something which is beyond your reach, you may listen to it, you may gather it in your memory, you may talk about it, but nothing happens. You remain the same. Your information is increased, but not your being. Your knowledge goes on increasing, but your being remains the same poor mediocrity; nothing happens to it.

Remember, body is what is in your reach; just now you can do something with it and change your mind through the body. By and by you will become a master of the body, and then you will become a master of the mind. And when you become a master of the mind, you will change the mind by and by and you will be moving beyond it. If the body changes, you move beyond body. If the mind changes you move beyond mind. And always do something which you CAN do.

For example, you may not be capable of becoming a master of anger like a Buddha just now. How can you ? But you can change your breathing and then you can feel the subtle effect, the change. Do it. If you feel filled with passion, sexual passion, take a few deep breaths and feel the effect: the passion will have dispersed.

Aldous Huxley's wife, Laura Huxley, has written a beautiful book — just simple devices about doing certain things. If you feel angry, Laura Huxley, says just tighten up your face. You can tighten in such a way, for example, in your closet, so that one will be able to see — or just under your desk or table; then no one will see.

A person is sitting just beyond, in front of you. You feel angry, so just tighten up your face. Go on tightening it as much as you can, and then suddenly relax and feel the difference. The anger will have gone. Or if it has not gone, do it again. Go on doing it — twice, thrice. What happens? If you tighten your face muscles and you go on tightening and tensing them, the energy that was going to become anger moves into the face.

And it is very easy to move into the face. When you are angry, how do you feel? You feel you want to beat someone with your fists. The energy is there so use it. If you can use it, it is dispersed. Your face will become relaxed, and the other person will not even be able to know that you were angry. It will appear as if nothing has happened to you. And once you know these things, you become more and more aware that energy can be transformed, diverted, checked, released, or prevented from release, or used in a different way. If you can use your energy you become the master. Then one day you may not use it at all; you may preserve it.

This exercise is not good for a Buddha — to clench the fists. This is not good for a Buddha because this is wasting energy. But this is good for you. At least the other is saved from you, and a vicious circle is saved. If you get angry he will get angry, and there is no end to it. It may disturb your whole night, and it may continue as a hangover for a week. And then, because of this hangover, you may do many things you never intended to do. Do not say that this is just physiological. You are physiological, so what can be done? You are a physique; you cannot deny that fact. Use your energy. There is no need of denying it.

If you close your eyes sometimes you may feel a certain tension gathering there or an uneasiness. That is due to certain reasons. One, when you close your eyes do not become tense about it. Let them be relaxed. You can close your eyes forcibly: then you will get tense. Then your eyes will get tired and inside you will feel uneasiness. Relaxedly, relax the face, relax the eyes, and let them be closed. I say "Let them be closed"; do not close them. Relax! Feel relaxed. Drop the eyelids and let the eyes be closed. Do not force them! If you force them, that is not good.

If you cannot feel the difference, then do this: first force them to close. Let your whole face become tense, strained, and then close your eyes forcibly. For a few moments remain strained; then relax. Then again close your eyes, relaxedly. Then you will feel the difference. This difference is to be felt, and this should be done relaxedly. Do not strain to do anything: that will tire you.

Two, when the eyes are closed and your face is relaxed, look as if everything has become dark. A deep darkness is around you. Imagine you are amidst darkness, in a deep velvety darkness, surrounded in it, in a deep dark night. Go on feeling this darkness. That will help your eyes to stop their movements. With nothing to be seen, the eyes will stop. Be in darkness.

You can do it in a dark room. Open your eyes, look at the darkness, then close them and feel the darkness. Again open your eyes, feel the darkness; close your eyes, feel it inside. Darkness is deeply relaxing. Darkness is outside and inside you; everything is dead — dark and dead. Both are related. That is why we paint death as black, dark. All over the world death is painted as black, and people fear darkness.

While doing this method, feel darkness, love darkness, and feel inside that you are going to die. Darkness is all around, and you are dying. The eyes will stop. You will feel that they cannot move: they will have stopped. In that stopping, suddenly the energy will go up and start hammering the third eye. When it starts hammering, you will hear it, you will feel it. A warmth will come, a fire will flow — a liquid fire trying to find a new path.

Do not be afraid. Help it; cooperate with it; let it move; become it. And when the third eye opens for the first time, the darkness will disappear and there will be light — light without a source. You have seen light, but always with a source. Either it comes from the sun or from the stars or from the moon or from the lamp. Some source is there.

When your energy moves through the third eye, you will come to know a light without source. It is not coming from any source: it is simply there, not coming from anywhere. That is why the

Upanishads say that God is not like the sun or like a flame. He is sourceless light. There is no source anywhere. Simply, light is there just as if it is morning. The sun has not arisen, but the night has disappeared. In between there is the dawn — the pre-dawn.

Or in the evening, the sun has set and the night has not yet come. Just in between there is the margin. That is why Hindus have chosen *"sandhya"* as a proper time for meditation. *"Sandhya"* is the in-between time — neither night nor day, just the line that divides. Why? just as a symbol. The light is there, but without a source. The same will happen inside. Light will be there without a source. Wait for it; do not imagine it.

The last thing to be remembered: you can imagine anything, so it is dangerous to tell you many things. You can imagine them. You will close the eyes and you will feel and imagine that now the third eye has opened or is opening, and you can imagine light also. Do not imagine. Resist imagination. Close your eyes. Wait! Whatsoever comes, feel it, cooperate with it, but wait. Do not jump ahead; otherwise nothing will happen. You will be having a dream — a beautiful, spiritual dream, but nothing else.

People go on coming to me. They say, "We have seen this and we have seen that," but they have imagined — because if really they have seen, they would be transformed. But they are not transformed. They are the same persons, only now a spiritual pride is added. They have some dreams — beautiful, spiritual dreams: someone seeing is Krishna playing on his flute, someone is seeing light, someone is seeing kundalini rising. They go on seeing things, and they remain the same — mediocre, stupid, dull. Nothing has happened to them, they go on relating that this is happening, that is happening, but they remain the same — angry, sad, childish, stupid. Nothing has changed.

If you really see the light which is there waiting for you to be seen through the third eye, you will be a different person. And then you need not tell anyone. People will come to know you are a different person. You cannot even hide it; it will be felt. Wherever you will move, others will feel that "something has happened to this man".

So do not imagine; wait and let things take their own course. You do the technique, and then wait. Do not jump ahead.

7
Several More "Looking" Methods

December 16, 1972, Bombay, India

SUTRAS:

9. Simply by looking into the blue sky beyond clouds, the serenity.

10. Listen while the ultimate mystical teaching is imparted. Eyes still, without winking, at once become absolutely free.

11. At the edge of a deep well look steadily into its depths until — the wondrousness.

12. Look upon some object, then slowly withdraw your sight from it, then slowly withdraw your thought from it. Then.

We live on the surface of ourselves — just at the fringe, the boundary. Senses are just on the boundary and your consciousness is way deep down at the center. We live in the senses; that is natural. But that is not the ultimate flowering. It is just the beginning. And when we are living in the senses, we are basically concerned with objects, because senses are irrelevant unless there is concern with some object of enjoyment. For example, eyes are useless unless there is something to be seen, ears are useless unless there is something to be heard, and hands are useless unless there is something to be touched.

We live in the senses: therefore, we have to live in the objects. Senses are just on the boundary of the being, in the body, and objects are not even on the boundary: they are beyond the boundary. So three points have to be understood before we enter the techniques. First, the consciousness is at the center. Second, the senses through which the consciousness moves out are at the boundary, and the objects in the world to which the consciousness moves through the senses are beyond the boundary. These three things have to be remembered: consciousness at the center, senses at the boundary and objects beyond the boundary. Try to understand it clearly, because then the techniques will be very simple.

Look at it from many directions. One: senses are just in between, just in the middle. At one side is consciousness, at another side is the world of objects. Senses are just in the middle — between the two. From the senses you can move either way. Either you can go to the objects or you can go to the center, and either way the distance is the same. From the senses, doors open both ways. Move to the objects or move to the center.

You are at the senses. That is why one of the most famous Zen Masters, Bokuju, has said that Nirvana and the world are at the same distance. So do not think that the Nirvana is very far away. The world and the Nirvana, this world and that other world, are both at the same distance.

This saying has created much confusion because we feel that Nirvana is very, very far away — that "Moksha" (Liberation), The Kingdom of God, is very, very far away. We feel that the world is just near, just here. But Bokuju says, and he says rightly, that both are at the same distance.

The world is here, and the Nirvana is also here. The world is near, and the Nirvana is also near. For Nirvana you have to move inwards, for the objects you have to move outwards. The distance is the same. From my eyes, my center is just as near as you are near me. I can see you if I move outward, I can see myself if I move inward. And we are at the doors of the senses, but, naturally, bodily needs are such that consciousness moves outwards naturally. You need food, you need water to drink, you need a house where to live. These are your bodily needs and these can only be found in the world, so quite naturally, consciousness moves through the senses toward the world. Unless you create a need which can only be fulfilled when you move inward, you will never move inward.

For example, if a child were born self-sufficient, if he didn't need any food, he would not look at his mother at all. The mother would become irrelevant, meaningless, because for the child mother is not the meaning: food is the meaning. The mother is his first food, and because the mother gives him food and satisfies a basic need without which he will die, he starts loving the mother. That love comes secondly as a shadow because the mother is fulfilling a basic need.

So those mothers who are feeding their children through bottles should not expect much love because for the child food is the need, not the mother. The mother will come into his being, enter into his being, only through food. That is why food and love are deeply related — very, very deeply related. If your love need is fulfilled, you will need less food. If your love need is not fulfilled, you will need more food. So those who love and who are loved will not gather much fat. There are other reasons also, but this is one of the most basic. They will not eat much. If love is not fulfilled, then food becomes a substitute. Then they will eat much.

For the child food is the basic need. But if a child should be born who can be self-sufficient, who does not need any food, who does not need any outward help to be alive, he will not move in the world at all. Do you think he will move? There would be no need. And unless a need is there, the energy will never move. We move outwardly not because we are sinners. We move outwardly because we have needs which can be fulfilled only through objects — objects which can be gained if we move in the world of objects.

Why do you not move inward? Because you have not yet created the need to move inward. Once the need is there, it is as easy to move inward as to move outward. What is that need? That need is concerned with religion. You cannot be religious unless that need is there. How is that need created? By what process does one become aware of a deep need which helps you move inward?

Three things are to be remembered: firstly, death. Remember, all life needs force you to move outward. If you want to move inward, death must become a basic concern; otherwise you cannot move inward. That is why it happened that persons like Buddha, who became deeply conscious of death, started moving inward. Only when you become aware of death will you create the need to look back.

Life looks outward. Unless you become aware of death, religion is meaningless for you. That is why animals have no religion. They are alive: they are as much alive as man or even more. But they cannot be conscious of death, they cannot conceive of death, they cannot see death in the future. They see that others are dying, but it never occurs to the animal mind that this death is an indication of his death also.

For the animal mind death always occurs to others. And if for you also, death is just something which happens to others, you still live in the animal mind. If you are not aware of death you have not yet become man. That is the basic difference between animal and man — because animals cannot be aware of death; only man can be. If you are not aware of death you are not a man yet, and only man creates the need to move inward.

To me "man" means awareness of death. I am not saying become afraid of death; that is not awareness. Just be aware of the fact that death is coming nearer and nearer and you have to be prepared for it.

Life has its own needs, death creates its own needs. That is why younger societies are irreligious — because younger societies are not yet aware of the phenomenon of death; it has not become a central concern for them. An older society, for example — India, one of the oldest societies in existence, is too much aware of death. Because of that awareness, deep down India is religious. So the first thing: become aware of death. Think about it, look at it, contemplate it. Do not be afraid, do not escape the fact. It is there and you cannot escape it! It has come into existence with you.

Your death is born with you; now you cannot escape it. You have hidden it in yourself. Become aware of it. The moment you become aware that you are going to die, that death is certain, your total mind will start looking in a different dimension. Then food is a basic need for the body, but not for the being, because even if you get food death will occur. Food cannot protect you from death. Food can only postpone. Food can help you to postpone. If you get a good shelter, a good house, it will not protect you from death. It will only help you to die conveniently, comfortably, and death, whether it happens comfortably or uncomfortably, is the same.

In life you may be poor or rich, but death is the great equalizer. The greatest communism is in death. Howsoever you live, it makes no difference. Death happens equally. In life, equality is impossible; in death inequality is impossible. Become aware of it. Contemplate it. And it is not only that death is certain somewhere in the future: with the idea that it is very far away, you will again not be able to contemplate it. The mind has a very small range; the focus of the mind is very small. You cannot think beyond thirty years. After thirty years there will be death. It is as if you are not going to die. Thirty years is so long, the distance is so much, it is as if death is not going to occur.

If you want to contemplate death, know another fact about it: it can occur the next moment; it is possible the very next moment. You may not be able to hear my whole sentence. I may not be able to complete it. My mother's father used to tell me that when I was born he consulted one astrologer, one of the best known astrologers of those days. The astrologer was to make my *kundali* (birth chart). But the astrologer studied it and he said, "If this child survives after seven years, only then will I make the chart. It seems impossible that he can survive for more than seven years, so it is useless. If the child is going to die in seven years it is useless to make the *kundali*. It will be of no use. And it has been my habit," the astrologer said, "that unless I am certain that the *kundali* will be useful I never make it." So he didn't make it.

Fortunately or unfortunately, I survived. Then my mother's father went to the astrologer, but he was dead. So he never could make my *kundali*. He was dead, and I have been constantly wondering about this. He was aware of the fact that this child may die, but he was not aware of the fact that he may die. He was not aware! It seems that he was absolutely unconcerned, and he was no ordinary man. But no one is concerned with his own death. Knowingly, cunningly, we are not concerned with it because it creates a fear. So I have always suspected that that astrologer might have never looked at his own *kundali;* otherwise he would have become aware.

Death is possible the very next moment, but the mind will not believe it. I say it and your mind will say, "No ! How is it possible the next moment ? It is far away." But that is a trick. If you postpone, you cannot contemplate. It must be so near that you can focus on it. And when I say that the next moment it is possible, I mean it. It can happen, and whenever it will happen it will be the next moment. Just before it, you could not have conceived that it was going to happen.

A person is dying: just a moment before he could never have thought that death is so near. It always happens in the next moment — remember. It has always happened that way, and this will be the way always. It always happens in the next moment. Bring it near so that you can focus on it. And that very focusing will help you to enter in. A new need will be created.

Secondly, you go on living. You go on creating artificial meanings and purposes for this very moment. You never think of your life as a whole, whether it has any meaning or not. You go on creating new meanings, and you pull on with those meanings. That is why a poor man lives a more meaningful life than a rich man — because a poor man has many things to get. That gives a meaning to his life. If you are really rich, it means you have everything that is possible and this world cannot offer anything to you. Then your life becomes meaningless. Now you cannot create any meaning for this moment, for this day, to help you live. That is why the richer a society, the more affluent a culture, then the more meaninglessness is felt. Poorer societies never feel meaninglessness.

A poor man is concerned with having a house. For years together he will work for it. His life has a meaning; something has to be achieved. And when he gets the house he will be happy for a few days at least, but then bigger houses are there. So he will go on moving, doing this and that, never thinking about his life as a whole, whether it has any meaning or not. He never takes life as a whole.

Just imagine that you have everything — the house, the car that you long for, and all your dreams are fulfilled. So now what? Just imagine — whatsoever you need is there; you have it. Now what? Suddenly meaning disappears. You are standing on an abyss; nothing can be done. You become meaningless. You are already meaningless, just not aware. Even if you get the whole world, then what? What is fulfilled?

Alexander was coming to India, and he met a great saint — Diogenes. Diogenes was one of the most penetrating minds ever born. He lived naked like Mahavir. He is the Mahavir of Greek civilization and culture. He left everything, renounced everything — not because through renouncing things he was going to get anything: that is not real renouncing, not authentic renunciation. If you renounce something to get something, that is a bargain. If you think that you are going to have some reservation in heaven and that is why you renounce, it is not renunciation. If you renounce the bodily pleasures to have spiritual pleasures, this is not renunciation.

Diogenes renounced everything — not because out of it he was going to get something: he renounced just to see if when he has nothing, whether there is any meaning or not. He thought that if one possesses nothing, if even then one has a meaning, a purpose, a destiny, then death cannot annihilate anything because death can annihilate only possessions — and the body is also a possession. He left everything. He had only one thing: a wooden bowl out of which to drink water. He thought this is not much of a possession. Then one day he saw a child drinking water with his hands. He immediately threw the bowl. He said, "If a child can drink water with his hands, am I more weak than a child?"

When Alexander was coming to India to win, to make a world empire, somebody informed him that just on the way, where he would be stopping, there lived a great sage who was just contrary to him. He was told, "You are going to make a world empire, and he has even thrown his bowl because he says that as he is happy without it, why carry this burden. And you say that unless the whole world becomes your empire, you cannot be happy. So he is just at the opposite pole, and it would be good if you meet him."

Alexander was fascinated. It happens that the opposite always fascinates. The opposite always fascinates; it has a deep sexual attraction. Just as man is attracted to woman or woman is attracted to man, there is the same attraction with the opposite. Alexander could not by-pass Diogenes. It was not good for him to go to Diogenes, and it was impossible that Diogenes would come to him. There was no end.

Diogenes was informed. Many, many messengers came to inform him that "The Great Alexander is passing this way. It would be good if you meet him." He said, "The Great Alexander? Who has said this to you! I think he himself. So tell your Great Alexander that he has nothing to give to me, and there is no need for him to meet me — and I am a very small man." He used to say, "Really, I am a dog, not a man at all — just a dog, so there is no need. It is below his dignity to meet this dog."

Then Alexander had to come. Diogenes is reported to have said, "I hear you are going to win the whole world, so I thought, I closed my eyes and thought, Okay! If I have won the whole world, then what? This has been my problem constantly. If I have won the whole world, then what?" It is reported that Alexander, after hearing this, became very sad. "Then what?" he said to Diogenes. "Do not talk such things. You make me very sad."

Diogenes said, "But you will become very sad when you win the whole world. What can I do? I am just imagining, and I have come to conclude that this is useless. You are after a suicidal effort. You yourself are trying to win the whole world, so then what? If you succeed, 'then what?'"

Alexander returned from Diogenes very disturbed, upset, sad. He said to his companions, "This man is very dangerous. He has shattered my dreams." And he could never forget, could never forgive Diogenes. The day he died, he remembered him again, and he said, "It may be that fellow was right. 'Then what ?' "

So the next thing is to remember always that whatsoever you are doing, whatsoever you are achieving, remember to ask, "If I succeed, then what ?" Is there any meaning in it all or is there just some artificial meaning given by you only to divide, to create an illusion around you so that you feel you are doing something worthwhile, and all the time you are really wasting life and energy, not doing anything worthwhile ! There is only one thing worthwhile: if you can become happy without any-thing — without any dependence, if you can be blissful alone — totally alone, if nothing is needed for your bliss, only then can you be blissful; otherwise you will be in misery — always in misery.

Dependence is misery, and those who depend on possessions, those who depend on accumulated knowledge, those who depend on this or that, they are helping their own misery to become accumulated more and more. So the next point to remember is to ask whether you have any meaning or whether you are just floating along without any meaning. Are you just making believe that this or that is the meaning of your existence ?

One man used to come to me. He used to say that if his son gets into college, that would be all and he would be very happy. He was a poor man, a very ordinary clerk, and that was the only dream — that his son would get into college. Then the son got into college. Now the son has become a forest official. A few months back he was here and he told me, "I am getting only 600 rupees per month. I have two children and this is my only dream — that they can get a good education; that is all. I am working hard. If they can be well educated and if I can send one of my children to some foreign country to study, that is all I ask."

His father is no more; he has died. This was his meaning in life, his purpose — to make his boy educated and well placed. Now the boy is well placed, and now the boy has the same purpose — to help his children become educated and well placed. And he will die, and those children will go on doing the same nonsense.

What is the meaning of all this ? What are you doing ? Just passing time ? Just destroying life ? Or have you got some authentic meaning which you can say makes you happy, blissful ! This is the second consideration which will turn you inward.

And thirdly: man goes on forgetting. You go on forgetting things. You were angry yesterday, and you repented it. Now you have forgotten. And if the same stimulus is given again, you will be angry again. This has been so for your whole life. You go on repeating the same things. It is said that it is very extraordinary to find a man who learns through life — very rare. Really, no one learns. If you learn, then you cannot commit the same mistake twice. But you go on committing the same thing again and again. Rather, the more you commit, the more you become prone to commit it. You are angry again and again, and again and again you repent it, and you have not learned anything.

Given the stimulus, you will be angry, and you will do the same madness, and then you will repent again: that is also part of it. And then you will again be ready to be stimulated and to be angry. The third thing: if you want to turn in, learn ! Whatsoever you are doing, learn through it. Take the essential out of it. Look back at what have you been doing with your life and your energy and your time. The same mistakes, the same foolishnesses, the same stupidities, again and again.

So you move in a wheel. However, it is not good to say that you move the wheel: rather, the wheel moves you. Mechanically, you go on and on and on. That is why in India we have called the world *"sansar"*. *Sansar* means the wheel which goes on, and you are just clinging to some spoke on it and you go on moving.

Unless you learn something about this wheel, this vicious circle, this *sansar*, unless you learn something about it, you will not leave the spoke and jump out of it. So three words, three key words: "Death": make it a constant contemplation; "meaning":

go on searching for it in your life; and "learn": learn through your life because there is no other learning. Scriptures won't give you anything.

If your own life cannot give you something, nothing can give it to you. Learn through your own life, conclude through it. What have you been doing with yourself? If you are in a wheel, jump out of it. But to know that you are in a wheel, you will have to go deep into understanding and learning. These three things will help you to turn in.

Now the techniques: *"Simply by looking into the blue sky beyond clouds, the serenity."*

That is why I said so many things — because the techniques are very easy, and you can do them and nothing will result. Then you will say, "What type of techniques are these? We can do them. They are so simple. Simply by looking into the sky, the blue sky, beyond the clouds, the serenity: one will become silent and serene — fulfilled."

You can look at the blue sky beyond the clouds and nothing will happen. Then you will say, "What type of technique is this? Shiva is not talking rationally, reasonably. He is saying anything, whatsoever comes to his mind. What kind of technique is this — 'Simply by looking into the blue sky, beyond clouds, the serenity': one will become serene!"

But if you remember, "death, meaning, learning," this technique will help you immediately to turn in: "Looking into the blue sky beyond clouds" — just looking, not thinking. The sky is infinite; it ends nowhere. Just look into it. There is no object; that is why the sky is chosen. The sky is not an object. Linguistically, it is; existentially, the sky is not an object because an object begins and ends. You can go around an object; you cannot go around the sky. You are in the sky, but you cannot go around it. So you may be the object for the sky, but the sky cannot be your object. You can look into it, but you cannot look at it, and that looking into it goes on and on: it never ends.

So look into the blue sky and go on looking. The object is infinite. There is no boundary to it. Do not think about it; do not say it is beautiful; do not say, "How lovely!" Do not appreciate the color; do not start thinking. If you start thinking, you have stopped. Now your eyes are not moving into the blue, the infinite blue. Just move, just look: do not think. Do not create words; they will become barriers. Not even "blue sky" should be said. Do not verbalize. There should be just a pure innocent look into the blue sky. It never ends. You will go on and on and on and on and suddenly, because there is no object, just a vacuum, suddenly you will become aware of yourself. Why? Because if there is any vacuum your senses become useless. Senses are only useful if there is an object.

If you are looking at a flower, then you are looking at "something": the flower is there. The sky is not there. What do we mean by a sky? That which is not there. "Sky" means the space. All objects are in the sky, but the sky is not an object. It is just the vacuum, the space, in which objects can exist. Sky itself is just pure emptiness. Look at this pure emptiness. That is why the sutra says "beyond the clouds" — because clouds are not the sky. They are objects floating in the sky. You can look at the clouds, but that will not help. Look into the blue sky — not at the stars, not at the moon, not at the clouds, but at objectlessness, emptiness. Look into it.

What will happen? In emptiness, there is no object to be grasped by the senses. Because there is no object to be grasped, clung to, senses become futile. And if you are looking into the blue sky without thinking, WITHOUT thinking, suddenly you will feel that everything has disappeared; there is nothing. In that disappearance you will become aware of yourself. Looking into this emptiness, you will become empty. Why? Because your eyes are like a mirror. Whatsoever is before them is reflected. I see you; you are sad. Then a sudden sadness enters into me. If a sad person enters into your room, you become sad. What has happened? You have looked at sadness. You are like a mirror: the sadness is reflected in you.

Someone laughs heartily: suddenly you feel a laughter coming to you also. It has become infectious. What has happened?

You are like a mirror. You are reflecting things. You look at a beautiful object: it is reflected in you; you look at an ugly object: it is reflected in you. Whatsoever you are seeing penetrates deep into you. It becomes part of your consciousness.

If you are looking into the emptiness, there is nothing to be reflected — or, only the blue infinite sky. If it is reflected, if you feel the blue infinite sky within, you will become serene, you will find serenity. That is there. And if really you can conceive of emptiness — where sky, blue, everything disappears: just at emptiness — inside also emptiness will be reflected. And in emptiness, how can you be worried, how can you be tense ?

In emptiness, how can the mind function ? It stops; it disappears. In the disappearance of the mind — the mind that is tense, worried, filled with thoughts that are relevant, irrelevant — in that disappearance of the mind, "the serenity."

One thing more. Emptiness, if reflected in, becomes desirelessness. Desire is tension. You desire and you become worried. You look at a beautiful woman: a sudden desire arises. You look at a beautiful house: you want to possess it. You look at a beautiful car just passing by your side: you want to be in it, you want to drive it. A desire has come in, and with the desire mind becomes worried: "How to get it ? What to do to get it ?" The mind becomes frustrated or hopeless or hopeful, but it is all dreaming. Many things can happen.

When desire is there, you are disturbed. The mind is shattered into fragments, and many plans, dreams, projections start; you become mad. Desire is the seed of madness.

But emptiness is not an object; it is just emptiness. When you look at emptiness, no desire arises. It cannot arise. You do not want to possess emptiness, you do not want to love emptiness, you do not want to make a house out of it. Emptiness ? You cannot do anything with it ! All movement of the mind stops; no desire arises. With the non-arising of desire, "the serenity." You become silent, serene. A sudden peace explodes in you. You have become like the sky.

Another thing: whatsoever you contemplate, you become like it. You become that because mind can take infinite forms. Whatsoever you desire, your mind takes its form. You become it. That is why a person who is just after riches, gold, after money, his mind becomes just a treasure — nothing else. Shake him, and you will feel the rupees inside — the sound of rupees, nothing else. Whatsoever you desire, you become that. So be conscious of what you are desiring because you are becoming that.

The sky is the most empty thing. It is just near you and it costs nothing, and you do not have to go somewhere — to the Himalayas or to Tibet — to find the sky. They have destroyed everything: technology has destroyed everything. But the sky is still there; you can use it. Use it before they destroy it. Any day they will destroy it. Look, penetrate into it — and the look must be a non-thinking one, remember this. Then you will feel the same sky within, the same dimension within, the same space and blueness and emptiness. That is why Shiva says, "simply": Simply by looking into the blue sky beyond clouds, the serenity.

The next technique: *"Listen while the ultimate mystical teaching is imparted. Eyes still, without winking, at once become absolutely free."*

"Listen while the ultimate mystical teaching is imparted": This is a secret method. In this esoteric tantra, the Teacher, the Master, gives you the teaching secretly, the doctrine secretly — or, the mantra secretly. When the disciple is ready, then the mantra, or the supreme secret, will be imparted, communicated to him, privately. Just in his ear it will be whispered. This technique is concerned with that whispering: "Listen while the ultimate mystical teaching is imparted."

When the Teacher has decided, the Master has decided, that now you are ready and the secret of his own experience can be communicated, when the moment has come when he can say to you that which is unsayable, then this technique has to be used. "Eyes still, without winking, at once become absolutely free." When the Guru, when the Master, is imparting his secret to you in your ear, whispering it, let your eyes be totally still:

165

no movement of the eyes. That means the mind should be quiet, thoughtless.

No winking — not even a slight movement, because that will show a disturbance within. Just become an empty ear with no movement within. The consciousness is just waiting to be impregnated, just open, receptive, passive, no activity on its own part. And when this will happen — this moment when you are totally empty, not thinking anything but just waiting, not waiting for something because then it will become thinking, not waiting for something but just waiting; when this static moment, this non-dynamic moment will happen; when everything has stopped: time is not flowing and mind is totally vacant; it becomes "no-mind". Only into a no-mind can a Teacher impart.

And he is not going to give a very long discourse: he will give just one or two or three words. In that silence those one, two or three words will penetrate to your very core, to the very center, and they will become a seed there. In this passive awareness, in this silence, "at once become absolutely free."

One can become free only by becoming free of the mind. There is no other freedom. Freedom from the mind is the only freedom. Mind is the bondage, the slavery, the servitude. So a disciple has to wait with his Master for the right moment when he will call and impart. He is not to ask, because asking means desire. He is not to expect, because expectation means conditions, desire, mind. He is just to wait. And when he will be ready, when his waiting will become total, the Master can do anything.

Sometimes the Master can do very trivial things, and the thing will happen. And, ordinarily, even if a Shiva goes on talking about 112 methods, nothing will happen because the preparation is not there. You can throw seeds on stones, but nothing will happen. The fault is not of the seeds. You can throw a seed out of season, but nothing will happen. The fault is not of the seed. The right season is needed, the right moment is needed, the right soil is needed. Only then will the seed become alive and transform.

So sometimes very trivial things work: for example, Lin-chi became Enlightened while he was just sitting on his Guru's verandah — on the verandah of his Master, and the Master came out and just laughed. He looked at Lin-chi — into his eyes — and laughed uproariously. Lin-chi started laughing, bowed down and left. But he was waiting there for six years: that verandah was his abode for six years.

The Master would come day after day, month after month, and he would not even look at him. And Lin-chi was waiting there. Then, after two years, for the first time he looked at him. Then two more years passed, and for the first time he patted him. Then Lin-chi waited and waited, and after six years, one day suddenly he came out, stared into Lin-chi's eyes, and Lin-chi must have done this technique: "Listen while the ultimate mystical teaching is imparted. Eyes still, without winking, at once become absolutely free."

The Master looked and used laughter as a medium. He was a great Master. Really, words were not needed — just laughter. Suddenly there was that laughter, and something happened in Lin-chi. He bowed down, laughed, left and told everyone that now he was no more, that he was liberated, free. He was no more: that is what liberation means. YOU are not liberated. You are liberated FROM YOURSELF.

Lin-chi used to tell how it happened. For six years he was waiting. It was a long waiting, a patient waiting. He was just waiting on the verandah, and every day the Master would come and he would wait for the right moment. When he would become ready, then the Master would do something. Just by waiting for six years, you will fall into meditation. What can you do? He might have thought for a few days about old things, but if you do not give new food every day to the mind, by and by it stops. How much can you chew again and again the same thing?

He might have been thinking about past things, and by and by, because no new stimulus was given, thinking stopped. He was not allowed to read, he was not allowed to talk, he was not allowed to move and meet anyone. He was just allowed to fulfill the basic bodily needs and wait on the verandah.

Silently he waited, day after day, day in, day out, day and night; summer would come and pass away and winter would come and pass away, and there would be rain and it would pass away: he must have forgotten time. He must have forgotten for how many days he had been there. And then one day suddenly the Master appeared, and he looked deeply into his eyes. Lin-chi's eyes must have suddenly become static, non-dynamic. This was the moment. Six years were wasted for this. There was no movement of the eyes, because a single movement and he may miss. Everything must have become silent — and then suddenly, the uproarious laughter: The Master began laughing madly. That laughter must have been heard deep down at the very core. It must have reached.

So when Lin-chi was asked, "What happened to you?" he said, "When my Master laughed, suddenly I recognized that the whole world was just a joke. In his laughter, this was the message: 'The whole world is just a joke, just a drama.' All seriousness disappeared. And if the whole world is just a joke, who is in bondage? And who needs to be free?" So Lin-chi said, "There was no bondage at all. I was thinking that I was bound, and that is why I was trying to be free, and then suddenly the Master laughed, and the bondage fell down."

Sometimes it has happened with such things, you can never conceive of how it was possible. There are many Zen stories. One Zen Master became aware when the gong was beaten. Just while he was hearing the gong beaten, the sound, something shattered in him. One Zen nun became aware, Enlightened, while she was carrying two pails of water. Suddenly the bamboo broke, and the earthen pots fell down. The sound, the breaking of the pots and the water flowing out of them, and she became Enlightened.

What happened? You can break many pots, but nothing will happen. A right moment had come. She was coming back. Her Master had said, "This night I am going to give you the secret, so go and take a bath, and bring two pails of water for me. I will take a bath and impart to you the secret for which you have been waiting." She must have felt ecstatic. The moment had come. She took a bath, filled the pots and carried them back.

It was a full-moon night, and just when she was passing from the footpath, from the river to the Ashram, suddenly the bamboo broke. And when she reached, the Master was waiting. He looked at her and he said, "Now there is no need. It has happened. Now I have nothing to convey. You have already received."

That old nun used to say, "With that bamboo breaking, something broke in me, something broke in me also. Those pails falling down, those broken, earthen pots, and I saw my body broken. I looked at the moon. Everything was silent, serene, and I became silent and serene. From that moment, I have not been, I am no more." This is what Liberation, freedom means.

The next technique: *"At the edge of a deep well look steadily into its depths until — the wondrousness."*

The techniques are similar, with a slight difference. "At the edge of a deep well look steadily into its depth until — the wondrousness": Look into a deep well. The well will be reflected in you. Forget thinking completely; stop thinking completely. Just go on looking into the depth. Now they say mind has its own depth like a well. Now in the West, they are developing depth psychology. They say mind is not just a surface. It is just a beginning. There are depths — many depths, hidden depths.

Look in a well without thinking. The depth will be reflected in you. The well will become just an outer symbol of the inner depth. And go on looking "until — the wondrousness", until you feel wonder-filled.

Do not stop before this moment. Go on looking, go on looking, go on looking, day after day, month after month. Just go to a well, look deep, with no thoughts moving in the mind. Just meditate. Just meditate in the depth: meditate the depth. Become one with it; go on meditating. One day your thoughts will not be there. Any moment it can happen. Suddenly you will feel you have the same well within you, the same depth. And then a strange, very strange, feeling will come to you: you will feel wonder-filled.

Chuang Tzu was passing though a bridge with his Teacher, Lao Tse. Lao Tse is reported to have said to Chuang Tzu, "Remain here. Go on looking down from this bridge to the river until the river stops and the bridge starts flowing. Then come to me." The river is flowing. The bridge never flows. But Chuang Tzu was given this meditation — to wait on this bridge. It is said he made a hut on the bridge and remained there. Months passed. He would just sit on the bridge, looking down for the moment when the river would stop and the bridge would flow. Then he would go to the Teacher.

One day it happened. The river stopped and the bridge started flowing. How can it happen ? If thought stops completely, then anything is possible, because, really, it is fixedness of thought which says that the river is flowing and the bridge is static. This is just relative — just relative !

Einstein says and physics says that everything is relative. You are travelling on a train, a fast train. What happens ? The trees flow by: they run by. And if the train is really smooth and you do not feel that the train is running, you are just looking through the windows, trees are moving, not the train.

Einstein has said that if in space two trains are running, or two spaceships are running side by side with the same speed, you would not be able to feel that they are moving. You can feel a moving train because you see the static things by the side. If there is nothing — for example, if the trees are also moving in the same direction with the same speed — you will feel static. Or, when a train passes in the opposite direction, your speed is double. You feel your train has become fast.

It has not become fast. It is the same train with the same speed, but a train going in the opposite direction gives you the feeling of double speed. If speed is relative, then it is just a fixedness of the mind to think that the river is flowing and the bridge is static.

Continuously meditating, meditating, meditating, Chuang Tzu came to realize that everything is relative. The river is flowing because you take the bridge as static. The bridge is also flowing deep down. Nothing is static in this world. Atoms are moving, electrons are moving, the bridge is a constant movement within. Everything is flowing; the bridge is also flowing.

Chuang Tzu must have had a glimpse of the atomic structure of the bridge. Now they say this wall which looks static is not static. Movement is there; every electron is running. But the movement is so fast you cannot see it. That is why you feel it as static.

If this fan goes on with a faster movement, faster and faster, you will not be able to see its wings, the spaces. You will not be able to see this. And if it moves with the speed of light, you will see simply one circular disc that is static. Nothing will be moving in it because eyes cannot catch that fast movement.

So Chuang Tzu must have had a glimpse of the atomic structure of the bridge. He waited and waited, and the fixed mind dissolved. Then he saw that the bridge is flowing — and the movement was so fast that the river is just static in comparison to it. He came running to Lao Tse and Lao Tse said, "Okay! Now do not ask me. The thing has happened to you." What had happened? No-mind had happened.

In this technique, "At the edge of a deep well look steadily into its depth until — the wondrousness." When you feel wonder-filled, when the mystery descends upon you, when mind is no more but simply mystery — a milieu of mystery, then you will be capable of knowing yourself.

Another technique: *"Look upon some object, then slowly withdraw your sight from it, then slowly withdraw your thought from it. Then."*

Look upon some object. Look at a flower, but remember what that look means. Look! Do not think. I need not repeat it. Always remember that "look" means look; do not think. If you think, it is not a look. Then you have contaminated everything. It must be a pure look, a simple look.

Look upon some object: look at a flower — a rose flower. Then slowly withdraw your sight from it — very slowly. The flower is there: first look at it. Drop thinking; go on looking. When you feel that now there is no thought, simply the flower is there in your mind — nothing else, now slightly move your eyes away. By and by the flower recedes, goes out of focus. But the image will remain with you. The object will have gone out of focus; you will have turned your look away. The image, the outer flower, is no more there, but it is reflected — reflected in your mirror of consciousness. It will be there! Then slowly withdraw your sight from it, then slowly withdraw your thought from it.

So first, withdraw from the outer object. Then only the inner image remains — the thought of the rose flower. Now withdraw that thought also. This is very difficult — the second part: but if the first part is done exactly as it is said, it will not be so difficult. First withdraw your mind from the object, your sight. Then close your eyes, and just as you have removed your eyesight from the object remove .yourself from the image. Withdraw yourself; become indifferent. Do not look at it inside. Just feel that you have gone away from it. Soon the image will also disappear.

First the object disappears, then the image disappears. And when the image disappears, Shiva says, "Then." Then you are left alone. In that aloneness one Realizes oneself, one comes to the center, one is thrown to the original source.

This is a very good meditation. You can do it. Take any object, but let the object remain the same every day so that the same image is created inside and you remove yourself from the same image. Images in the temples were used for this technique. Images are there, but the technique is lost. You go to a temple: this is the technique to do. Look at the statue of Mahavir or Buddha or Ram or Krishna or any: look at the statue, concentrate on it. Focus the whole mind so that the statue becomes an image inside. Then close your eyes. Remove your eyes from the statue, then close them. And then remove the image, wipe it out completely. Then you are there in your total loneliness, in your total purity, in your total innocence. Realizing that is freedom, realizing that is Truth.

8

Doubt Or Faith, Life Or Death: The Bases Of Different Paths

December 17, 1972, Bombay, India

QUESTIONS:

1. Should a "mixed type" do two different kinds of techniques?

2. As tantra is life affirmative, how can death orientation be used?

3. How can the mind be transformed only by bringing the body to a death-like state?

The first question : *"I feel that neither am I a feeling type altogether, nor am I the intellectual type. I am a mixed type. Should I do two different kinds of techniques alternatively? Please guide."*

This is a significant question. Many things will have to be understood. One — whenever you feel that you are neither the intellectual type nor the emotional type, know well that you belong to the intellectual type because confusion is part of it. The emotional type is never confused. One who belongs to the emotional type will not feel such confusion. Emotion is always total and whole. Intellect is always fragmented, divided, confused. That is the very nature of intellect. Why? Because intellect depends on doubt and emotion depends on faith. Wherever doubt is, division will be, and doubt can never be total. How can it be? The very nature of doubt is doubting. It can NEVER be total! You cannot doubt a thing totally. If you doubt a thing totally, it becomes faith.

Doubt is always confusion, and basically, when you doubt, you also doubt your doubt. You cannot be certain about it. A doubting mind cannot be even certain about doubt. So layers of confusion will be there, and each layer will be based on another layer of doubt and confusion.

The intellectual type always feels this way: the feeling will always be there that "I am nowhere, I do not belong anywhere" or "Sometimes I am here and sometimes there, sometimes this and sometimes that". But the emotional type is at ease with himself. Because trust is the base, emotion is not divided. It is whole, individual. So if you have any doubt, if you cannot feel certain to what type you belong, know well you belong to the intellectual type. Then practise techniques which are meant for the intellectual type. If you do not feel any confusion, then only do you belong to the emotional type, the feeling type.

For example, a Ramakrishna: he is a feeling type. You cannot create doubt in him; that is impossible, because a doubt can be created only when basically the doubt exists already. No one can create doubt in you if it is not already hidden there. Others can only help it to come out. They cannot create it. Neither can faith be created. That too others can help to manifest, to come out.

Your basic type cannot be changed, so it is very essential to know your basic type — because if you are doing something which doesn't suit you, fit with you, you are wasting time and energy. And you will get more and more confused because of your wrong efforts. Neither can doubt be created in you nor faith. You already have the seed of either this or that. If you have doubt, then it is better not to think of faith at all because that will be a deception and hypocrisy. If you have doubt, do not be afraid. Even doubt can lead to the Divine. You have to use it.

I will repeat, even doubt can lead to the Divine — because if your doubt can destroy the Divine, then it is stronger, more powerful than the Divine. Even doubt can be used. It can be made a technique. But do not deceive. There are persons who go on teaching that if you have doubts, you can never reach to the Divine. So what to do? Then you have to force it under, suppress it, hide it, create a false belief. But that will be only on the surface. It will never touch your soul. Deep down you will remain in doubt, and just on the surface a façade will be created of belief.

That is the difference between faith and belief. Belief is always false. Faith is a quality; belief is a concept. Faith is the quality of your mind; belief is just acquired. So those who have doubt and are afraid of it, they cling to beliefs. They say, "I believe," but they have no faith. Deep down they know their doubt. They are always afraid of it. If you touch, criticize their belief, they will immediately get angry. Why? Why the anger, this irritation? They are not irritated by you. They are irritated by their own doubt which you are helping to come up. If a man of faith is there you can criticize him; he is not going to get angry because you cannot destroy faith.

A Ramakrishna is the type, or a Chaitanya or a Meera — they are feeling types. One of the most beautiful minds of Bengal, Keshav Chandra, went to meet Ramakrishna. He went not just to meet him, but to defeat him, because Ramakrishna was just an illiterate, not a scholar at all. And Keshav Chandra was one of the greatest minds ever born on Indian soil, one of the most keen, logical intellects. It was certain that Ramakrishna would be defeated. When Keshav Chandra came, all the intellectuals of Calcutta gathered at Dakshineshwar just to see Ramakrishna defeated. Keshav Chandra started arguing, but he must have felt very awkward because Ramakrishna enjoyed his arguments very much — rather, too much. When he would propose some argument against God, Ramakrishna would start jumping, dancing.

He felt very awkward, so he said, "What are you doing? You have to answer my arguments." Ramakrishna is reported to have said, "By my seeing you, my faith is strengthened. Such an intellect is impossible without God." That is how a feeling type looks at things. "And I predict," said Ramakrishna, "that sooner or later you will be a greater devotee than me because you have a greater mind. With such a mind, how can you fight the Divine? With such a keen mind? Even a fool, an idiot like me, has reached. How can you remain without reaching?"

He was not angry, not arguing, but he defeated Keshav Chandra. Keshav Chandra touched his feet and he said, "You are the first theist I have met with whom argument is futile. Looking at your eyes, looking at you and the way you have behaved with me, this is the first glimpse for me that the Divine is possible. You are the proof without giving any proof." Rama-krishna became the proof.

The intellectual type has to proceed through doubt. Do not force any belief upon yourself; that will be deceiving yourself. You cannot deceive anyone else. You can only deceive yourself. Do not force; be authentic. If doubt is your nature, then proceed through doubt. Doubt as much as possible, and do not choose any technique which is based on faith. That is not for you. Choose some technique which is scientifically experimental. No need to believe.

There are two types of methods. One is experimental. You are not told to believe. You are told to do it, and the consequence will be the belief, the faith. A scientist cannot believe. He can take a hypothesis to work out, to experiment with. If the experiment comes out right, if the experiment proves that the hypothesis is right, then he reaches to a conclusion. Faith is achieved through experiment. So there are tecniques in these 112 techniques which do not require any faith on your part.

That is why Mahavir, Buddha, they are intellectual types, just as Ramakrishna and Chaitanya are feeling types. Because of this Buddha says that there is no need to believe in God; there is no God. He says, "Do what I say. Do not believe in me. Experiment with what I say, and if your experience proves it right then you can believe it." Buddha says, "Do not believe in me, do not believe what I say. Do not believe something because I have said it. Experiment with it, go through it, and until you achieve your own conclusion remain in doubt. Your own experience will become your faith." Mahavir said, "No need to believe in any-one — not even in the Guru, in the Teacher. Just do the technique."

Science never says to believe. It says do the experiment, go to the lab. This is for the intellectual type. Do not try faith before you do the experiment. You cannot try it. You will falsify everything. Be real unto yourself. Remain real and authentic.

Sometimes it has happened that even atheists have reached the Divine because of their truth about themselves. Mahavir is an atheist; he doesn't believe in God. Buddha is an atheist; he doesn't believe in any God. So a miracle happened with Buddha. It is said about him that he was the most godless man and the most godlike. Both — godless and godlike. He was absolutely intellectual, but he reached because he never deceived himself. He went on doing experiments. For six years continuously he was doing this experiment and that and that, and he did not believe. Unless something were proven true by experience, he would not believe it. So he would do something, and if nothing happened he would leave it.

One day he reached. Just by doubting and doubting and doubting, experimenting, a point came: a point came when nothing remained to be doubted. Without any object, the doubt fell. There was no object to doubt now. He had doubted everything, and even doubt became futile. Doubt dropped, and in that dropping he Realized. Then he realized that the doubt was not the real thing: rather, the doubter was, and you cannot doubt the doubter. The doubter is there to say, "No, this is not right."

It may not be right, it may be right, but who is it who is saying that this is not right or this is right? That source of saying is right, is true. You can say there is no God, but you cannot say, "I am not," because the moment you say "I am not" you have accepted yourself. Who is making this statement? You cannot deny yourself without at the same time recognizing yourself. That is impossible. Even to deny you have to be there. You cannot say to someone, some guest who is knocking on the door, that "I am not in the house". How can you say this? This is absurd because your saying that "I am not in the house" proves that you are there.

Buddha doubted everything, but he could not doubt himself. When everything was doubted and became useless, ultimately he was thrown to himself. And there doubt was impossible, so doubt fell. Suddenly he was awakened to his own reality, to his own source of consciousness, the very ground of consciousness.

So he was godless, but he became godlike. Really, on this earth a more godlike person has never walked. But his instinct was intellectual.

Both types of techniques are there. If you feel you are intellectual, confused, doubting, do not try faith techniques. They are not for you. Every technique is not for everyone. If you have faith, there is no need to try any other method — no need! If you have faith, then try those methods which require faith as a presupposition. But be authentic; that is basic. That is a very essential thing to remember continuously.

It is very easy to deceive — VERY easy to deceive, because we imitate. You may start imitating Ramakrishna without knowing that you are not of that type. If you imitate, you will be an imitation; nothing real will happen to you. You can imitate Buddha. This is happening every day because we are born into religions. Because of that, much nonsense continues. You cannot be born into a religion: you have to choose. Religion has nothing to do with blood, bones, birth — nothing!

Someone is born a Buddhist. He may be a feeling type, but he will follow Buddha. Then his whole life will be wasted. Someone is born an intellectual type. He may be born a Mohammedan or he may be born into a devotion cult. His life will be wasted and he will become false. The whole world is irreligious because religion is foolishly associated with birth. There is no relationship at all. You have to choose consciously, because first you have to understand your type and then you have to choose. The world will be deeply religious the day we allow everyone to choose his religion, method, technique, path.

But religion has become organizational, politically organizational. That is why the moment a child is born we force religion upon him. We condition him into a religion. The parents are afraid that he may move into another organization. Before he becomes conscious he must be destroyed, crippled, forced. Before he becomes conscious and can think about things, his mind must be conditioned so that he cannot think freely. You cannot think freely because whatsoever you think has been pre-conditioned.

I was reading Bertrand Russell. He says, "Intellectually, I conceive of Buddha as being greater than Jesus. But deep down in my heart, that is impossible: Jesus is greater than Buddha. At the most, if I force myself, then I will put them parallel, equal. Intellectually, I feel Buddha is a giant. Jesus is nothing before him."

Why this feeling? Because Bertrand Russell is himself the intellectual type, so Buddha has appeal for him, Jesus has no appeal. But the mind has been conditioned into Christianity. This is not truth because these comparisons are meaningless. They simply show something about Bertrand Russell — neither about Buddha nor about Jesus, because no comparison is possible. For someone who is of the feeling type, Jesus will look greater than Buddha. But if he is a Buddhist, if he is born a Buddhist, it will be difficult. His own mind will feel uneasy if he thinks that someone is greater than Buddha. It is difficult, impossible in a way, because whatsoever you think has been fed into you: it has been already fed.

Your mind is something like a computer. The information has been fed, evaluation has been fed. You are already based on some nonsensical concepts, traditions. You cannot throw them away easily; that is why religion is just a word. Very few people can become religious because very few people can rebel against their own conditioning. Only a revolutionary mind can become religious — a mind which can see a thing, the facts of it, and then decide what to do.

But feel your type: try to feel your type. It is not difficult. The first thing: if you feel confused, you are the intellectual type. If you feel certain, trusting, then proceed with the different techniques which require trust as a basic thing. And secondly, remember, never do both the techniques. That will create more confusion in you. Nothing is wrong; both are right. Ramakrishna is right, Buddha is right. Remember one thing: in this world, many things can lead you to Truth — many paths. There is no monopoly. Even contradictory paths, absolutely contradictory paths, can lead you to the same point.

There is no one path. On the contrary, if you go deep and Realize, you will come to know that there are as many paths as there are travellers because each individual has to proceed from the point where he is standing already. He cannot use a ready-made path. Basically, you create your path by your movement. There is no ready-made path already there. There are no highways that are ready-made. But every religion tries to force this idea, that the path is ready and you have just to travel over it. That is wrong. This inner search is more like the sky than the earth.

A bird is flying: he will leave no footprints in the sky. The sky will remain a vacuum. The bird has flown; he has not left any footprints. No bird can follow in his footprints. The sky is always empty. Another bird, any bird who has to fly, will create his own path.

Consciousness is like a sky, not like the earth. A Mahavir moves, a Buddha moves, a Meera moves, a Mohammed moves. You can see their movement, you can see their achievement, but the moment they move the path disappears. You cannot follow deadlike, you cannot imitate. You have to find your own path.

First think about your type and then choose methods. In these hundred and twelve methods, many are for the intellectual type, many are for the emotional type. But do not think that because you are a mixed type you have to follow both. That will create more confusion, and you will be divided so deeply that you may even go mad, schizophrenic; you may become split. Do not do that.

The second question : *"To know death is certain, you said yesterday. This seems to be the approach of Buddha who was life-negative. But tantra's approach is life-affirmative, not negative, so how can this death orientation be used in tantra?"*

Buddha is not really life-negative. He appears so: he appears to be life-negative because he focuses on death. To us he appears to be in love with death, but he is not. On the contrary, he is in love with eternal life. To find that life which is deathless, he focuses on death. Death is not his love. He has to focus on death just to find something which is beyond death. And Buddha says that if there is nothing beyond death, than life is futile, but only then is life futile. He never says life is futile. He says that if nothing is beyond death, then life is futile. And your life is futile, he says, because your life is not beyond death. Whatsoever you think is your life is just a part of death. You are fooled by that. You think it is life and it is nothing but death on its way.

A man is born: he is on his way to die. Whatsoever he becomes, whatsoever he achieves, possesses, nothing will help. He is moving toward death. This so-called life is moving toward death. How can we call it life ? That is Buddha's question. A life which moves toward death, how we can call it life ? Life which implies death inevitably is just hidden death, not life. It is gradual death. By and by you are dying, and you go on thinking that you are living.

Right now you feel you are living, but you are dying. Every moment you are losing life and gaining death. A tree is known by its fruits, Buddha says, so your tree of life cannot be called life because death is the fruit. A tree is known by its fruit, and if on your tree of life only fruits of death come, then you were deceived by the tree. And another thing: if a tree gives a particular fruit, it shows that that particular fruit was the seed of the tree; otherwise that particular fruit could not come out of the tree. So if life gives the fruit of death, death must have been the seed.

Let us understand it. You are born, and you think that birth is the beginning. It is not. Before this birth, you died in another life. That death was the seed of this birth, and then again, death will become the fruit. And that fruit will become the seed for another birth.

Birth leads to death, death precedes birth. So if you want to see life as it really is, it is rounded on both the sides by death. Death is the beginning and death is again the end, and life is just the illusion in between. You feel alive between two deaths.

The passage joining one death to another you call life. Buddha says this is not life. This life is *dukkha* — misery. This life is death. That is why he appears to us who are deeply "life-hypnotized", obsessed to be alive in any way, as life-negating. To us, just to be alive seems to be the end. We are so much afraid of death, that Buddha appears in love with death and that looks abnormal. He seems to be suicidal. This is what many have criticized Buddha for.

Albert Schweitzer has criticized Buddha because he feels that Buddha is obsessed with death. He is not obsessed with death. We are obsessed with life. He is simply analyzing things, finding out what are the facts. And the deeper you go, the more you will find he is right. Your life is just false, fake, overtaken by death, just a dressing. Inside there is death. Buddha focuses on death because he says, "If I can find out what death is, only then can I find out what life is. And if I can know what both death and life are, then there is a possibility that I may transcend both and know something which is beyond birth and death, beyond both." He is not negative, not life-denying, but he appears so.

Tantra appears life-affirmative, but that again is our interpretation. Neither is Buddha life-denying, nor is tantra life-affirmative. The source is the same. Buddha focuses on death, tantra focuses on life. And both are one, so wherever you want to start, start. But go so deeply that you come to know the other also.

Buddha focuses at the end — death. Tantra focuses on the beginning — life. That is why Buddha seems to be too much in love with death and tantra seems to be too much in love with sex, love, body, life. In the end there is death and in the beginning there is sex. Because tantra focuses itself on the beginning, sex becomes very important. So how to go deep and know what sex is, how to reveal the mystery of love, how to penetrate into the beginning, into the seed, so that you can go beyond: that is tantra's approach.

Buddha focuses on death, and he says to meditate deeply on death, move into it and know the whole reality of it. Both are two ends of the same thing. Sex is death, and death is very sexual.

It will be difficult to understand. There are many insects which die with their first intercourse. The first sex act, and death occurs. There is a species of spider in Africa in which the male dies in copulation. He cannot come down from the copulation. He is just on the female, and he dies there. The first copulation becomes death, and it is very horrible. At the moment of ejaculation he dies. Actually, he is not even really dead: he is still in the pangs of death. The moment the spider, the male spider, ejaculates, death starts and the female starts eating him. He never dismounts. The female starts eating him, and by the time the sexual act is finished he is half eaten.

Sex and death are so interconnected. Because of this man became afraid of sex. Those who want to live more, who are fascinated with long life, they will be always afraid of sex, and those who think that they can become immortal, *brahmacharya* (celibacy) will be their cult. No one has yet been immortal and no one can be because you are born out of sex. If you were born out of *brahmacharya*, then it could be possible. If your father and mother were celibates, then, then only, can you be immortal.

Sex has already entered with your birth. Whether you go into sex or not makes no difference: you cannot escape death. Your very being starts with sex, and sex is the beginning of death. Because of this Christians say Jesus was born from a virgin mother. Just to say that he is no mortal, no ordinary mortal, they say he was born to a virgin mother. "He is no ordinary mortal": just to say this, just to say that death has no power over him, they had to create this myth.

This is a part of a long myth. If he was born out of sex, then death would have its power over him. Then he could not escape death as with sex death enters. So they say that he was born without any sex act; he was not a sexual by-product. They say that because he was the son of a virgin mother, he could revive again — resurrect. They crucified him, but they could not kill him. He remained alive because he was not a sexual by-product.

They could not kill. If really Jesus was born out of a virgin mother, it is impossible to kill him. It is impossible to kill him! Death is impossible! When the beginning is not, how can the end be? If he was not born out of a virgin mother, then death will be the certain, inevitable end.

So the whole myth has to be maintained. If you say that he was not born out of a virgin mother, then the second part of the myth, resurrection, becomes false. If you say he resurrected, that he denied death, escaped death, that death could not kill him, that he could not be crucified really, that those who were crucifying him were deceived, that he was alive and he remained alive, then you have to maintain the first part of the myth.

I am not saying anything for or against. I am simply saying that the WHOLE myth has to be maintained. One part cannot be maintained. If sex is there before birth, then death will be there. Because of this deep association, many times many societies have become afraid sex. That fear is of death. Even if you accept sex, a certain fear remains there. Even if you move in sex, a certain fear remains there. No one allows himself a total let-go in it. The fear is there; you are on guard. You cannot go into it totally; you cannot let yourself go completely because that let-go is just like death.

Neither is tantra for your idea of life nor is Buddha against the real life. Tantra starts from one part — the beginning; Buddha starts with the end. And tantra is more scientific than Buddha, because it is always good to begin at the beginning. You are already born; death is far away. Birth has occurred; you can work on it more deeply. Death has to occur. It is still in the imagination; it is not reality to you. And when you see someone die, you never see death. You see someone dying, never the death — the process which happens to him inside. You cannot see it. It is invisible; it is individual. And the individual himself cannot say anything because the moment he goes through the process he is no more. He cannot come back; he cannot step back and tell what has happened.

So whatsoever is known about death is just inference. No one knows anything about death actually. Unless you can remember your past lives, you cannot actually know anything about death. You have died many times; that is why Buddha had to revive many techniques about remembering past lives. Because your death of this life is in the future, how can you concentrate on it ? How can you meditate on it ? It has not happened yet. It is very vague, dark, unknown. What can you do ? You can only think about it, but that thinking will also be borrowed. You will be repeating what others have said. Someone has said something about death, and you will be repeating it. How can you meditate on death ? You can see others dying, but that is not a real entry into it. You are just an outsider.

It is just as if someone is eating a sweet. You look at him, but how can you feel what is happening to him, what taste, what sweetness, what fragrance is happening to him ! What is going on in him you cannot know. You can just look at his mouth, his behaviour, or you can see the expression on his face — but this is all inference, not actual experience.

You cannot know what is happening to him unless he says something, but whatsoever he says will be words to you, and again not an experience. Buddha talked about his past deaths, but no one believed him. If I tell you something about my past deaths, deep down you will not believe it. How can you believe it ? You do not have any access to the reality of it. You are just closed at this birth, and the death of this life has not come yet. It always happens to others; it has not happened to you yet.

It is difficult to meditate on death. As a base, you will have to move into past lives. You will have to go digging into past memories. Buddha, Mahavir, they both used the technique of *jati-smaran* — the technique of going into past lives. Only then can you meditate on death.

Tantra is more scientific. It starts with life, with birth, with sex, which is a fact to you. Death is still a fiction. But, remember, the end of both is the same. They both are in search of eternal life — life which is deathless. Either transcend the beginning or transcend the end. Either jump from one pole or from another, and, remember, you can jump out of it only from a pole. You cannot jump from the middle.

If I want to jump out of this room, either I have to move to this side to the extreme or to that side to the extreme. I cannot jump out from the middle of the room because jumping is possible only from the extreme pole. And there are two extreme poles in life — birth and death. Tantra starts from birth. It is more scientific, more real. You are already in it, so you can meditate upon it. Sex is a fact, so you can meditate upon it: you can move deep within it.

Death is not a fact. A very rare mind is needed to conceive of death; a very keen intellect is needed to penetrate into the future. Rarely, it happens that a Buddha will conceive of death so deeply that the future becomes the present. But it is always for rare individuals.

Tantra can be used by anyone who has any interest, who has any desire to search in order to know what real life is. But tantra also uses death just to help you move inwards — not for you to meditate on it, not for you to jump out of it, but to help you move inwards.

Buddha also talked about birth just to make it a part of the meditation on death. The other part can be used as a help, but is not the center. Tantra says if you can think about death, your life will take a different meaning, shape and significance. Your mind will start thinking in new dimensions which without death would be difficult or even impossible. The moment you begin to feel that this life is going to end in certain death, death becomes a certainty and you cannot cling to this life. Mind starts moving beyond. That is what I was saying yesterday.

If you think about just this life, your mind will go outwards: it will go out and out and out to the objects. If you begin to look and see that death is hidden everywhere, then you cannot cling to objects. Your mind will start moving inwards.

Just the other day a young girl came to me. She is an Indian girl who fell in love with an American boy. But after she fell in love and they were just thinking and planning to get married, the boy fell ill and it was discovered, diagnosed, that he had a certain type of cancer that is incurable. Death was certain. He could be alive two or three or four years at the most. The boy tried to persuade the girl not to marry him now. He said, "Death is so certain, why waste your life with me?"

But the more he insisted (this is how the mind functions), the more the girl became adamant about wanting to marry him. This is how mind works in paradoxes. If I would have been in the place of that boy, I would have insisted on marrying. Then the girl would have escaped. Then there was no possibility of marriage. Then I would not have seen that girl again. But the boy insisted — out of his love, but out of a foolish mind, without knowing how mind functions — that she should not marry him. Anyone would have done the same, and because he was insisting the girl felt it to be a matter of conscience: she insisted to marry.

Then they got married. Now, after marriage, the girl is surrounded constantly by death. She is sad; she cannot love the boy. It is easy to die for anyone. It is very difficult to live. It is very easy to die. To be a martyr is such an easy thing. It is such an easy thing to be a martyr because it is a momentary thing: you can do it in a single moment.

If you love me and I say, "Jump out of this building," you can jump because you feel you love me. But if I say, "Okay, now live with me for thirty years," it is very difficult — VERY difficult!

You can become a martyr in a single moment. To die for someone, for something, is the easiest thing in the world; to live for something is the most arduous and difficult thing. She became a martyr, but now she has to live enclosed in death's presence. She cannot love. She cannot see the face of her husband because the moment she feels it the cancer is there, the death is there just by the corner. Any moment it can happen, so she is in constant agony.

190

What has happened? Death has become a certainty. Now life has no interest for her. Everything has dropped and has become death. She came just to meet me from America. She wants to meditate because life seems futile. Life has become equivalent to cancer, so now she has come here to ask me, "Teach me meditation. How can I move beyond life?" Unless life becomes futile you never think about moving beyond it.

I told her that apparently her marriage looks very unfortunate, but it may prove very fortunate. Everyone's husband is going to die, but it is "not certain". Everybody's wife is going to die, but it is "not certain". Death is certain; only the date is not certain. And who knows, even the date may be certain: you do not know. That is why ignorance is very blissful. She could have loved that boy if still they were ignorant; apparently nothing is wrong. But now love has become impossible, life has become impossible. Death is always there, constantly present between the two.

So I asked her, "Why are you not loving him more because he is going to die? Love him more." She said, "How can I love? We are always three; the privacy is lost. I am there and my husband is there, and between we two, the death. There is no privacy left."

Death is too much; it is impossible to live with. It can become a turning. If you can become aware of death, says tantra, use it as a turning inwards. No need to go into details about death, no need to go on contemplating about it. Do not make it an obsession. Just awareness that death is there will help you to move inwards, to be meditative.

The third question: *"How can the mind be transcended and transformed only by bringing the body to a deathlike state?"*

The mind is constantly active. While you are active meditation is impossible because meditation means a deep inactivity. You can know yourself only when everything has become still, silent and quiet. Only then, in that silence, do you happen to encounter yourself. Otherwise, in activity you are so much occupied with something or other, you cannot feel your own presence. You go on forgetting yourself. Continuously, with this or that object, you go on forgetting yourself.

"Activity" means being related with something outside. You are active because you are related with something outside, doing something outside. "Inactivity" means you have returned home; you are not doing anything. In Greek language, leisure is called "scholē". The English word "school" comes from the Greek word. "School" means leisure. You can learn something only when you are at leisure; learning happens in leisure. If you are active, doing this and that, you cannot learn.

Schools were for the leisure class — those who could afford leisure. Their children were sent to schools, to places of leisure. They are not to do anything but to learn. They were allowed total inactivity as far as the world is concerned. They were freed from all worldly activity, and then they could learn.

Similar is the phenomenon if you want to learn about your own presence: you will have to be completely inactive — COMPLETELY inactive, just being, not doing anything. All the ripples must cease, all activity must evaporate. You are simply: YOU ARE! In that moment, for the first time, you become aware of your own presence. Why? Because the presence is so subtle. Occupied with a gross object, engaged with gross activity, you cannot become aware of such a subtle presence. It is a very silent music, your presence. And you are so much filled with noise (and every type of noise is occupying you) that you cannot hear that still small voice within.

Cease being engaged in outward noises and activities. Then that still, small voice, for the first time, is heard; that soundless sound, that soundless music, is felt. You enter the subtle and leave the gross. Activity is gross; inactivity is subtle. And your presence is the most subtle thing in the world. To feel that you will have to cease; you will have to be absent from everywhere so that your total presence comes in and you can encounter yourself. That is why in many techniques it is suggested to make your body as if it is dead. It means simply being inactive like a dead man.

While you are meditating, let your body enter death. It will be imagination, but even that will help. Do not ask how imagination can help. Imagination has its own function. For example, now scientific experiments are available. You sit down. There is a doctor, and he is observing your pulse rate. Inside, you just start being angry; you imagine that you are fighting, angry. Your pulse rate will go high.

Inside, just imagine you are dying, that you are just going to die. Become silent and feel death descending. Your pulse rate will come down. The pulse rate is very physical, and you were just imagining. Imagination is not unreal. It is also real. If you can really imagine, even real death can occur. If you can really imagine, you can affect physical things.

You might have observed some display of hypnosis. Or if not, you can do this easily at home. It is not difficult; it is very easy. Use your child as the medium. If the child is a girl, it is better than using a boy, because a boy is more doubting than a girl and a boy is always in a fighting mood instead of a cooperative mood. A boy means that — a fighting mood.

Cooperation is needed. Just tell the child to relax, and go on suggesting, "You are going into a deep trance, going into a deep trance, going into a deep trance, falling asleep. Your eyelids are becoming heavy, heavy, heavier." And use a monotonous voice: "Heavier, heavier, heavier." Let your voice be monotonous, as if you are also becoming sleepy.

Within five minutes the child will be fast asleep. This is not ordinary sleep. This is a hypnotic trance. It is basically, qualitatively different from sleep, because now the child can hear only your voice. There is nothing else that he can hear or she can hear. If someone else talks, the child is deaf. If you talk (the person who has hypnotized him), he can still hear: he will follow your orders.

Try to do some experiments. Say to the child, "This is a burning hot coal that I am putting in your hand. You will be burned." Put any ordinary thing in the child's hand — a piece of stone that is cold with nothing hot about it. The child will throw it immediately because the mind has the suggestion that it is a burning coal, hot, and that his or her hand is going to be burned. He will throw it. He will scream as if something hot has touched.

But a miracle happens. Really, you will come to know that his hand is burned. What is happening? There was no possibility of burning by a cold stone, but the child is burned exactly as if there was a burning coal put in his hand. It was just imagination. That is why those who have penetrated the human mind, they say that imagination is a fact as real as anything. Imagination is not JUST imagination, because it results into actual fact.

Do this experiment: Fall down on the ground, lie still, and feel you are going to die. The body is becoming dead. By and by you will feel a heaviness coming over the body. The whole body will become a dead weight, a lead weight. Tell yourself that "Even if I want to remove my hand from the position where it is, I cannot move it". Then try to remove it, and you will not be able to do so. Now the imagination is working.

In this state where you feel the body has become a dead weight, you can cut yourself off from the world of activity easily. That is why this is suggested. You can now become inactive because you are dead. Now you can feel that everything has died and the bridge from you to the world is broken. The body is the bridge. If the body is dead, you cannot do anything. Can you do anything without the body? You cannot do anything without the body.

Any activity is through the body. Mind can think about it but cannot do it. You have become impotent; you cannot do anything. You are inside, the world is outside, the vehicle is dead and the bridge is broken. In this state of the body being dead and the bridge being broken, your energy will start moving inwards because there is no way to move out. The outer way is closed and blocked, so now move inwards. See yourself standing at the heart center; look within at the details of the body. You will feel very strange when for the first time you can look from within your own body.

Tantra, yoga, ayurveda, all the old physiologies, all the old physiological doctrines, their work was revealed and made known through such inner meditative techniques. Modern physiology is known through dissection, but ancient physiology was known through meditation, not dissection. And now there is a school, a school of very avant-garde medical thinkers who say that when you dissect a body and come to know something, you come to know something which is dead — and whatsoever is inferred from a dead part is irrelevant to a live body.

They may be right. If you take my blood out and then examine it, you are examining dead blood. It is not the same blood which was in me. Outwardly it is the same, but in me it was a live process, a live current, alive, part of a mechanism, of an organic whole. Now it is dead. It is as if you pull my eyes out and then examine them. When they were with me I was behind them and in them. Now they are dead stones, and whatsoever you come to know about those eyes is not about my eyes, because the basic, essential part is missing: I am not there. Those eyes were part of a big whole.

Their whole quality consisted in being part of a big whole. Now they are independent, not part of anything. The pattern is lost, the live contact is lost. All the traditions of yoga and tantra say that unless you can come to know the living body, your knowledge is false. But how to come to know the living body? There is only one way: if you enter in yourself and move within to see the details of the body. A different world was revealed through these techniques, an alive world.

So the first thing: Be centered at the heart, look around at your body, move. Two things will happen. One: you will not feel now that you are the body. You cannot feel it. You are the observer — one who is aware, alert, looking at, not being looked at. For the first time body will become just a clothing; you will be different from it. And the second thing: immediately you will feel, "I cannot die."

This will seem strange, using a method, an imaginary method, of death, and then coming to the deathless point. You will come to know suddenly, "I cannot die." You have seen others who had died. What had happened to them ? Their bodies became dead; that is why you inferred they are dead. Now you can see that the whole body is lying dead, and you are alive.

So bodily death is not your death. The body dies, and you move on. And if you persist in this technique, the time is not very far away when you can come out of your body and look at your body from without, at your body lying dead just before you. It is not very difficult. Once you experience this, you will not be the same person again. You will be reborn; you will become *dwij* — twice born. Now a new life starts.

I was telling you yesterday about one astrologer who had promised to work on my life's birth chart. He died before it, so his son had to prepare the chart. But he was also puzzled. He said, "It is almost certain that this child is going to die at the age of twenty-one. Every seven years he will have to face death." So my parents, my family, were always worried about my death. Whenever I would come to the seven-year age barrier, they would become afraid, and he was right. At the age of seven I survived, but I had a deep experience of death — not of my own, but of the death of my maternal grandfather. And I was so much attached to him that his death appeared to be my own death.

In my own childish way I imitated his death. I would not eat for three days continuously, would not drink water, because I felt that if I did so it would be a betrayal. I loved him so much, he loved me so much, that when he was alive I was never allowed to go to my parents. I was with my maternal grandfather. He said, "When I die, only then can you go." He lived in a very small village, so I couldn't go to any school because there was no school. He would never leave me, but then the time came when he died. He was part and parcel of me. I had grown with his presence, his love.

When he died I felt that it would be a betrayal to eat. Now I didn't want to live. It was childish, but through it something very deep happened. For three days I remained lying down: I would not come out of the bed. I said, "When he is dead, I do not want to live." I survived, but those three days became a death experience. I died in a way, and I came to realize (now I can tell about it, though at that time it was just a vague experience), I came to feel, that death is impossible. This was a feeling.

Then at the age of fourteen, my family again became disturbed that I would die. I again survived, but then I again tried consciously. I said to them, "If death is going to occur as the astrologer has said, then it is better to be prepared. And why give a chance to death? Why should I not go and meet it half the way? If I am going to die, then it is better to die consciously."

So I took leave from my school for seven days. I went to my principal and I told him, "I am going to die." He said, "What nonsense you are talking! Are you committing suicide? What do you mean you are going to die!"

I told him about the astrologer's prediction that the posssibility of death would confront me every seven years. I told him, "I am going into retreat for seven days to wait for death. If death comes, it is good to meet it consciously so that it becomes an experience."

I went to a temple just outside of my village. I arranged with the priest that he should not disturb me. It was a very lonely, unvisited temple — old, in ruins. No one ever came to it. So I told him, "I will remain in the temple. You just give me once a day something to eat and something to drink, and the whole day I will be lying there waiting for death."

For seven days I waited. Those seven days became a beautiful experience. Death never came, but on my part I tried in every way to be dead. Strange, weird feelings happened. Many things happened, but the basic note was this — that if you are feeling you are going to die you become calm and silent. Nothing creates any worry then because all worries are concerned with life. Life is the base of all worries. When you are going to die anyway one day, why worry?

I was lying there. On the third or fourth day a snake entered the temple. It was in view; I was seeing the snake. But there was no fear. Suddenly I felt very strange. The snake was coming nearer and nearer, and I felt very strange. There was no fear. So I thought, "When death is coming, it may be coming through this snake, so why be afraid? Wait!"

The snake crossed over me and went away. Fear had disappeared. If you accept death, there is no fear. If you cling to life, then every fear is there.

Many times flies came around me. They would fly around, they would creep over me, on my face. Sometimes I felt irritated and would have liked to throw them off, but then I thought, "What is the use? Sooner or later I am going to die, and then no one will be here to protect the body. So let them have their way."

The moment I decided to let them have their way, the irritation disappeared. They were still on the body, but it was as if I was not concerned. They were as if moving, as if creeping on someone else's body. There was a distance immediately. If you accept death, a distance is created. Life moves far away with all its worries, irritations, everything.

I died in a way, but I came to know that something deathless is there. Once you accept death totally you become aware of it.

Then again, at the age of twenty-one, my family was waiting. So I told them, "Why do you go on waiting? Do not wait. Now I am not going to die."

Physically, someday I will die, of course. However, this prediction of the astrologer helped me very much because he made me aware very early about death. Continuously, I could meditate and could accept that it was coming.

Death can be used for deep meditation because then you become inactive. Energy is released from the world; it can move inwards. That is why a deathlike posture is suggested, Use life, use death, for discovering that which is beyond both.

9
From Words To Pure Sounds To Being

January 22, 1973, Bombay, India

SUTRAS:

13.   Devi, imagine the Sanskrit letters in these honey-filled foci of awareness, first as letters, then more subtly as sounds, then as most subtle feeling. Then, leaving them aside, be free.

14.   Bathe in the center of sound, as in the continuous sound of a waterfall. Or, by putting the fingers in the ears, hear the sound of sounds.

Jean Paul Sartre wrote an autobiography. He has called it "Words". The name is very meaningful. It is the autobiography of every man — words and words and words: you are filled with words, and this process of words continues the whole day, even in the mind. When you are sleeping, you are still filled with words, thoughts.

The mind is just an accumulation of words, and everyone is too much obsessed with the mind. That is why Self-knowledge becomes more and more impossible. The Self is beyond the words, or behind the words, or below the words, or above the words, but never in the words. You exist not in the mind, but just below the mind, behind the mind, above the mind — never in the mind. You are focused in the mind, but you are not there. Standing out, you are focused in the mind. Because of this constant focusing, you have become identified with the mind. You think you are the mind: this is the only problem, the basic problem, and unless you are aware that you are not the mind, nothing meaningful can happen to you. You will live in misery.

This identification is the misery. It is as if one is identified with a shadow. Then the whole life becomes false. Your whole life is false, and the basic error is that you are identified with the mind. You think you are the mind: this is the ignorance. You can develop your mind, but in that way ignorance will not be dissolved. You can become very intelligent, you can become very talented, you may even become a genius. But if the identification with the mind is there, you remain basically mediocre because you remain identified with a false shadow. How does it happen ? Unless you understand the mechanism of how it happens you cannot go beyond it, and all the techniques of meditation are nothing but processes to go beyond: to go beyond the mind.

Meditation techniques are not against the world. They are against the mind — and not really against the mind, but against identification. How are you identified with the mind ? What is the mechanism that works ? Mind is a need — a great need, particularly for humanity, and that is the basic difference between man and the animal. Man thinks, and he has used thinking as a weapon for his struggle to survive. He could survive because he could think; otherwise he is more helpless than any animal, more weak than any animal. Physically, it was impossible for him to survive. He could survive because he could think. Because of thinking, he has become the master of the earth.

If thinking has been so deeply helpful, then it becomes easy to understand why man has become identified with the mind. You are not so much identified with the body. Of course, religions go on saying do not be identified with the body, but no one is really identified with the body — no one ! You are identified with the mind, not with the body, and this identification with the body is not so fatal as the identification with the mind — because body is more real. Body exists: it is related to existence very deeply. Mind is just a shadow.

Identification with the mind is more subtle than identification with the body, but we are identified with the mind because mind has been such a great help to survive — not only against animals, against nature, but against other human beings also. If you have a keen intelligent mind, you will win against other human beings as well. You will succeed, you will become more rich, because you will be more calculating and more cunning.

Against other human beings also, mind is the weapon. That is why we are so much identified — remember this.

Against death, against disease, against nature, against animals, against other human beings, mind has been your protection, your security. And mind has done much, so obviously we think of ourselves as mind. If someone says that your body is ill you do not feel offended, but if someone says that your mind seems ill you do feel offended. If your body is ill, you do not feel offended. Why? You are not identified with the body. But if your mind is ill and someone says you are psychologically ill, mentally ill, insane, you feel offended. Now this is something about "you", not about your body.

You behave with the body as if it is a vehicle, something you possess, but not so with the mind. With the mind, you are the mind; with the body, you are the master. The body is a slave: you possess it. This mind has created a division in your being also, and that is the second basic cause of why we are identified with it. You think not only about external things: you think about internal things also. For example, the body has many instincts. You think about your instincts also. Not only do you think: you fight against your instincts. So there is a constant internal fight. There is sex: the mind fights it or tries to mould it in its own way. It suppresses it, perverts it, tries to control it.

The mind is fighting inside also. That fight creates a division between you and your body. And, really, you start thinking that the body is something inimical — not a friend, because the body goes on doing things which the mind is against. The body is not going to listen to the mind, so the mind feels offended, defeated. It attacks the body, and then a division is created. And you are always identified with the mind, never with the body.

The mind is your ego. That is your "I". If the body feels sexuality, you can divide. You can say, "This is the body, not me. I am against it. I have taken a vow of celibacy. I am against it. This is the body; this is not me." Then who are you? The mind which has taken a vow? This mind is your ego, and you go against the body because the body is very much ego-destroying. Whatsoever you decide, it never listens.

All the ascetic nonsense was born because of this: the body will not listen. The body is nature; the body is a part of the Cosmic Whole. The body has its own Laws. Those Laws are unconscious; it functions according to them. The mind tries to create its own Laws over and above the body. Then a conflict is created. Then the mind starts fighting the body. Then the mind will starve the body. It will try in every way to kill it.

That is what has happened in the past: so-called religious people have been really mad against their bodies. And whatsoever they were doing was less for God and more against body. Really, to be in search of God became synonymous with being against the body. Religious persons took the attitude of "kill the body, destroy the body. The body is the enemy." And, really, this is not a religious attitude, but one of the most irreligious attitudes because it is most egoistical. This is the ego: the ego feels offended.

You decide not to be angry again, and then anger comes: your ego feels defeated. Your decision is thrown overboard, and the anger comes. And when the anger comes you feel this is coming from the body. You decide against sex and sex comes: you feel offended, so you try to punish the body. Asceticism is nothing but punishment — punishing your own body in order to force it to behave according to the ego.

This mind, this process of thinking, this ego, is just a fragment of your whole total being, and this fragment is trying to be the sovereign. This is not possible. The fragment cannot be the sovereign. It is going to fail; that is why there is so much frustration in life. You can never succeed: you are trying the impossible. The fragment cannot be the sovereign. The whole is bigger and the whole is more powerful.

It is just as if a branch of a tree tries to control the whole tree, even the roots. How can a branch control the whole tree and how can it force the roots to follow it ? That is impossible. Whatsoever it thinks, it is mad: the branch has gone mad. It may go on thinking and dreaming, conceiving of some future where the tree will be following it, but it is not possible. It is not possible! It will have to follow the tree because it is alive only because of the tree and the roots. And the roots were before it. The roots are the source of it also.

Your mind is just a fragment of your body; it cannot control it. The very effort to control the body will create frustration and failure. And the whole humanity has been a failure because of this. Everyone is suffering, in conflict, in anguish, in anxiety, trembling because the impossible is being tried. But the ego always likes to try the impossible. The possible has no challenge for it; the impossible is a challenge. And if the impossible can be done, then the ego will feel very good because this "cannot" be done. You can try to do it, but you will waste your life trying that which "cannot be done".

Because of this inner effort to become the master, you are identified with the mind. Who would like to be identified with a slave: Who would like to be identified with the unconscious? It is useless. The unconscious is negated because it cannot be grasped. And with the unconscious there is no ego: you cannot feel "I".

Try to understand it in this way: when sex overpowers you, really, you cannot say "I". It is as if something greater than you has taken possession — as if you are in a strong current. You are no more; something else is driving you. That is why these words are meaningful: that is why those who are against sex will say, "Sex possessed me."

Anger possesses you, hunger possesses you: they are something greater than you, and you are just taken by the current. It is fearful. It is VERY fearful because then you are no more. It is a sort of death. That is why you are so much against sex: it is a sort of death. And those who are against sex will always be afraid of death, and those who are not against sex and can flow in it easily, spontaneously, will never be afraid of death. See the association: those who are against sex will always be afraid of death and those who are afraid of death will be always against sex.

Those who are afraid of death will always create theories of immortality; they will always think about life beyond death. Those who think about immortality will always be against sex. These are alternatives. Sex gives you a fear. What is the fear? You are no more in it. Something greater than you possesses you. You are thrown overboard; you are no more in it.

So even those who are not against sex, they too never move really deep into sex. They never move; they are always holding back trying to remain there, not allowing themselves, not ready for a let-go. That is why orgasm, such a natural thing, has become so impossible for man and woman. A deep orgasm means you have been in something which was greater than you. You have been in something where you were not: the ego was not.

The ego is struggling to control everything, and mind helps you. In the effort you become identified with the mind, and this identification is the misery: it is a false shadow. Mind is a very utilitarian instrument. You have to use it, but do not become identified with it. It is a good instrument — necessary. Use it! But do not feel that YOU are the mind, because once you start feeling you are the mind you cannot use it. The mind starts using you. Then you are simply drifting with the mind.

All the meditation techniques are an effort to give you a glimpse of that which is not mind. So how to go beyond it? How to leave it and look at it even for a single moment?

The first technique: *"Devi, imagine the Sanskrit letters in these honey-filled foci of awareness, first as letters, then more subtle as sounds, then as most subtle feeling. Then, leaving them aside, be free."*

Words are sounds. Thoughts are words in sequence, in logical sequence, in a particular pattern. Sound is basic. With sound words are created, and then with words thoughts are created, and then with thoughts religion and philosophy, everything. Deep down is the sound.

This technique uses a reverse process. Shiva says, "Devi, imagine the Sanskrit letters in these honey-filled foci of awareness, first as letters, then more subtly as sounds, then as most subtle feeling. Then, leaving them aside, be free."

We live in philosophy. One is a Hindu, one is a Mohammedan, one is a Christian, or something else. We live in philosophies, systems of thought, and they have become so important that we can die for them. Man can die for words, for mere words. Someone calls his absolute, his conception of the absolute, a lie, and someone calls Ram or someone calls Christ or something else a lie: then man can fight for a mere word; he can kill the other. The word has become so important. This is nonsense, but this is history and this is how we are still behaving.

A single word can create such a disturbance in you, you are ready to kill or to die for it. We live in philosophies, systems of thoughts. What are philosophies ? Thoughts arranged logically, systematically, in a pattern. And what are thoughts ? Words arranged in a system, meaningfully. And what are words ? Sounds upon which it is agreed that they mean either this or that. So sounds are basic. They are the basic structure of the mind. Philosophies are the peak, but the bricks by which the whole structure is raised are sounds.

What is wrong ? A sound is just a sound, and the meaning is given by us, agreed upon by us. Otherwise it has no meaning. The meaning is invested by us, projected by us; otherwise, "Ram" is just a sound: it is meaningless. We give it a meaning, and then we create a system of thoughts around it. Then this word becomes very significant. Then we make a philosophy around it. Then you can do something — anything. You can die or you can live for it. If someone insults this sound "Ram", you can become infuriated. And what is this ? Just an agreement, a legal agreement, that this word means this. No word means anything in itself. It is simply a sound.

This sutra says to go in a reverse order — back. Come to the sounds, then, more basic than sounds, a feeling is somewhere hidden. This has to be understood. Man uses words. Words mean sounds with meanings that are agreed upon. But animals, birds, use sounds without any linguistic meaning. They do not have any language, but they use sounds with feeling. A bird is singing: it has a "feeling" meaning in it. It is indicating something. It may be a call for the partner, for the beloved, or it may be a call for the mother, or the child may be feeling hungry and just showing his distress. It is indicating a feeling.

Above sounds there are words, thoughts, philosophies; below sounds are feelings. And unless you can get below feelings, you cannot get below mind. The whole world is filled with sounds. Only the human world is filled with words, and even a child who cannot use language uses sounds. Really, the whole language developed because of particular sounds that every child is using all over the world.

For example, in any language, the word "mother" is somehow related with "ma". It may be "mater", it may be "muhter", it may be "mata", it may be "ma", anything, but somewhere it is related with the sound "ma" — in all the languages more or less. The child can utter "ma" most easily. The first sound which the child can utter is "ma". Then the whole structure is based on this "ma". A child utters "ma" because it is the first sound which is easy for the child to utter. This is the case anywhere, in any part of the world, in any time. Just because of the structure of the throat and the body, "ma" is the easiest sound to utter.

And the "mother" is the nearest and the first person who is meaningful. So the first sound becomes associated with the first person who is meaningful, and then "mother," "mater," "mata," "ma," all the other words, are derived. But when the child for the first time utters "ma", he has no linguistic meaning for it, but a feeling is there. And because of that feeling the word becomes associated with the mother. That feeling is more basic than the sound.

So this sutra says first to imagine the Sanskrit letters. Any language will do. Because Shiva was talking to Parvati, that is why he said Sanskrit. You can use English or Latin or Arabic:

any language will do. Sanskrit has no meaning except in that Shiva was talking to Parvati in Sanskrit. It is not that Sanskrit is something superior to any other language — no! Any language will do. First feel inside, in your consciousness, "the honey-filled foci of awareness" filled with letters — A, B, C, D — any letters of any language. This can be done, and it is a very beautiful exercise. If you want to do it, close your eyes and just see your consciousness inside being filled with words.

Think of consciousness as a blackboard, then "A, B, C": visualize all the words, all the letters. Visualize these letters first as letters. "A": look at it as "A" as you write it. Write it with consciousness and look at it. Then, by and by, forget the letter "A" and just remember the sound of "A" — just the sound. Start with visualization — because eyes are predominant for us. Ears are not so predominant. We are eye-oriented, eye-centered. Again, the same is the reason: because eyes help us to survive more than anything else, our consciousness is 90% in the eyes.

Conceive of yourself without eyes, and your whole life goes dead. Then a very minor part remains. So first visualize. Use your eyes inwards and see the letters. Letters are more related to ears than eyes because they are sounds, but for us, because we are reading, reading, reading, they have become associated with eyes. Basically, they are associated with ears. They are "sounds". Start with the eyes, then forget the eyes by and by. Then move away from the eyes to the ears. First imagine them as letters, then see them, hear them "more subtly as sounds, then as most subtle feeling". And this is a very beautiful exercise.

When you say "A", what is the feeling? You may not have been aware of it. What is the feeling inside you? Whenever you use any sound, what type of feeling comes into existence? We are so feelingless that we have simply forgotten. When you see a sound, what happens inside? You go on using it and the sound is even forgotten. You go on seeing it. If I say "A", you will see it first. In your mind, "A" will become visible: you will visualize it. When I say "A", do not visualize it. Just hear the sound "A", and then go and find out what happens in your feeling center. Does nothing happen ?

Shiva says move from letters to sounds, uncover sounds through the letters. Uncover sounds, and then, through the sounds also, uncover feeling. Be aware of how you feel. They say that man has now become very insensitive: he is the most insensitive animal on earth now.

I was reading about one poet, a German poet, and he relates one incident of his childhood. His father was a lover of horses, so he had many horses at the house — a big stable, but he would not allow this child to go to the stable. He was afraid, as the child was very small. But when the father would not be there the child would sometimes steal into the stable where he had a friend — a horse. Whenever the child would go in, the horse would make some sounds.

And the poet has written, "Then I also started making sounds with the horse because there was no possibility of language. Then, in communication with that horse, for the first time I became aware of sounds — their beauty, their feeling."

You cannot be aware with a man because he is dead. A horse is more alive, and he has no language. He has pure sound. He is filled with his heart, not with his mind. So that poet remembers, "For the first time, I became aware of the beauty of sounds and their meaning. This was not the meaning of words and thoughts, but a meaning filled with feeling." If someone else was there, the horse would not make those sounds, so the child could understand that the horse meant, "Do not come in. Someone is here and your father will be angry."

When there was no one, the horse would make the sounds, meaning, "Come in. There is no one." So the poet remembers that "It was a conspiracy, and he helped me very much: that horse helped me very much. And when I would go and love that horse, he would move his head in a particular way when he liked it. When he did not like it, he would not move his head in that way. When he liked it, then it was a different thing. He would express it. When he was not in the mood, then he would not move in a certain way." And this poet says, "This continued for years. I would go and love that horse, and that love was so deep that I never felt any affinity with anyone else so deeply.

"Then suddenly, one day when I was stroking his neck and he was moving and enjoying it ecstatically, suddenly for the first time I became aware of my hand, that I am stroking, and the horse stopped: now he would not move his neck." And that poet says, "Then for years I tried and tried, but there was no response. The horse would not reply. Only later on did I become aware that because I became aware of my hand and myself, the ego came in and the communication broke. I couldn't recapture again that communication with the horse."

What happened? That was a feeling communication. The moment ego comes, words come, language comes, thought comes, then the layer is changed completely. Now you are above sounds, then you were below sounds. Those sounds are feelings, and the horse could understand feelings. He couldn't understand, so the communication broke. The poet tried and tried, but no effort is successful because even your effort is the effort of your ego.

He tried to forget his hand, but he couldn't forget. How can you forget? It is impossible. And the more you try to forget it, the more you remember. So you cannot forget anything with effort. Effort will simply emphasize the memory more. The poet says, "I became fixed with my hand; I couldn't move that horse. I would go up to my hand, and then there was no movement. The energy would not move into that horse and he became aware of this."

How did the horse become aware? If I suddenly start speaking some other language, then the communication is broken. Then you will not be able to understand me. And if this language were not known to you, you would suddenly stop because now the language is unknown to you. Thus, the horse stopped.

Every child lives with feeling. First comes sounds, then those sounds are filled with feeling. Then comes words, then thoughts, then systems, religions, philosophies. Then one goes farther and farther away from the center of feeling.

This sutra says come back, come down — down to the state of feeling. Feeling is not your mind: that is why you are afraid of feeling. You are not afraid of reasoning. You are always afraid of feeling because feeling can lead you into chaos. You will not be able to control. With reason, the control is with you. With the head, you are the head. Below the head you lose the head. You cannot control, you cannot manipulate. Feelings are just below the mind — a link between you and the mind.

Then Shiva says, "Then, leaving them aside, be free." Then leave the feelings. And, remember, only when you come to the deepest layer of feelings can you leave them. You cannot leave them just now. You are not at the deepest layer of feelings, so how can you leave them? First you have to leave philosophies — Hinduism, Christianity, Mohammedanism. First you have to leave philosophies, then you have to leave thoughts, then you have to leave words, then you have to leave letters, then you have to leave sounds, then you have to leave feelings, because you can leave only that which is there. You can leave that step upon which you are standing; you cannot leave that step upon which you are not standing.

You are standing at the step of philosophy, the farthest away one. That is why I insist so much that unless you leave religion you cannot be religious.

This sutra, this technique, can be done very easily. The problem is not with feelings: the problem is with words. You can leave a feeling, just as you can undress — as you can go out of your dress. You can throw your clothes; you can leave feelings simply in that way. But right now you cannot do it, and if you try to do it, it will be impossible. So go step by step.

Imagine letters — A, B, C, D — then change your emphasis from the written letter to the heart sound. You are moving deep. The surface is left behind. You are sinking deep. Then feel what feeling comes through a particular sound.

Because of such techniques, India could discover many things. It could discover sounds which are related to particular feelings. Because of that science, mantra was developed. A particular sound is related to a particular feeling, and it is never otherwise. So if you create that sound within you, that feeling will be created. You can use any sound, and then the related feeling will be created around you. That sound creates the space to be filled by a particular feeling.

So do not use any mantra. That is not good; it may be dangerous for you. Unless you know, or unless a person who gives you the mantra knows what particular sound creates what particular feeling, and whether that feeling is needed by you or not, do not use any mantra. There are mantras which are known as death mantras. If you repeat them, you will die within a particular time. Within a particular period you will die, because they create in you a longing for death.

Freud says that man has two basic instincts: libido (Eros) — the will to live, the will to be, the will to continue, the will to exist, and Thanatos — the will to die. There are particular sounds which, if you repeat them, the will to die will come to you. Then you would like just to drop into death. There are sounds which give you Eros — which give you more libido, which give you more lust to live, to be. If you create those sounds within you, that particular feeling will overwhelm you. There are sounds which give you a feeling of peace and silence, there are sounds which create anger. So do not use any sound, any mantra, unless it is given to you by a Master who knows what is going to happen through it.

When you come down from sounds, you will be aware. Each sound has its counterpart in feeling. Each sound has a corresponding feeling that goes with it, just hidden behind it. Then move to the feeling: forget the sound. Move to the feeling! It is difficult to explain, but you can do it. And there were techniques for this. Particularly in Zen, there were techniques. A particular mantra would be given to a seeker. If he was doing it rightly inside, the Master could know from the face. The Master could know from the face whether he was doing it rightly or not because a particular feeling would come. If the sound is created, then the feeling is bound to come. And it will be on the face. You cannot deceive a Master. He knows by your face what is happening inside.

Dozo was a great Master, but he himself was very much disturbed when he was a disciple about how his Master came to know what he was experiencing. And the Zen Master moved with his staff and he would hit you immediately. If something goes wrong with your sound inside, he will hit you immediately. So Dozo asked, "But how do you know? And you hit me exactly in the right moment. How do you know?" The face expresses the feeling, not the sound. The sound cannot be expressed by the face, but the face is bound to express the feeling. And the deeper you move, the more your face becomes flexible to express, the more liquid. It immediately shows what is happening inside. This face which you have right now will drop because this is a mask: this is not a face. When you move in, masks fall down because they are not needed. Masks are needed for others.

Because of this, old Masters insisted on moving away from the world. This was so that you could move away from the mask easily. Otherwise others will be there, and because of them you have to carry masks. You do not love your wife or your husband, but you have to carry a mask — a loving face, a false loving face. The moment you enter the house, you arrange the face: you come in and you start laughing. This is not your face.

Zen Masters insisted that first one should attain the original face because with the original face everything becomes easy. Then the Master can simply know what is happening. So Enlightenment was never reported. If some seeker attained Enlightenment, he was not to report to the Master that he has attained because the Master will simply know. He will tell the disciple. No disciple was allowed to tell the Master, "I have attained." There was no need. The face will show, the eyes will show, the very movement, the walking, will show. Whatsoever he does, every gesture will show that he has attained.

When you move from sounds to feelings, you move in a very, very ecstatic world, an existential world. You move away from the mind. Feelings are "existential"; that is what the word means: you feel them. You cannot see them, you cannot hear them: you simply feel them.

When you come to this point, you can take the jump. This is the last step. Now you are standing near an abyss; you can jump.

And if you jump from the feelings, you jump into yourself. That abyss is you — not as your mind, but as your Being; not as the accumulated past, but as the present, here and now.

You move from the mind to the Being, and the bridge, the link, is the feeling. But to come to the feeling you will have to leave many things — words, sounds, the whole deception of mind. "Then, leaving them aside, be free": You ARE free. This saying, "be free," doesn't mean that you have to do something to be free. "Then, leaving them aside, be free" means you are free! Being is freedom; mind is bondage. That is why it is said that mind is the *sansar*, the world.

Do not leave the world: you cannot leave it. If the mind is there, you will create another. The seed is there. You can move to a mountain, to a retreat, but you move with the mind: you cannot leave it here. The world moves with you; you will create another world. Even in your retreat you will start creating it again because the seed is there. You will create relationship again. It may be with the trees, it may be with birds, but you will create relationship again, you will create expectation again, and you will go on spreading the net because the seed is there. You will again be in a "world".

Mind is the world, and you cannot leave mind anywhere. You can leave it only if you move within. So the only Himalaya is this; no other Himalaya will do. If you move within from words to feelings and from feelings to Being, you are moving away from the world. And once you know this inner abyss of Being, then you can be anywhere, even in hell. Then it makes no difference. It makes no difference then! If you are without mind hell cannot enter you, and with mind ONLY hell enters. The mind is the door to hell.

"Leaving them aside, be free": but do not try directly with feelings. You will not succeed. Try first with words. But with words also you will not succeed if you do not leave philosophies, if you do not leave thoughts. Words are just units — and if you give significance to words you cannot leave them.

Know well that language is a human creation. It is utilitarian, necessary, and the meanings we have given to sounds are our own creation. If you can understand this well, then you can move easily. If someone is saying something against the Koran, or against the Vedas, how do you feel? Can you laugh about it or does something clench within you? Can you laugh about it? Someone is insulting the Gita or someone is saying some derogatory thing against Krishna or Ram or Christ: can you laugh? Can you see through the words — that these are mere words? No, you will be hurt. Then it is difficult to lose words.

See that words are just words — noises with agreed-upon meanings and nothing else: be convinced of it. And it is so! First become detached from words. If there is detachment from words, then you can understand that these are just noises. It is just like in the military where they use numbers. One soldier is "number 101": he can become identified with 101. And if someone says something derogatory against number 101, he will feel insulted, he will start fighting. And 101 is just a number, but he has become identified with it. Your name is just a number, just an index number. Things will be difficult otherwise, so we have labelled you. That is just a label; any other label may do the same work. But it is not just a label for you: it has gone deep. Your name has become the center of your ego.

So they say, the so-called wise ones, they say, "Live for your name. See that your name remains pure. Respectability of your name must be there, and even if you die your name will live." It was never there. It is just a code number. You will die and the name will live. When you yourself cannot live, how is the label going to live?

Look at words — at their futility, their meaninglessness, and do not become attached to any word. Only then can you do this technique.

The second technique : *"Bathe in the center of sound, as in the continuous sound of a waterfall, or by putting the fingers in the ears, hear the sound of sounds."*

This technique can be done in many ways. One way is to begin by just sitting anywhere. Sounds are always present. It may be in a market or it may be at a Himalayan retreat: sounds are there. Sit silently, and with sound there is something very special. Whenever there are sounds, you are the center. All the sounds come to you from everywhere, from all directions.

With sight, with eyes, this is not so. Sight is linear. I see you, then there is a line toward you. Sound is circular; it is not linear. So all sounds come in circles and you are the center. Wherever you are, you are always the center of sound. For sounds, you are always "God", the center of the whole universe. Every sound is coming to you, moving toward you, in circles.

This technique says, "Bathe in the center of sound." Wherever you are, if you are doing this technique, just close your eyes and feel the whole universe filled with sound. Feel as if every sound is moving toward you and you are the center. Even this feeling that you are the center will give you a very deep peace. The whole universe becomes the circumference, and you are the center and everything is moving toward you, falling toward you.

"As in the continuous sound of a waterfall": If you are sitting by the side of a waterfall, close your eyes, and feel the sound all around you, falling on you, from every side, creating a center in you from every side. Why this emphasis on feeling that you are in the center ? Because in the center there is no sound. The center is without sound; that is why you can hear sounds. Otherwise, you could not hear them. A sound cannot hear another sound. Because you are soundless at your center, you can hear sounds. The center is absolute silence: that is why you can hear sounds entering you, coming to you, penetrating you, encircling you.

If you can find out where is the center, where is the field in you to where every sound is coming, suddenly sounds will disappear and you will enter into soundlessness. If you can feel a center where every sound is being heard, there is a sudden transference of consciousness. One moment you will be hearing the whole world filled with sounds, and another moment your awareness will suddenly turn in and you will hear the soundlessness, the center of life. Once you have heard that, then no sound can disturb you.

It comes to you, but it never reaches you. It comes to you, it is always coming to you, but it NEVER reaches you. There is a point where no sound enters. That point is YOU. Do it in a market: there is no other place like a market. It is so much filled with sounds — mad sounds. But do not start thinking about sounds — that this is good and this is bad and this is disturbing and that is very beautiful and harmonious. You are not supposed to think about sounds. You are simply supposed to think of the center. You are not supposed to think about every sound moving toward you — whether it is good, bad, beautiful. You are just to remember that you are the center and all the sounds are moving toward you — every sound, whatsoever the sort.

In the beginning you will get dizzy because you are not hearing whatsoever is happening all around. Your hearing is selective, your seeing is selective. And now scientific research says that 98% is not heard, only 2% of whatsoever is happening all around you. Otherwise, if you hear 100% you will go mad. If you hear 100% of what is happening all around you, you will simply go mad. Previously, it was thought that senses are the doors, the openings, the windows, to get the outside to enter inside. Now they say they are not doors, and they are not so open as it was thought: they are NOT open. Rather, they are like a watchman, a censor, who is every moment watching what is to be allowed in or not.

Only 2% happenings are allowed in, and you are already mad with 2%. With 100% — with a total opening, with everything opened, every sense opened, functioning, and everything being allowed in — you will go mad. So when you try this method, in the first step you will feel a dizziness coming to you. Do not be afraid. Go on feeling the center — and allow everything, whatsoever is happening. Allow everything to move in.

Relax yourself, relax your watch towers — your senses, relax everything; let everything enter you. You have become more liquid, open: everything is coming to you, coming to you; all sounds are moving toward you. Then move with the sounds, and come to the center where you hear them.

Sounds are not heard in the ears. They are NOT heard in the ears; ears cannot hear them. They only do a transmission work, and in the transmission they cut out much which is useless for you. They choose, they select, and then those Sanskrit sounds enter you. Now find out within where is your center. Ears are not the center. You are hearing from somewhere deep down. The ears are simply sending you selected sounds. Where are you? Where is your center?

If you are working with sounds, then sooner or later you will be surprised — because the center is not in the head. The center is NOT in the head! It appears in the head because you have never heard sounds: you have heard words. With words the head is the center; with sounds it is not the center. That is why in Japan they say that man thinks not through the head, but through the belly — because they were working with sounds since long.

You have seen in every temple a gong. That was placed there to create sounds around a seeker. Someone would be meditating, and the gong would be sounded or a bell would be rung. The very disturbance seems to have been created by the sound of the bell. Someone is meditating, and this bell or gong seems disturbing. This seems disturbing! In a temple, every visitor who comes will hit the gong or ring the bell. With someone meditating there, this would seem to be a constant disturbance. It is not — because the person is waiting for this sound.

So every visitor is helping. Again and again the bell is hit, and the sound is created and the meditator again enters himself. He looks at the center where this sound goes deep. There is one hit at the bell: the visitor has done that. Now the second hit will be inside the meditator, somewhere inside. Where is it ? The sound always hits at the belly, at the navel, never in the head. If it hits in the head, you can understand well that it is not sound: it is words. Then you have started thinking about the sound. Then the purity is lost.

Now there is much research about children who are in the womb. They are also hit by sounds and they react to sounds. They cannot react to language. They have no head yet, they have no reasoning, and they do not yet know language and the agreed-upon customs of the society. They do not know about language, but they hear the sounds. And every sound affects the child more than it affects the mother, because the mother cannot hear the sounds: she hears the words. And we are creating mad sounds, chaotic, and those sounds are hitting the unborn children. They will be born mad. You have already disturbed them too much.

Even plants are affected by sound. They grow more if some musical sounds are created around them; they grow less if some chaotic sounds are created around them. You can help them to grow. You can help them in many ways through sounds.

Now they say that because of traffic noises which are not harmonious and cannot be, man is going mentally insane and it seems that the limit has come. If it grows more, then there is no hope for man. These sounds are hitting you continuously — but if you think about them they will hit your head, and that is not the center: the navel is the center. So do not think about them.

All the mantras are meaningless sounds. And if some Guru or some Master says that "this" is the meaning of this mantra, then it is not a mantra at all. A mantra needs to be, of necessity, without meaning; it has no meaning. It has some work, but no meaning. It has to do something within you, but it has no meaning because it has just to be a pure sound within you. That is why we evolved the mantra "AUM". It is meaningless; it has no meaning. It is just a pure sound. If this pure sound is created within you, if you can create it within, then too the same technique can be used.

"Bathe in the center of sound, as in the continuous sound of a waterfall. Or, by putting the fingers in the ears, hear the sound of sounds." You can create the sound just by using your finger, or with anything which closes your ears forcibly. Then a certain sound is heard. What is that sound and why do you hear it when the ears are closed, when the ears are plugged ?

It happened in America, in a certain city, that a train was passing through a certain neighbourhood. This was in the middle of the night, somewhere about two a.m. A new line was inaugurated and the train stopped moving from the old route. But a very strange phenomenon happened. The people who were living in that neighbourhood where the train had stopped moving complained to the police that at about two a.m. something mysterious was heard. And there were so many reports, so it had to be investigated what was the matter. Strange sounds were heard at about two. They were never heard when the train was passing; the people had become accustomed to the train. Now suddenly the train stopped. They were waiting to hear it in their sleep; they had become accustomed to it, conditioned. They were waiting, and the sound was not there: absence was heard, and this absence was something new. They felt uneasy about it. They couldn't sleep.

So for the first time it was understood that if you are constantly hearing something and it stops, you will hear the absence of it. So do not think that you will simply not hear it. You will hear the absence: the negative part of it will be heard. It just as if I look at you, and then, if I close my eyes, I see your negative. If you look at the window and then close your eyes you will see the negative of the window, and the negative can be so forceful that if you suddenly look at the wall the negative will be projected on the wall. You will be seeing the negative.

Just as there are negatives of photographs, there are negative sounds. Not only can the eyes see the negative: the ears can even hear the negative. So when you close your ears, you hear the negative world of sounds. All the sounds have stopped. Suddenly a new sound is heard. This sound is the absence of sound. A gap has come in. You are missing something, and then you hear this absence. "Or, by putting the fingers in the ears, hear the sound of sounds": That negative sound is known as the sound of sounds — because it is not really a sound, but its absence. Or, it is a natural sound because it is not created by anything.

All sounds are created. The sound you hear when you close your ears is not a created sound. If the whole world becomes absolutely silent, then you will hear the silence also. Pascal is reported to have said, "The moment I think about the infinite cosmos, the silence of the infinite cosmos makes me very much afraid." The silence makes him afraid because sounds are only on the earth. Sounds need atmosphere. The moment you go beyond the earth's atmosphere there are no sounds — only absolute silence. That silence you can create even on earth, if you close both of your ears completely. You are on the earth, but you have moved. You have dropped below sounds.

Astronauts are being trained for many things, and one thing is to be in the silence. They have to be trained in silent chambers so that they become accustomed to soundlessness; otherwise they will go mad. Many problems face them, and this is one of the deepest problems: how to be away from the human world of sounds. Then you become isolated.

If you are lost in the forest and you hear a certain word, you may not know the source but you are less afraid: someone is there. Someone is there! You are not alone! In soundlessness, you are alone. Just in a crowd, if you close both of your ears totally and move in, you are alone: the crowd has disappeared because it was through sounds that you could know others were here.

"Putting the fingers in the ears, hear the sound of sounds": This absence of sound is a very subtle experience. What will it give to you? The moment there are no sounds, you fall back upon yourself. With sounds we move away; with sounds we move to the other. Try to understand this: with sounds we are related to the other, we communicate with the other.

So even a blind man is not in so much difficulty as a man who cannot speak, who is dumb. Observe a person who is dumb: he looks inhuman. A blind man never looks inhuman, but a dumb person looks inhuman; the face gives a feeling of something which is not human. And a dumb person is in more difficulty than a blind man. With the blind man the problem is that he cannot see, but he can communicate. He can become a part of a greater humanity, he can become a part of society, of a family: he can love, he can speak. A dumb man is suddenly out of society. He cannot speak, he cannot communicate, he cannot express.

Try to imagine yourself in an air-conditioned glass room, a soundproof room. No sound can enter you and you cannot scream; you cannot do anything to express. Then the sound will not go out. In a glass room you can see the whole world moving around you, but neither can you speak to them nor can they speak to you. You will feel hopelessly frustrated, and the whole thing will become a nightmare.

A dumb man is in a nightmare continuously. Without communicating he is not part of humanity. Without expression he cannot flower. He cannot reach anyone and no one can reach him. He is with you and far away, and the gap is unbridgeable.

If sound is the vehicle to move to the other, then soundlessness becomes the vehicle to move to oneself. With sound you communicate with the other, with soundlessness you fall down into your own abyss, into yourself. That is why so many techniques use soundlessness to move within.

Become absolutely dumb and deaf — even if only for a few moments. And you cannot go anywhere else than to yourself: so suddenly you will find that you are standing within; no movement will be possible. That is why silence was practised so much. In it, all the bridges for moving to the other are broken.

Gurdjieff used to give long silent periods to his disciples, and then he would insist that not only is language not to be used, but there was to be no communication, no gesture — neither with the eyes nor the hands. No communication was to be used. Silence means NO communication. So he would force the group to live in a house — twenty, thirty or forty people in one bungalow, in one house — and then he would say, "Remain here in this house as if you are alone. You cannot go out." Forty persons would be there, and he would say, "Move in the house, live in the house, as if you are alone. No communication! Do not recognize that the other is, not even by the eyes. Move completely as if you are the only person residing in the house. With three months of living in this way, absolutely dumb and deaf with no possibility of communicating, there would be no possibility to move away.

I do not know whether you have observed or not, but in society those who can talk much become prominent; those who can communicate their thoughts easily become leaders — religious, political, literary, any type. Those who can communicate their thoughts, those who can talk efficiently, they become leaders. Why? They can reach more people, they can reach to greater masses.

Have you ever heard of any dumb person becoming a leader? You can find a blind man becoming a leader; there is no problem. And sometimes he may become a great leader, because all that his eyes are not doing, all those energies, will be transferred to his ears. But a dumb man cannot become a leader in any walk of life. He cannot communicate, he cannot become social.

Society is a language. Language is basic to social existence — to relationship. If you leave language, you are alone. The world may be filled with millions, but if you lose language you are alone.

Meher Baba stayed continuously for forty years in silence. What was he doing in silence? Really, you cannot do anything in silence because every act is somehow related with others. Even in imagination, if you do something you will have to imagine others; you cannot do it alone. If you are absolutely alone, action becomes impossible. Even the imagination to act becomes impossible. Acting is related to others. If you drop language inside, all doing drops. You are, but you are not doing anything.

Meher Baba would tell his disciples (by writing a note), "Now, on this particular date, I am going to break my silence," and then he would not break it. This continued for forty years, and then he died in silence. What was the problem? Why should he say, "Now, this year, on this day, on this date, I am going to speak"? And why should he postpone it again? What was happening inside? Why would he not keep his promise?

Once you know silence for such a long time, you cannot fall back to sounds again; it becomes impossible. There is a rule, and he didn't follow the rule so he could not come back. There is a rule that one should not remain silent more than three years. Once you cross the limit, you cannot come back to the world of sounds. You may try, but it is impossible. It is easy to move from sounds to silence, but it is very difficult to move from silence to sounds. Beyond three years many things simply become impossible. The mechanism cannot function the same way again. It has to be used continuously. At the most, one can remain silent for three years. Beyond that, if you remain silent the mechanism which can produce sounds and words cannot be used again: it becomes dead.

Secondly, the person becomes so much silent remaining with himself alone that it will now be a misery to communicate. Then to say something to someone will be like talking to a wall, because the person who has remained silent for such a long time knows that you cannot understand whatsoever he is saying. Regardless of what he is saying, he knows he is not saying that which he wants to say. The whole thing has gone. After such a deep silence, he cannot move again to the world of sounds.

So Meher Baba tried and tried, but he couldn't bring himself to speak again. And he wanted to say something and he had something worth saying, but the mechanism and the movements necessary to come back to a lower realm was impossible. Thus, he died without saying what he wanted to say.

It will be helpful to understand this: whatsoever you are doing, always go on doing the opposite with it. Go on changing to the opposite always. Remain silent for a few hours, then talk. Do not become fixed in anything. You will be more alive and more moving. Do meditation for a few days, and then stop suddenly and do everything that can create tension in you. Then move again to meditation.

Go on moving between the opposites. You will be more alive and dynamic. Do not get fixed. Once you get fixed, you will not be able to move to the other extreme. And the ability to move to the other means life. If you are not able to move, you are already dead. This movement is very good.

Gurdjieff advised his disciples for sudden changes. He would insist on fasting and then he would say, "Now eat as much as you can." Then suddenly he would say, "Go on a fast." Then again he would say, "Start eating." He would say, "Be awake for a few days and nights continuously, then fall asleep for a few nights. This movement between the polar opposites gives you a dynamism, an aliveness.

"Or, by putting the fingers in the ears, hear the sound of sounds": In one technique two opposites have been shown. "Bathe in the center of sound, as in the continuous sound of a waterfall": this is one extreme, "Or, by putting the fingers in the ears, hear the sound of sounds": this is another extreme. One part is to hear the sounds coming to your center, another part is to stop all sounds and feel the soundless center. These both have been given in one technique for a special purpose — so that you can move from one to another.

The "Or" is not a choice to do this or that. Do both! That is why both have been given in one technique. First do one for a few months, then do the other for a few months. You will be more alive, and you will know two extremes. And if you can move to the two extremes easily, you can remain young forever. Those who get fixed to any extreme become old and die.

10
Tantra: An Acceptance Of The Peaks And The Valleys

January 23, 1973, Bombay, India

QUESTIONS:

1. *Should we consciously channelize and regulate instincts?*
2. *How to turn horrible noises into positive sound?*

The first question: *"Last night you discussed the censorship and suppression by the conscious mind of the unconscious instincts, and you said that the unconscious instincts belong to the animal heritage in man's evolution. Then is it not good to channelize and regulate them according to the intelligence, discrimination and art of living which belong to the conscious mind?"*

Man is an animal, but not only an animal: he is more also. But that "more" cannot deny the animal. It has to absorb it. Man IS more than an animal, but the animal cannot be denied. It has to be absorbed creatively. You cannot leave it aside: it is in your very roots. The animal cannot be left aside; you have to use it creatively. So the first thing to remember is not to be negative about your animal heritage. Once you start thinking in negative terms you will become destructive to yourself, because you are 99% animal.

If you create a division, you are fighting a losing battle; you cannot win. The result of your fight will be quite the opposite, because 99% is animal. Only 1% of the mind is conscious. This 1% cannot win against the 99%. It is going to be defeated. That is why there is so much frustration — because everyone is defeated by his own animal. You can never succeed. Of necessity you are going to be a failure, because that 1% cannot succeed against the 99% and that 1% really cannot even be divided from the 99%.

It is just like a flower: it cannot go against the roots; it cannot go against the whole tree. And while you are against your animal heritage you are being fed by it. You are alive because of it. If your animal dies this moment you will die immediately. Your mind exists as a flower; your animal heritage is the whole tree. Do not be negative. That is suicidal, and if you are divided against yourself you can never attain anything which is blissful.

You are creating a hell, and the hell is nowhere else but in a divided personality: in the split personality is the hell. And hell is not something geographical: hell is psychological and heaven also. The personality which is a whole, one unit with no inner division and conflict, is heaven.

So the first thing I would like to say is do not be negative. Do not divide yourself, do not go against yourself, do not become two. The animal that is there is not something bad. The animal is very much potential in you. That is your past and that is also your future, because much is hidden in it. Uncover it, develop, it, allow it to grow and go beyond it, but do not fight with it: that is one of the basic teachings of tantra.

Other traditions are divisive. They divide you; they create a fight within you. Tantra is not divisive; it doesn't believe in fight. Tantra is absolutely positive; it doesn't believe in saying "no". Tantra believes in saying "yes" — yes to the whole life. And through "yes" the transformation happens and through "no" only disturbance: no transformation is possible. Against whom are you fighting? Against yourself? How can you win? And your major part is from the animal, so the major part will win. So those who fight, they are creating their own defeats. If you want to be defeated, fight. If you want to win, do not fight.

Victory needs knowledge, not fight. Fight is a subtle violence. And this is strange, but this has happened: those who talk about non-violence to others are very much violent against themselves. There are teachings and traditions which say do not be violent to anyone, but those same teachings are very much violent as far as you are concerned inwardly. They teach you to be violent with yourself but not to be violent with others.

All types of asceticism, renunciation, negative attitudes, life-denying philosophies, they are based on maintaining a violent attitude toward yourself. They tell you to be violent with yourself.

Tantra is absolutely non-violent — ABSOLUTELY NON-VIOLENT! Tantra says if you cannot be non-violent with yourself you cannot be non-violent with anyone else; that is impossible. A person who is violent to himself will be violent to everyone. In his non-violence also he will be just hiding his violence. Aggression can be turned against yourself, but that aggressive attitude is destructive.

But that doesn't mean to remain the animal which you are. The moment you accept your heritage, the moment you accept your past, the future becomes an opening. Through acceptance is the opening. The animal is the past; it need not be the future. There is no need to go against the past, and you cannot go. Use it creatively.

What can be done to use it creatively ? The first thing is to be profoundly aware of its existence. Those who fight, they are not aware of it. Because they are afraid, they push the animal behind, they push the animal into the unconscious. Really, there need not be any unconscious. Because of suppression the unconscious is created. You feel many things within which you condemn without understanding them. A man who understands condemns nothing; there is no need. He can even use poison as a medicine because he knows. Everything can be used creatively. Because you do not know, in ignorance poison is poison. With wisdom it can become the elixir.

The person who is fighting against his sex, anger, greed, against the animal, what will he do ? He will suppress. Fighting is suppression. He will push down anger, sex, greed, hatred, jealousy. He will push everything down somewhere — underground, and he will create a false structure above ground. The structure will be false because energies have not been transformed which can make it real. The structure is phony. Underground the real energies have been repressed. Those real energies will always remain there working: any moment they can explode. You are just sitting on a volcano, and every moment that volcano is trying to erupt. If it does, your structure will be shaken.

Whatsoever you have built in the name of religion, morality, culture, is a phony structure that is above — just a false façade. Underground the real man is hiding. So your animal is not very far away; your façade is just skin deep. Someone insults you, and the gentleman disappears and the animal comes out. The gentleman is just skin deep; the volcano is just near. Any moment it can be brought out, and when it comes out, your intelligence, your morality, your religion, your so-called being above animal things, simply disappear. When the real asserts, the false disappears. Only when the real goes again back into the underground does the false come again.

When you are angry, where is your mind, where is your consciousness, where is your morality, where are your vows that you have taken so many times that now "I am not going to be angry again"? When anger comes they all simply disappear. When anger has moved again to its cave, its underground cave, you start repenting. Those phony fellows have gathered again. They start talking, condemning, and planning for the future, and again in the future the same will happen: when anger will come the shadows will disappear.

Your consciousness right now is just a shadow. It is not a real thing; it has no substance in it. You can take a vow of *brahmacharya* — of celibacy. It makes no difference to your sex instinct. It simply goes underground, and when it comes up, your vows of *brahmacharya*, of celibacy, will prove to be made of just very dreamlike stuff. They cannot face the real thing.

So these are the two attitudes: you can either suppress sex. Then you will never go beyond it. Or, you can use your sex energy in a creative way — not saying "no" to it, but giving it a deep "yes"; not forcing it to the underground, but creating a structure above ground with it. Then you will be a real man. It will be difficult, obviously. That is why we choose the easier path. It is easier to have a false structure because nothing is needed. Only one thing is needed: to deceive yourself; that is all. If you can deceive yourself, you can create a false structure very easily. Nothing will change really, but you will go on thinking that everything has changed. This is easy — to create an illusion.

To create reality is a difficult task. It is arduous. But it is worthwhile, because once you have created something with real energies your structure cannot be shattered. If sex is above ground, then you can create something out of it — for example, love. Take love, for example: if sex is transformed, it becomes love; if it is suppressed, it becomes hatred.

You become afraid of love if you suppress sex. A person who has suppressed sex will always be afraid of love because the moment love comes sex will follow. Love is the soul and sex is the body, so love cannot be allowed to happen because then sex will follow. It will be just somewhere near the corner. So a person who has suppressed sex cannot be loving. He may show, he may pretend that he is very loving, but he cannot be because he is so afraid. He cannot touch you with a loving hand because the fear is there. The loving hand can any moment turn to be a sexual touch. So he will be afraid; he will not allow you to touch him.

He may create many justifications for it, but the real thing is fear — fear of the instinct which he has repressed. And he will be filled with hatred, because any energy that is repressed reverses itself and goes to its original nature.

Sex moves easily toward love; that is a natural flow. If you prevent it, if you create hindrances to its path, it will become hatred. So your so-called saints and so-called moral teachers, if you look deep into them you will find them filled with hatred, and that is bound to be; it is natural. Sex is hidden there. Any moment it can erupt. They are sitting on a dangerous volcano. If you push down energies, you are just postponing a task. And the more it is postponed, the more difficult it will be.

Tantra says create your life with real energies — and real energies are all animal energies. But when I say "animal", there is no condemnation in it. The word "animal" for me is not condemnatory as it is for you. The animal is beautiful in itself. The animal in itself is nothing to be condemned. The animal within you is pure energy, moving according to natural laws. It has been asked, "What should we do consciously? Should we not channelize? Should we not control?" No! Your consciousness is not to control, your consciousness is not to channelize.

Your consciousness can do only one thing: your consciousness is to understand, and understanding in itself becomes the transformation.

Tantra will say understand sex; do not try to channelize it. If you do not understand it every effort is bound to be a failure, and harmful. So do not do anything. First understand it, and through understanding the path will be revealed. You are not to force your energies on that path. Through understanding you come to know the law, just like in science. What are you doing in science? You come to understand a law; a natural mystery is revealed. Once the natural mystery is revealed, you can use the energy creatively.

Without your knowing the inherent law, all efforts are doomed. So tantra says understand the animal, because in the animal is hidden the potential for your future. Really, it can be said that in the animal God is hidden. The animal is your past, God is your future — but the future is hidden in your past, in seed form. Understand whatsoever your natural forces are. Accept them; understand them. Your mind is not to be there mastering; it is not there to control them and fight with them. It is there to understand them.

Really, if you understand them, you are using your mind rightly. Understand sex, understand anger, understand greed. Be alert; try to find out their ways — how they work, what are their functions. And be constantly aware of the very movement of these animal instincts within. If you can be conscious of these animal instincts, there will be no division. You will not have an unconscious mind. If you can move with these instincts deep within, you will have only a conscious mind; there will be no unconscious.

The unconscious is there because of repression. You have closed the major part of your being to consciousness because you are afraid. You cannot look at your own reality. You are so afraid that you have already moved out of the house. You just live on the verandah; you never go in because the fear is there. If you come face to face with yourself, all your imagination, all your illusions about yourself, will fall down.

You think yourself to be a saint, you think yourself to be a religious person, you think yourself to be this and that. If you face your reality, all these illusions will evaporate. And everyone has created an image of himself. That image is false, but we cling to the image and this clinging becomes the barrier toward moving within.

So the first thing is to accept the animal. It is there, and nothing is wrong about it. It is your past, and you cannot deny your past. You can only use it. If you are wise, you will use it and create a better future out of it. If you are foolish you will fight with it, and through fight the future will be destroyed. Fight with a seed, and you will destroy it. Use it, give it soil, help it, protect it so that the seed becomes a tree, an alive tree, and the future blossoms through it.

The animal is your seed. Do not fight with it. Tantra has no condemnation against it, simply love for it because whole future is hidden in it. Know it well, and then you can use it and you can thank it.

I have heard that when St. Francis died, when he was just on his dying bed, suddenly he opened his eyes and thanked his body before going to his death. Before moving to the other world, he thanked his body. He said, "Much was hidden in you, and you helped me so much. And I was so ignorant, and there were times when I even fought with you. There were times I even thought about you in inimical terms. But you were always a friend, and it is because of you I could move to such a state of consciousness."

This thanksgiving to the body is beautiful. But St. Francis could understand it only in the end. Tantra says try to understand in the beginning. When you will be dying, even if you thank your body it is of no use. It is a treasury of hidden forces, of mysterious possibilities. Tantra says that in your body is the whole cosmos in miniature: it is just a miniature of the whole cosmos. Do not fight with it. What is your sex if the body is a miniature? If really this is so, that your body is the whole cosmos in miniature, what is sex? That which is creation in the cosmos is sex in you. Throughout the whole cosmos, creation is going on every moment: that is sex in you. And if there is so much force in it, it is because you are needed to be a creator.

If sex is so powerful, it only means for tantra that you cannot be allowed to be non-creative. You must create. If you cannot create something greater, then at least create life. If you cannot create anything better than you, then at least create someone who will replace you when you die. Sex is so forceful because the cosmos cannot allow you to be non-creative, and you are fighting with it. Use it.

There is no need to use sex only in reproduction. In every creation sex is used. That is why a great poet, a great painter, may not feel so much of an urge of sex. But the reason is not that he is a saint. The reason is simply this, that he is creating something greater and the need is fulfilled.

A great musician is creating music. No father can feel so much fulfilled as a musician feels when great music is created, and no son can give so much happiness to any parent as a great piece of music can give to the musician or great poetry can give to the poet. Because he is creating on higher realms, nature relieves him of lower creation. The energy has moved higher. Tantra says do not fight with the energy: allow the energy to move higher. And there are many realms of higher movement and many dimensions.

Buddha is neither a painter, nor a musician, nor a poet, but he has gone beyond sex. What has happened to him? The highest creation is the creation of oneself. The highest creation is the creation of total consciousness within, creation of a whole within, oneness. That is the peak, the Himalayan peak. Buddha is at that peak; he has created himself. When you move in sex, you create your body; the replica is created. When you move higher, you create spirit, you create soul. Or, if you allow me the expression, you create God.

You have heard that God created the world, but I say to you that you have the potentiality to create God — and unless you create him you will never be fulfilled. So do not think that God is in the beginning. Rather, it will be better to think that God is in the end. God is not the cause of the world, but the teleology, the very end, the very peak. If you flower in your totality, you will become a god. That is why we call Buddha a god — and he never believed in God. This is very paradoxical. He never believed in God; he is one of the deepest atheistic minds ever born. He says there is no God, but we called Buddha himself Divine.

H. G. Wells has written that Gautam Buddha was the most godless man and the most god-like. What had happened to this Gautam ? He had created, he had given birth, to the highest peak, the highest possibility. The Ultimate had happened in him; then he was no longer creating anything. There was no need. It would have been futile for Buddha to write poetry, it would have been futile for him to paint. It would have been childish. He created the Ultimate; he had given himself a new birth. The old has been used completely to give birth to the new. And because it is an ultimate phenomenon the whole past had been used. The past disappeared, the animal was no more, because when the tree is born the seed disappears. The seed cannot be there.

Jesus says unless a seed of corn falls to the ground and dies, nothing can happen. Once the seed falls to the ground and dies, the new life bubbles up through it. The death is only a death of the seed, of the past, but there can be no death without "giving birth to a birth". Something new will come out of it.

Tantra says do not try to control. Who are you to control and how will you be able to control? Your control will be just illusory. Try to understand. Try to understand the inner nature, the phenomenon, the dynamics of the energies, and that understanding will automatically change you. Change is not an effort. If change is an effort, then it cannot create bliss.

Bliss never happens through effort. Effort is always tension creating; it gives anguish. Effort is always ugly because you are forcing something. Understanding is not an effort. It is beautiful: it is a spontaneous happening. Do not control. If you try, you will be a faiure, and you will destroy yourself. Understand! Let understanding be the only law, the only *sadhana* (spiritual practice). Leave everything to understanding. If understanding cannot do anything, then it cannot be done so forget it. All that can be done can be done through understanding.

So tantra says accept things because acceptance will be needed to understand. You cannot understand anything if you deny. If I hate you, I cannot look into your eyes, I cannot see your face. I will turn about; I will escape from you; I will not look at you directly. When I love you, only then can I look into your eyes. When I love you deeply, only then can I see your face.

Only love sees a face. Otherwise you never see faces. You move, you look, but that look is just casual, not deep. It touches, but it never penetrates. But when you love, then your whole energy becomes your eyes. Then the energy moves, touches deep, goes deep down into the other person, meets at his center of being. Then only can you see and know.

That is why, in the old Biblical language, they have used the word "know" for sex, for love — for deep love. It is not coincidental. In the Bible it is reported that "Adam knew his wife Eve and then Cain was born". Adam "knew" his wife Eve and then Cain was born. This use of "know", "to know," for deep love, for sex, is strange, but very meaningful, because when you "know" someone it means you have loved someone. There is no other way to know.

And it is not only with persons: it is so with energies also. If you want to know your inner being and the multi-dimensional phenomenon of energies, love! Do not hate the animal. Love! And you are not unrelated to it. You are part of it, and the animal has pushed you to this point where you have become man. Be grateful to it.

It is sheer ungratefulness when people go on condemning the animal — condemning the animal in man. This is sheer ingratitude. The animal has pushed you to this point where you have become man, and the animal can push you to the point where you can become God. It is the animal that is pushing you. Understand it — its ways, how it works — and that understanding will become transformation.

So no control, no effort to become the boss — no! Why are you so afraid of your animal? Because your mind is really impotent; that is why you are so afraid. Why do you want to control it? If you are really the master, the animal will follow you. But you know well that "The animal is the master and I have to follow him". That is why there is this whole effort to become the master.

You know very well that anything real that happens, happens through the animal, and anything bogus that happens, happens through the mind. This awareness creates fear. That is why you want to try to become the master, but a master is never born out of effort. Only slaves try to become masters. A master is simply a master. He is the master.

I will tell you one story. It happened in the house of a great warrior. One night he suddenly became aware of a mouse. He was a great warrior, a great swordsman. He became very much angry because the mouse was sitting just in front of him and looking into his eyes. No one had ever dared so much as the mouse was daring. So he pulled his sword, but the mouse would not run. Then he attacked the mouse, but suddenly the mouse jumped and the sword was broken in pieces. It fell on the stone, on the floor.

Of course, the warrior became just mad. He tried and tried, and the more he tried, the more he was defeated. It is difficult to fight with a mouse, and once you have started fighting you have accepted defeat. The mouse became bold. With every failure of the warrior, the mouse became bold. He simply jumped on his bed. The warrior went out and asked his friends what to do. "This has never happened in my life," he said. "No one can dare so much as an ordinary mouse! But it seems miraculous. I am totally defeated." So the friend said, "It is nonsense to fight with a mouse. It is better to bring a cat."

But the rumour went out that the warrior had been defeated — and even cats heard it, so no cat was ready to come. All the cats gathered. They elected a leader and said, "You go, because it is not an ordinary mouse. The warrior has been defeated. And we are ordinary cats, and this is a great warrior. If he is defeated, where are we? So we will wait outside and let the leader go in."

The leader became afraid. Leaders are always afraid. They are leaders because cowards are there, and those cowards choose them. They are leaders of the cowards. If there were no cowards, there would not be any leaders. Basically, they are chosen by cowards, so they are leaders of cowards.

The cat had to go, as every leader has to go — because the followers were pushing. Now that the leader was chosen, nothing could be done. The cat had to go. She entered, afraid, trembling, nervous. The mouse was sitting on the bed, The cat had never seen such a mouse: he was just sitting on the bed. She started thinking what to do, what method to apply, and while she was thinking what to do, what method to apply, what technique, about old experiences and memories, about what to do with this situation, while she was thinking, the mouse suddenly attacked. The cat ran away because this had never happened in the past! There was no mention in history of a mouse attacking a cat!

She came out and fell dead, so the warrior was advised by the neighbourhood that "Now ordinary cats won't do. You go to the palace. Bring the King's cat. Only a royal cat can do something. This is not an ordinary case." So the warrior had to go to the King and ask for the cat. The cat from the palace came. The warrior was very much afraid when the cat was coming with him because that cat looked very ordinary — just ordinary. He was afraid that this was again going to be a failure, because the cat who had died was bigger, greater, a great leader. And this ordinary cat? It seemed that the King was just joking. This cat won't do, but the warrior couldn't say anything to the King. The King said, "Go!"

He came with that ordinary cat. The cat entered, killed the mouse and came out. All the cats were waiting. They gathered around and they said, "What is the trick? Our leader has died. The warrior has been defeated by the mouse, and you simply killed him. You came with the dead mouse. The cat said, "I am a cat and he is a mouse. There is no other technique. I am a cat: that is enough. What is the use of any technique? Being a cat is enough. When I entered, it was enough that a cat should enter. I am a cat!"

Really, this is a Zen story. Really, if your mind is the master, there is no need for effort. Every effort is just to deceive yourself. You are not the cat, and you are fighting with the mouse. Become a master. But how to become a master? Tantra says understanding will make you a master; nothing else can make you a master. Understanding is the secret of all mastery. If you know it well, you are the master. If you do not know, you will go on fighting. Then you will remain the slave, and the more you fight, the more you will be defeated. You are fighting with a mouse.

The second question: "Are there no horrible noises if we listen from the center of the body? What about the screeching city noises that have been a source of irritation to us all of our lives: Can we turn these into positive sound?"

This always remains a basic question — how to change something else, how to change negative sounds into positive ones. You cannot! If you are positive, then nothing is negative for you. If you are negative, then everything will be negative for you. You are the source of all that exists around you; you are the creator of your own world. And we are not living in one world, remember. There are as many worlds as there are minds. Each mind is living in its own world. It creates the world.

So if everything looks negative and everything looks destructive and everything looks inimical, against you, it is because you do not have the positive center in you. So do not think about how to change negative noises. If you feel negativity all around you, it simply shows you are negative within. The world is just a mirror, and you are reflected in it.

I was staying in a rest house, in a village rest house. It was a very poor village, but the village was filled with many dogs. They all gathered in the night around the rest house. It may have been their usual habit. The rest house was a good place — big trees, shadow, and they might have been resting there every night. So I was staying there, and one minister of a particular state was staying there. The minister became very much disturbed because the dogs were barking, creating much nuisance. Half the night passed and the minister couldn't sleep, so he came to me.

He said, "Are you asleep?" I was fast asleep, so he came near me, made me wake up and asked me, "Please tell me how you could fall into sleep amid such noises all around. At least twenty to thirty dogs are there, and they are fighting and barking and doing everything that dogs ordinarily do. So what to do? I cannot sleep, and I am so tired of the whole day's journey. If I cannot sleep, it will be difficult for me. The next day I have to go again on a tour. I will leave early in the morning. Sleep doesn't seem to come, and I have tried all the methods I have learned and heard about — chanting mantra, praying to God, etc. I have done everything, but nothing happens, so what to do now?"

So I told him, "Those dogs are not gathered here for you or to disturb you. They are not even aware that a minister is staying here; they do not read newspapers. They are completely ignorant; they are not here purposefully. They are not concerned with you. They are doing their work. Why are you getting disturbed?" So he said, "Why should I not? How not to? With so much barking, how can I go into sleep?"

So I told him. "Do not fight with the barking. You are fighting: that is the problem — not the noise. The noise is not disturbing you. You are disturbing yourself because of the noise. You are against the noise, so you have a condition. You are saying, 'If the dogs stop barking, then I will sleep.' The dogs won't listen to you. You have a condition. You feel that if the condition is fulfilled, then you can sleep. This condition is disturbing you. Accept dogs! Do not make a condition that 'If they stop barking then I will sleep'. Just accept.

"Dogs are there and they are barking: do not resist; do not fight; do not try to forget those noises. Accept them and listen to them: they are beautiful. The night is so silent, and they are barking so vitally. Just listen. This will be the mantra — the right mantra: just listen to them."

So he said, "Okay! I do not believe that this will help, but as there is nothing else to do, I will try." He fell asleep, and dogs were still barking. In the morning he said, "This is miraculous. I accepted them; I withdrew my condition. I listened. Those dogs became very musical, and their barking, their noise, was not disturbing. Rather, it became a sort of lullaby, and I fell into deep sleep because of it."

It depends on your mind. If you are positive, then everything becomes positive. If you are negative, then everything turns negative, everything turns sour. So please remember this — not only about noises, but about everything in life. If you feel that something negative exists around you, go and find the cause within. It is you. You must be expecting something; you must be desiring something; you must be making some conditions.

Existence cannot be forced to go according to you. It flows in its own way. If you can flow with it, you will be positive. If you fight with it, you will become negative and the whole thing, the whole cosmos around you, will turn negative.

It is just like a person who is trying to float upstream: then the stream is negative. If you are trying to float upstream in a river, then the river will seem negative and you will feel that the river is fighting you — that the river is pushing you downwards. The river is trying to move you downstream, not upstream, so it will seem as if the river is fighting you. The river is completely unaware of you, blissfully unaware. And it is good; otherwise the river will go to a madhouse. The river is not fighting with you: you are fighting with the river. You are trying to float upstream.

I will tell you one anecdote. A great crowd gathered around Mulla Nasrudin's house, and they said, "What are you doing? Your wife has fallen into the stream and the river is in a flood. Go immediately; otherwise the stream will take your wife to the sea." The sea was just near, so Mulla came running to the bank, jumped into the stream and started swimming upstream to find where his wife was.

So the crowd screamed, "What are you doing, Nasrudin? Your wife couldn't have gone upstream. She has gone downstream." So Mulla said, "Do not disturb me. I know my wife very well. If anyone else had fallen into the stream, he would have gone downstream. Not my wife, however. She must have gone upstream. I know my wife well. I have lived with her forty years."

The mind is always trying to go upstream, to move upstream. Fighting with everything, you create a negative world around you. Obviously, this has to happen. The world is not against you. Because you are not with the world, you feel it is against you. Float downstream, and then the river will help you to float. Then your energy will not be needed. The river will become a boat: it will take you. You will not lose any energy floating downstream because once you float downstream you have accepted the river, the current, the flow, the direction, everything. Then you have become positive to it. When you are positive, the river is positive to you.

You can turn everything positive only by turning yourself positive toward life. But we are not positive toward life. Why? Why are we not positive toward life? Why are we negative? Why this constant struggle? Why can we not have a total let-go with life? What is the fear?

You may not have observed: you are afraid of life — very much afraid of life. It may sound odd to say that you are afraid of life, because ordinarily you feel that you are afraid of death — not of life. This is the usual observation, that everyone is afraid of death. But I tell you, you are afraid of death only because you are afraid of life. One who is not afraid of life will not be afraid of death.

Why are we afraid of life? Three reasons: firstly, your ego can exist only if it floats upstream. Downstream, your ego cannot exist. Your ego can exist only when it fights, when it says "no"! If it says "yes", always "yes", it cannot exist. The ego is the basic cause of saying "no" to everything.

Look at your ways, at how you behave and react. Look at how the "no" comes immediately to the mind and how "yes" is very, very difficult — because with "no" you exist as an ego, with "yes" your identity is lost. You become a drop in the ocean. "Yes" has no ego in it. That is why it is so difficult to say "yes" — very difficult.

You understand me? If you are floating upstream, you feel YOU are. If you just let go and you start floating with the stream wheresoever it leads, you do not feel that you are. Then you have become part of the stream. This ego, this thinking yourself to be isolated as an "I", creates the negativity around you. This ego creates the ripples of negativity.

Secondly, life is unknown, unpredictable, and your mind is very narrow: it wants to live in the known, in the predictable. Mind is always afraid of the unknown. There is a reason: it is because mind consists of the known. Whatsoever you have known, experienced, learned, mind consists of that. The unknown is not part of the mind. The mind is always afraid of the unknown. The unknown will disturb the mind, so the mind is closed for the unknown. It lives in its routine, it lives in the pattern. It moves into particular grooves, known grooves. It goes on moving, moving just like a gramophone record. It is afraid to move into the unknown.

Life is always moving into the unknown, and you are afraid. You want life to go according to your mind, according to the known, but life cannot follow you. It always moves into the unknown. That is why we are afraid of life, and whenever we get any chance we try to kill life, we try to fix it. Life is a flux. We try to fix it because with the "fixed" prediction is possible.

If I love someone immediately my mind will start working on how to marry, because marriage fixes things. Love is a flux, love cannot be predicted. No one knows where it will lead or whether it will lead anywhere. No one knows! It is floating with the stream, and you do not know where the stream is going. It may not be there the next day, the next moment. You cannot be certain of the next moment.

But the mind wants certainty and life is insecurity. Because the mind wants certainty, the mind is against love. The mind is for marriage because marriage is a fixed thing. Now you have fixed things, so now the flux is broken. Now the water is not flowing: it has become ice. Now you have something dead; you can predict. Only dead things are predictable. The more something is alive, the more it is unpredictable. No one knows where life will move.

So we do not want life: we want dead things. That is why we go on possessing things. It is difficult to live with a person; it is easy to live with things. So we go on possessing things and things and things. It is difficult to live with a person. And if we have to live with a person, we will try to make a thing out of that person. We cannot allow the person. A wife is a thing, a husband is a thing. They are not persons: they are fixed things. When the husband comes to the house, he knows that the wife will be there waiting. He knows, he can predict. If he feels like loving, he can love. The wife will be available. The wife has become a thing. The wife cannot say, "No, today I am not in the mood to love." Wives are not supposed to say such things. Not in the mood? They are not supposed to have moods. They are fixed institutions — institutes. You can rely on the institute: you cannot rely on life. Thus, we turn persons into things.

Look at any relationship. In the beginning it is a relationship of "I" and "thou", and sooner or later it becomes a relationship of "I" and "it". The "thou" disappears, and then we go on expecting things. We say, "Do this. This is a duty of a wife and that is the duty of a husband. Do this!" You will have to do it. It is a duty; it has to be done mechanically. You cannot say, "I cannot do."

This fixedness is a fear of life. Life is a flux; nothing can be said about life. I love you this moment, but the next moment the love may disappear. The moment before it was not there; this moment it is there. And it is not because of me that it is there. It just happened. I couldn't have forced it to be here. It just happened, and that which has happened can unhappen at any moment; you cannot do anything. The next moment it may disappear; there is no certainty for the next moment.

But the mind wants certainty, so it turns love into marriage. The living thing becomes dead. Then you can possess it; then you can rely on it. The next day also there will be love. This is the absurdity of the whole thing: you have killed the thing in order to possess it, and then you can never enjoy it because it is no more. It is dead.

In order that you could possess the wife, she has been killed. The beloved has become a wife, and now you expect that the wife should behave like the beloved. That is absurd. The wife cannot behave like the beloved. The beloved was alive, the wife is dead. The beloved was a happening, the wife is an institution. And when the wife is not behaving like the beloved, then you go on saying, "Don't you love me? You loved me before." But this is not the same person. This is not even a person: this is a thing. First you killed her to possess her, and now you want aliveness out of her. Then the whole misery is created.

We are afraid of life because life is a flux. The mind wants certainty. If you really want to be alive, be ready to be insecure. There is no security and there is no way to create security! There is only one way: do not live; then you will be secure. So those who are dead, they are absolutely secure. An alive person is insecure. Insecurity ts the very central core of life, but the mind wants security.

Thirdly, in life, in existence, there is a basic duality. Existence exists as duality, and the mind wants to choose one part and deny the other. For example, you want to be happy, you want pleasure. You do not want pain, but the pain is part of pleasure, the other aspect of it. The coin is one. On one side is pleasure, on another side is pain. You want pleasure, but you do not know that the more you want pleasure, the more pain will follow, and the more you become sensitive to pleasure, the more you become sensitive to pain also.

So a person who wants pleasure should be ready to accept pain. This is just like valleys and hills. You want peaks, hills, but you do not want valleys. So where will the valleys go? And without the valleys, how can there be peaks? Without valleys there can be no peaks. If you love peaks, love valleys also. They become part of the destiny.

The mind wants one thing and it denies the other, and the other is part of it. The mind says, "Life is good, death is bad." But death is part — the valley part, and life is the peak part. Life cannot exist without death. Life exists because of death. If death disappeared, life would disappear, but the mind says, "I want only life. I do not want death." Then the mind moves in a dreamworld which exists nowhere, and it starts fighting with everything because in life everything is related to the opposite. If you do not want the opposite, a fight starts.

A person who understands this — that life is duality — accepts both. He accepts death — not as against life, but as part of it, as the valley part. He accepts night as the valley part of the day. One moment you feel blissful; the next moment you are sad. You do not want to accept the next moment: that is the valley part. And the higher the peak of bliss, the deeper will be the valley because deeper valleys are only created by higher peaks. So the higher you move, the lower you will be falling. And this is just like waves rising high: then there is a valley part.

Understanding means being aware of this fact — not only being aware, but a deep acceptance of the fact, because you cannot move away from the fact. You can create a fiction, and we have been creating fictions for centuries. We have put hell somewhere deep down and heaven high up somewhere. We have created an absolute division between them, which is nonsense because hell is the valley part of heaven. It exists with heaven: it cannot exist apart.

This understanding will help you to be positive; then you will be able to accept everything. By "positive" I mean that you accept everything because you know that you cannot divide Existence.

I take a breath in, and immediately I have to throw it out. I inhale and then exhale. If I were only to inhale and not to exhale, I would die; or if I were only to exhale and not to inhale, then too I would die: because inhaling and exhaling are part of one process — a circle. I can inhale only because I exhale. Both are together and they cannot be divided.

This is what a Liberated man is — undivided. It happens if this understanding comes to him. I call a man Liberated, Enlightened, who accepts the very duality of Existence. Then he is positive. Then whatsoever happens is accepted. Then he has no expectations. Then he makes no demands on Existence. Then he can float downstream.

11
Soundlessness, Soundfulness
And Total Awareness

January 24, 1973, Bombay, India

SUTRAS:

15. Intone a sound, as A-U-M, slowly. As sound enters sound-fulness, so do you.

16. In the beginning and gradual refinement of the sound of any letter, awake.

17. While listening to stringed instruments, hear their composite central sound; thus omnipresence.

I wonder whether or not you have heard about the concept of anti-matter. A new concept has entered recently in the world of physics — the concept of anti-matter. It has been felt always that nothing can exist in the universe without its opposite. It is impossible to conceive of anything which exists alone without its opposite. The diametrically opposite must be there whether known or not.

The shadow cannot exist without light, life cannot exist without death, morning cannot exist without night, man cannot exist without woman — or the same with anything you can think of.

The diametrically opposite pole is inevitably needed. This was always proposed in philosophy, but now this is a proposition of physics. And very absurd notions have developed because of this concept. Time moves from the past to the future, but now physicists say that if time moves from the past to the future there must be somewhere the opposite time process which moves from the future to the past; otherwise this time process cannot be, but it is. The opposite, the diametrically opposite, must be there somewhere — anti-time. Moving from the future to the past? It looks very absurd. How can something move from the future to the past?

They also say that matter exists, so anti-matter must be existing somewhere. What will be the anti-matter? Matter is density. Suppose a stone is here in my hand. What is that stone? Around it is space and in the space there is a density of matter.

That density is matter. What will be the anti-matter ? They say anti-matter will be just a hole in space. Density is matter, and there is also a hole in space with nothing in it. A space will be around it, but it will be just a hole of nothingness. They say anti-matter must exist to balance matter. Why am I talking on this ? Because these sutras which are to follow, they are based on this anti-phenomenon.

Sound exists, but tantra says sound can exist only because of silence. Otherwise sound will be impossible. Silence is anti-sound. So wherever there is sound, just behind it there is silence: just behind it ! It cannot exist without it; it is the other aspect of the same coin. So I utter a word, for example, Aum. The more I utter it, just side by side, just behind it is the anti-phenomenon, soundlessness. So if you can use sounds as a technique to enter soundlessness, you will enter meditation. If you can use a word to go beyond words, you will move into meditation. Look at it in this way: mind is the word; meditation is no mind. Mind is filled with sound and words and thought. Just by the corner is the other extreme — no-mind.

Zen masters have called meditation "the state of no-mind". What is mind ? If you analyze it, it is a process of thought. Or if you analyze it in terms of physics, then it is a process of sounds. This sound process is mind, then just near it the no-mind exists. And you cannot move into the no-mind without using the mind as the jumping board because you cannot even conceive of what no-mind is without understanding what mind is. Mind has to be used as a jumping board, and from that jumping board you can have a plunge into the no-mind.

There have been two opposing schools. One school is there. It is known as Sankya. Sankya says mind has not to be used, because if you use mind you cannot go beyond it. The same is the teaching of J. Krishnamurti. He is a "Sankya-ite". You cannot use mind. If you use mind you cannot go beyond it, because the very use of the mind will strengthen it, will make it more powerful. When you use it, you will be in its clutches. Using it, you cannot go beyond it. So don't use mind. That is why

Krishnamurti is against all techniques of meditation: because any technique is bound to use mind as a base. Mind has to be used if you are going to use a technique. Any technique is bound to be a sort of conditioning — or a reconditioning, or an unconditioning, or whatsoever name you give to it — but it is going to be with the mind.

"Sankya" philosophy says that mind cannot be used: just understand this and take a jump. But yoga says this is impossible. Even this understanding is to be done by mind. Even with this understanding — that you cannot use mind, that no technique will be of help, that every technique will become a hindrance and whatsoever you do will create a new conditioning — you will still be using mind, you will move within mind. This too has to be understood by mind.

So yoga says there is no way in which mind is not used. Mind will have to be used. It should not be used positively: it should be used negatively. It should not be used in such a way that it is strengthened: it should be used in such a way that it is weakened. And techniques are the ways to use the mind in such a way that you use it to jump beyond it. You use it just to go beyond it — as a jumping board. A jumping board can be used.

If mind can be used as a jumping board (and yoga and tantra believe that it can), then something which belongs to mind has to be trained. Sound is one of the basic things: you can use sound to go into soundlessness.

The third technique on sound: *"Intone a sound as AUM slowly. As sound enters soundfulness, so do you."*

"Intone a sound as AUM slowly": for example, take AUM. This is one of the basic sounds. A-U-M: these three sounds are combined in it. A-U-M are three basic sounds. ALL sounds are made of them or derived from them; all sounds are combinations of these three sounds. So these three are basic. They are as basic as the claim of physics that the electron, neutron and positron are basic. This has to be deeply understood.

Gurdjieff speaks of "the Law of the Three". He says Existence in the absolute sense is one. In the absolute sense, in the ultimate sense, there is only one Law. But that is absolute, and whatsoever we see is relative. Whatsoever we see is never absolute. The absolute is always hidden. It cannot be seen, because the moment we see something it is divided. It is divided in three: the seer, the seen and the relationship. I am seeing you: I am here, you are there, and between the two there is the relationship of knowledge, of seeing, of vision, of cognition. The process is divided into three. The absolute is divided into three; the moment it is known it becomes three. Unknown, it remains one. Known, it becomes three. The known is relative; the unknown is absolute.

So even our talk about the absolute is not absolute, because the moment we say "the absolute" it has become known. Whatsoever we know, even the word "absolute", is relative. That is why Lao Tse insists so much that Truth cannot be said. The moment you say it, it has become untrue because it has become relative. So whatsoever word we use — the Truth, the absolute, "Para-brahma," Tao — whatsoever word we use, the moment we use it, it has become relative and it has become untrue. The One has become divided into three.

So Gurdjieff says that the Law of the Three is basic for the universe we know. And if we go deep, we will find, we are bound to find, that everything will be reduced to three. This is the Law of the Three. Christians have called it the "Trinity" — God the Father, Jesus the Son, and the Holy Ghost. Indians have called it "Trimurti" — the three faces of Brahma, Vishnu, Mahesh (Shiva). Now physics says that if we move, if we go on moving through analysis to the very base, then matter will be reduced to three: the electron, neutron and positron.

Poets have said that if we go deep in search for human aesthetic feeling, emotion, then there is *satyam, shivam, sundaram* — the true, the good and the beautiful. Human feeling is based on these three. Mystics have said that if we analyze ecstasy — Samadhi, then there is *Satchitananda* — Existence, Consciousness and Bliss.

The whole human consciousness, in whatsoever dimension it works, comes to the Law of the Three. "AUM" is a symbol of the Law of the Three — A-U-M: These three are basic sounds. The atomic sounds you can call them. These three sounds have been combined in AUM, so AUM is just near the absolute: just behind it is the absolute, the unknown. And AUM is the last station as far as sounds are concerned. If you move beyond AUM, you move beyond sound. Then there is no sound. This is the last sound — AUM. These three are the last. They are the boundary of Existence. Beyond the three, you move into the unknown, into the absolute.

Physicists say that now we have come to the electron. It seems we have come to the limit, to the very limit, because the electron cannot be said to be matter. Electrons are not visible; they have no material property. And they cannot be called non-matter either because all matter consists of them, is constituted of them. If they are neither matter nor non-matter, what to call them ? No one has seen electrons. They are just inferred; it is mathematically assumed that they are there. Their effects are known, but they have not been seen. Now we cannot move beyond them. The Law of the Three is the limit. And if you move beyond the Law of the Three, you move into the unknown. Nothing can be said then. Even about electrons very little can be said.

AUM is the limit as far as sound is concerned. You cannot move beyond AUM. That is why AUM was used so much. And it has been used not only in India: it has been used all over the world. The Christian-Mohammedan "Amen" is nothing but AUM in a different form. The same basic notes are there. The English words "omnipresent, omnipotent, omniscient" contain it: the prefix "omni" is a derivation of AUM. So "omnipresent" refers to that which is present in the whole of the AUM, in the whole of Existence. "Omnipotent" means that which is absolutely potent. "Omniscient" means that which has seen the AUM, the Whole, the Law of the Three. The whole universe comes **under it.**

Christians, Mohammedans, they have been using after their prayers "Amen". But Hindus have made a complete science out of it — of the science of sound and the science of how to transcend sound. And if mind is sound, then no-mind must be soundlessness or (and both mean the same) soundfulness. This has to be understood. The absolute can be described in either of two ways — negative or positive. The relative has to be described in both the ways — negative and positive: it is a duality. When you try to express the absolute, you can use either positive terms or negative terms, because human languages have two types of terms — negative or positive. When you are going to describe the absolute, the indescribable, you have to use some terms symbolically. So it depends on the mind.

For example, Buddha liked to use negative terms. He would say "soundlessness"; he would never say "soundfulness". "Soundfulness" is a positive term. Buddha would say soundlessness, but tantra uses positive terms. The whole thinking of tantra is positive. That is why the term used here is "soundfulness": "enter soundfulness". Buddha describes his absolute in negative terms: *shoonya* — nothingness. The Upanishads describe the same absolute as the Brahman — absoluteness. Buddha will use nothingness and the Upanishads will use absoluteness, but both mean the same thing.

When words lose meaning you can use either negative or positive, because all words are either negative or positive. You have to choose one and that depends. You can say for a Liberated soul that he has become the Whole. This is a positive way of saying it. Or, you can say, "He is no more; he has become nothingness." This is a negative way of saying it.

For example, if a small drop of water meets the ocean, you can say that the drop has become nothingness, the drop has lost its individuality, the drop is no more. This is a Buddhist way of saying things. It is good, it is right as far as it goes, because no word goes very far. So as far as it goes, it is good. "The drop is no more": that is what is meant by Nirvana. The drop has become Non-Being: it is not. Or, you can use Upanishadic terms.

The Upanishads will say that the drop has become the ocean. They are also right because when the boundaries are broken, the drop has become the ocean.

So these are simply attitudes. Buddha likes negative terms because the moment you say anything positive it becomes limited, it looks limited. When you say that the drop has become the ocean, Buddha would say that the ocean is also finite. The drop remains the drop. It has become a little bigger; that is all. Howsoever bigger makes no difference. Buddha would say that it has become a little bigger, but it remains. The finite has not become infinite. The finite remains finite, so what is the difference ? A small drop and a big drop: for a Buddha, that is the only difference between "ocean" and "drop", and it is right. Mathematically it is so.

So Buddha says that if the drop has become the ocean, then nothing has happened. If you have become a god, then nothing has happened. You have only become a bigger man. If you have become the Brahman nothing has happened: you are still finite. So Buddha says that you have to become nothing, you have to become *shoonya* — empty of all boundaries and attributes, empty of everything that you can conceive of, just emptiness. But Upanishadic thinkers will say that even if you are empty YOU ARE ! If you have become emptiness YOU are still there, because emptiness exists, emptiness is. Nothingness is also a way of being, a way of existence. So they say why belabour the point and why unnecessarily use negative terms ? It is good to be positive.

It is your choice, but tantra almost always uses positive terms. The very philosophy of tantra is positive. It says, "Do not allow no, do not allow the negation." Tantrics are the greatest of yeasayers. They have said "yes" to everything, so they use positive terms. The sutra says, "Intone a sound, as A-U-M, slowly. As sound enters soundfulness, so do you ... Intone a sound, as A-U-M, slowly."

The intoning of a sound is a very subtle science. First you have to intone it loudly, outwardly. Then others can hear it, and it is good to start loudly. Why? Because you can also hear it clearly when you intone it loudly: because whatsoever you say, it is to others — and this has become a habit. Whenever you are talking you are talking to others, and you hear yourself talk only when you are talking to others. So start from the natural habit.

Intone the sound "Aum", then by and by, feel attunement with the sound. When you intone the sound Aum, be filled with it. Forget everything else. Become the Aum, become the sound. And it is very easy to become the sound because sound can vibrate through your body, through your mind, through your whole nervous system. Feel the reverberation of Aum. Intone it and feel it as if your whole body is being filled with it, every cell is vibrating with it.

Intoning is also "in-tuning". Tune yourself with the sound, become the sound. And then, as you feel a deep harmony between you and the sound and you develop a deep affection for it (and the sound is so beautiful and so musical — Aum), then the more you intone it the more you will feel yourself filled with a subtle sweetness. There are sounds which are bitter, there are sounds which are very hard. "Aum" is a very sweet sound, the purest. Intone it and be filled with it.

And when you begin to feel harmonious with it, you can drop intoning loudly. Then close your lips and intone it inwardly, but inwardly also first try loudly. Intone inwardly, but loudly so that the sound spreads all over your body, touches every part, every cell of your body. You will feel vitalized by it, you will feel rejuvenated, you will feel a new life entering you because your body is a musical instrument. It needs harmony, and when the harmony is disturbed you are disturbed.

That is why, when you hear music, you feel good. Why do you feel good? What is music but just some harmonious sounds! Why do you feel such a well-being when there is music around you? And when there is chaos, noise, why do you feel so disturbed? You yourself are deeply musical. You are an instrument, and that instrument reechoes things.

Intone "Aum" inside, and you will feel that your whole body dances with it. You will feel that your whole body is undergoing a cleansing bath; every pore is being cleansed. But as you feel it more intensely and as it penetrates you more, go on becoming more and more slow because the slower the sound, the deeper it can go. It is just like homeopathy. The smaller the dose, the deeper it penetrates — because if you want to go deeper, you have to go more subtly, more subtly, more subtly.

Crude, coarse sounds cannot enter your heart. They can enter your ears, but they cannot enter your heart. The passage is very narrow and the heart is so delicate, that only very slow, very rhythmic, very atomic sounds are allowed to enter it. And unless a sound enters your heart, the mantra is not complete. The mantra is complete only when the sound enters your heart — the deepest, most central core of your being. Then go on being more slow, more slow, more slow.

And there are also other reasons for making these sounds slower and more subtle: the more subtle a sound is, the more intense an awareness you will need to feel it inside. The more coarse the sound, the less need there is of any awareness. The sound is enough to hit you; you will become aware of it. But then it is violent.

If a sound is musical, harmonious, subtle, then you will have to listen to it inside and you will have to be very alert to listen to it. If you are not alert, you will go to sleep and miss the whole point. That is the problem with mantra, with any chanting, with any use of sound: it can create sleep. It is a subtle tranquilizer. If you continuously repeat any sound without being alert about it, you will fall asleep because then the repetition becomes mechanical. "Aum-Aum-Aum" becomes mechanical, and then repetition creates boredom.

Boredom is a basic necessity for sleep. You cannot get to sleep unless you are bored. If you are excited, you cannot get to sleep. That is why the modern life, the modern man, is becoming by and by incapable of going to sleep. What is the reason? There is so much excitement. It was never like this before.

In the old, past world life was a deep boredom, a repetitious boredom. If you go to a village hidden somewhere in the hills, there life is a boredom. It may not look to you like a boredom because you have not lived there, and on a holiday you may feel very much excited. But that excitement is because of "Bombay", not because of those hills. Those hills are completely boring. Those who are living there are bored and asleep. There is only the same thing, the same routine with no excitement, with no change, and nothing ever happens. There is no news. Things go on as they have always. They go on repeating in a circular way. As seasons repeat, as nature repeats, as day and night move in a circle, everything moves in a village, in an old village, in a circle. That is why villagers can fall to sleep so easily: everything is just boring.

Modern life has become so exciting, nothing repeats. Everything goes on becoming new, changing. Life has become unpredictable, and you are so excited you cannot fall asleep. Every day you can see a new film, every day you can hear a new speech, every day you can read a new book, every day something new is possible.

This constant excitement continues. When you go to your bed, the excitement is there. The mind wants to be awake; it seems futile to fall asleep. There are thinkers who are saying that this is pure wastage. If you live for sixty years, twenty years are wasted in sleep. Sheer wastage ! Life is so much excitement, why waste any of it ?

But in the old world, in the old days, life was not an excitement. It was a circular movement of the same repetition. If anything excites you, it means it is new. If you repeat a particular sound, it creates a circle within you. It creates boredom; it creates sleep. That is why Mahesh Yogi's Transcendental Meditation is known in the West as "a non-medical tranquilizer". It is because it is a simple repetition of a mantra. But if your mantra becomes just a repetition without an alert YOU inside, an alert YOU constantly listening to you, listening to the sound, it may help sleep, but it cannot help anything else.

As far as it goes, it is good. If you are suffering from insomnia, Transcendental Meditation is good; it helps: but not unless you use the mantra with an alert inner ear. And then you have to do two things: go on reducing the pitch of the mantra, reducing the sound, making it more slow and more subtle, and at the same time simultaneously go on becoming MORE alert, more alert. As the sound becomes subtle, become more alert. Otherwise, you will miss the whole point.

So two things have to be done: sound has to be slowed down and you have to become more alert. The more sound becomes subtle, the more alert you are. To make you more alert the sound has to be made more subtle, and a point comes when sound enters soundlessness, or soundfulness, and you enter total awareness. When the sound enters soundlessness or soundfulness, by that time your alertness must have touched the peak. When the sound reaches the valley, when it goes to the down-most, deepest center in the valley, your alertness has gone to the very peak, to the Everest. And there, sound dissolves into soundfulness or soundlessness, and you dissolve into total awareness.

This is the method: "Intone a sound, as A-U-M, slowly. As sound enters soundfulness, so do you." And wait for the moment when the sound has become so subtle, so atomic, that now, any moment, it will take a jump from the world of the Laws, the world of the Three, and it will enter the world of the One, the absolute. Wait! This is one of the most beautiful experiences possible to man — when sound dissolves. Then suddenly you cannot find where the sound has gone.

You were hearing it subtly, deep down: "Aum-Aum-Aum," and then it is no more there. You have entered the world of the One. The world of the Three is no more. This, tantra says, is soundfulness; Buddha says "soundlessness".

This is a way, one of the most used, one of the most helpful. Mantra became so important because of this. Because sound is already there and your mind is so filled with it, you can use it as a jumping board. But there are difficulties, and the first difficulty is sleep. Whosoever uses mantra must be aware of this difficulty. That is the hindrance — sleep. You are bound to fall into sleep because it is so repetitious, it is so harmonious, it is so boring. You will fall a victim. And do not think that your sleep is your meditation. Sleep is NOT meditation.

Sleep is good in itself, but beware. If you are using the mantra for sleep, then it is okay. But if you are using the mantra for spiritual awakening, then beware of sleep. For those who use mantra, sleep is the enemy — and it so easily happens and it is so beautiful, because it is a different type of a sleep: remember that too. This is not ordinary sleep. When it comes from mantra, this is NOT ordinary sleep. This is a different kind of sleep.

The Greeks have called it *"hypnos"*, and from *hypnos* the word "hypnotism" has been derived. In yoga, they call it *"yoga tandra"* — a particular sleep which happens to the yogi and not to the ordinary man. It is *hypnos* — an induced sleep, not an ordinary sleep. And the difference is very basic, so try to understand it — because if you try mantra, any sound, this is going to be your problem. The greatest problem to face is sleep.

Hypnosis uses the same technique — creating boredom. The hypnotist goes on repeating a certain word or certain sentences. He is continuously repeating, and you become bored. Or he gives you a light to concentrate on. Seeing a light continuously, you get bored.

In many temples, churches, people are fast asleep. Listening to scriptures, they fall asleep. They have heard those scriptures so many times, it has become a boredom. There is no excitement: they already know the story.

If you go on seeing the same film again and again, you will be fast asleep: no excitement for the mind, no challenge, and there is nothing to see. You have heard the Ramayana so many times, you can be asleep without any difficulty and you can go on hearing in your sleep. And you will never feel that you were asleep because you will never miss anything in the story: you know it already.

Preachers' voices are very deeply sleep inducing, monotonous. You can talk monotonously, in the same pitch, then sleep happens. Many psychologists advise their patients with insomnia to go and hear a religious talk. That gives sleep easily. Whenever you are bored, you will fall asleep, but that sleep is hypnosis, that sleep is *yoga tandra*. And what is the difference? That is not natural. That is NOT natural! It is unnatural, and with particular attributes.

One, when you fall asleep through mantra or through hypnosis, you can create any illusion easily and the illusion will be as real as possible. In ordinary sleep, you can create dreams, but the moment you are awake you will know that they were dreams. In *hypnos*, in *yoga tandra*, you can create visions, and when you will be out of it you will not be able to say that they were dreams. You will say that they were more real than the life around you: that is one of the basic differences.

You can create any illusion. So if a Christian falls into "hypnos", he will see Christ. If a Hindu falls, he will see Krishna playing on his flute. It is beautiful! And the quality of hypnosis is that you will believe that this is real. That is the danger, and no one can convince you that this is unreal. The feeling is such that you "know" this is real. You can say that the whole life is unreal, *maya*, illusion, but you cannot say whatsoever you have seen in *hypnos*, in *yoga tandra*, is unreal. It is so alive, so colourful, so attractive and magnetizing.

That is why, if someone says something to you while you are hypnotized, you will believe him absolutely. There can be no doubt; you cannot doubt him. You may have seen some hypnotic sessions. Whatsoever the hypnotist says, the hypnotized person believes and starts acting out. If he says to a man that "You are a woman, and now walk on the stage", the man will walk like a woman. He cannot walk like a man because *hypnos* is deep trust: it is faith. There is no conscious mind to think, no reason to argue. You are simply the heart; you simply believe. There is no way not to believe. You cannot question. The questioning mind is asleep: that is the difference.

In your ordinary sleep, the questioning mind is present. It is NOT asleep. In *hypnos* your questioning mind is asleep, and you are not asleep. That is why you can hear the hypnotist say anything to you. You will follow his instructions. In sleep you cannot hear: you are asleep, but your reasoning is not asleep. So if something happens which can be fatal to you, your sleep will be broken by your reason.

A mother is sleeping with her child: she may not hear anything else, but if the child gives even a very small sound, a small signal, she will be awake. If a child feels a little uneasy, she will be awake. The reasoning mind is alert.

YOU are asleep, but your reasoning mind is alert. So even sometimes in dreams, you can feel that they are dreams. Of course, the moment you feel this your dream will be broken. You can feel that this is absurd, but the moment you feel it the dream will be broken. Your mind is alert. A part is constantly watching.

But in hypnosis or in *yoga tandra* the watcher is asleep. That is the problem with all those who want to use sound to go into soundlessness or soundfulness, to go beyond. They must be aware that the mantra should not become an autohypnotic technique. It must not create autohypnosis.

So what can you do? You can do only one thing: while you are using your mantra, while you are intoning your mantra, do not simply intone it. At the same time be alert and listen to it also. Intone it and listen to it both. You have to do two things: intoning and listening. Otherwise, if you are not listening consciously, it will become your lullaby and you will fall into deep sleep. That sleep will be very good. You will feel refreshed after it, alive; you will feel a certain well-being. But this is not the point. You have MISSED the point!

The fourth technique on sound: *"In the beginning and gradual refinement of the sound of any letter, awake."*

Sometimes teachers have been using this technique very much. They have their ingenious uses. For example, if you enter a Zen Master's hut, he may suddenly give a scream. You will become startled, but if you know why he is doing this you know he is doing it just to make you awake. Any sudden thing makes you awake — any sudden thing! Any sudden sound can make you awake.

Suddenness breaks your sleep, and ordinarily we are asleep. Unless something goes wrong, we are not out of sleep: we go on sleepily, we go on doing things. That is why we never feel the sleep. You go to your office, you drive the car, you come back to your home, you love your children, you talk to your wife, so you think you are not sleepy at all. How can you do all of these things in a sleep? You think that isn't possible, but do you know anything about sleepwalkers — about those who walk in their sleep? Their eyes are open, and they are asleep, and they can do many things. But they will not remember in the morning that they have done them.

They may go to the police station and report that something is wrong, that someone came into their house at night and was creating mischief, and they themselves had been found to be responsible. But in the night, in their sleep, they walk and do certain things, and then they come back into their beds and fall asleep, and in the morning they cannot remember what has happened. They can open doors, they can use keys, they can do many things. Their eyes are open, and they are asleep.

In a deeper sense, we are all sleepwalkers. You can go to your office, you can come to your home, you can do certain things: you will repeat the same things you have always repeated. You will tell your wife, "I love you," and you will not mean anything by it. The words will be just mechanical. You are not even aware that you are telling your wife, "I love you." You are not aware! You are simply doing things as if fast asleep. This whole world is a world of sleepwalkers for a person who has become awakened. A Buddha feels that way, a Gurdjieff feels that way — that everyone is fast asleep and still doing things.

Gurdjieff used to say that whatsoever is happening in this world is absolutely what can be expected — wars, fights, riots, murder, suicide! Someone asked Gurdjieff, "Can something be done to stop wars?" He said, "Nothing can be done — because those who are fighting, they are fast asleep, and those who are pacifists — they are fast asleep, and everyone is going on in a sleep. These happenings are but natural, inevitable. Unless man is awake, nothing can be changed because these are all just by-products of his sleep. He will fight; he cannot be stopped from fighting. Only causes can be changed."

Once he was fighting for Christianity, for Islam, for this and that. Now he is not fighting for Christianity: now he is fighting for communism, for democracy. Causes will change, excuses will change, and the fight will continue because man is asleep and you cannot expect otherwise.

This sleepiness can be broken. You have to use certain techniques. This technique says, "In the beginning and gradual refinement of the sound of any letter, awake." Try with any sound, with any letter — Aum, for example. In the beginning, when you have not yet created the sound, "awake." Or, when the sound moves into soundlessness, then awake.

How can you do it ? Go to a temple. A bell is there or a gong. Take the bell in your hand and wait. First become totally alert. The sound is going to be there and you are not to miss the beginning. First become totally alert, as if your life depends on this, as if someone is going to kill you this very moment and you will be awake. Be alert — as if this is going to be your death. And if there is thought, wait, because thought is sleepiness. With thought you cannot be alert. When you are alert, there is no thought. So wait ! When you feel that now the mind is without thought, that there is no cloud and you are alert and then move with the sound.

Look when the sound is not there, then close your eyes. Then look when the sound is created, struck; then move with the sound. The sound will become slower and slower, subtler and subtler and subtler, and then it will not be there. Then go on with the sound. Be aware, alert. Move with the sound to the very end. See both the poles of the sound, both the beginning and the end.

Try it with some outer sound like a gong or a bell or anything, then close your eyes. Utter any letter inside — Aum or any —

and then do the same experiment with it. It is difficult; that is why we do it outwardly first. When you can do it outwardly, then you will be able to do it inwardly. Then do it. Wait for the moment when the mind is vacant, then create the sound inside. Feel it, move with it, go with it, until it disappears completely.

Until you can do this, it will take time. A few months will be needed, at least three months. In these three months, you will become more and more alert, more and more alert. The pre-sound state and the after-sound state have to be watched. Nothing is to be missed. Once you become so alert that you can watch the beginning and the end of a sound, through this process you will have become a totally different person.

Sometimes this looks very absurd. Such simple techniques, how can they change you? Everyone is so disturbed, in anguish, and the methods seem so simple. They seem like tricks. If you go to Krishnamurti and tell him that this is the method, he will say, "This is a mental trick. Do not be tricked by it. Forget it! Throw it!"

It looks so apparently. Obviously, it looks like a trick. How can you be transformed through such simple things? But you do not know. They are not simple. When you do them, then you know that they are very arduous. If you just hear me telling about them, they are simple. If I tell you that this is poison and if you take one drop of it you will die, if you do not know anything about poison you will say, "What are you talking about? Just a drop of this liquid, and a person like me who is healthy, strong, will die?" If you do not know anything about poison, then only can you say this. If you know something about it you cannot say it.

This seems to be very simple: intoning a sound and then becoming aware in the beginning and in the end. But awareness is VERY difficult, and when you try it then you will know that it is not child's play. You are not aware — and when you try it, for the first time you will know that you have been asleep your whole life. Right now you think you are already aware. Try this. With any small thing, try this.

Try this: tell yourself that "I will be awake, alert, for ten breaths", and then count the breaths. For ten breaths only, tell yourself, "I will remain alert, and I will count from one to ten, the incoming breath, the outgoing, the incoming, the outgoing. I will remain alert."

You will miss. Two or three, and you will have moved somewhere else. Then suddenly you will become aware that "I have missed. I am not counting the breaths." Or, you can count, but when you have counted ten, you will become aware that "I was counting in sleep. I was not alert."

Alertness is one of the most difficult things. Do not think that the methods are simple. Whatsoever the technique, alertness is the thing to be attained. All else is just a help.

And you can devise your own methods. But remember only one thing: alertness must be there. You can do anything in sleep; then there is no problem. The problem arises only when this is made a condition: "Do it alertly."

The fifth sound technique: *"While listening to stringed instruments, hear their composite central sound; thus omnipresence."*

The same! "While listening to stringed instruments, hear their composite central sound; thus omnipresence": You are hearing an instrument — a sitar, or anything. Many notes are there. Be alert and listen to the central core, the backbone of it around which all the notes are flowing, the deepest current which holds all the notes together — that which is central, just like your backbone. The whole body is held by the backbone. Listening to the music, be alert, penetrate the music, and find the backbone of it — the central thing which goes on flowing, holding everything together. Notes come and go and disappear, but the central core flows on. Become aware of it.

Basically, originally, music was used for meditation: particularly Indian music developed as a method for meditation. Indian dancing developed as a method of meditation. For the doer it was a deep meditation, and for the audience also it was a deep meditation. A dancer or a musician can be a technician. If there is no meditation in it, he is a technician. He can be a great technician. He can be a great technician, but then the soul is not there — only the body. The soul comes only when the musician is a deep meditator.

And music is just the outward thing. While playing on his sitar, one is not ONLY playing on his sitar: he is also playing on his alertness inside. The sitar goes on outwardly and his intense awareness moves inside. The music flows outwardly, but he is aware, constantly alert of the innermost core of it. And that gives Samadhi! That becomes ecstasy! That becomes the highest peak!

It is said that when the musician has really become the musician, he will break his instrument — because it is of no use. If he still needs his instrument, he is not a real musician yet. He is just learning — JUST LEARNING! If you can play with music, with meditation, sooner or later the inner music will become more important and the outer will become not only less important: ultimately it will become a disturbance. If your consciousness moves inside and can find the inner music, then the outer music will be a disturbance. You will throw the sitar, you will throw the instrument away from you, because now you have found the inner instrument. But it cannot be found without the outer; with the outer you can become alert more easily. Once you have become alert, leave the outer and move inwards. And for the listener also, the same!

But what are you doing when you listen to music? You are not meditating. On the contrary, you are using music something like alcohol. You are using it to be relaxed, you are using it for self-forgetfulness. This is the misfortune, the misery: the techniques which were developed for awareness are being used for sleep. And this is how man goes on doing mischief with himself.

If something is given to you which can make you awake, you will use it to make yourself more sleepy. That is why for millennia teachings were kept secret: because it was thought to be useless to give techniques to a sleepy man. He will use it for sleep; he cannot do otherwise. So techniques were given only to particular disciples who were ready to shake their sleep, who were ready to be shattered out of their sleepiness.

Ouspensky dedicates one book to George Gurdjieff as "the man who disturbed my sleep". Such people ARE disturbers. Persons like Gurdjieff or Buddha or Jesus, they ARE disturbers. That is why we take revenge upon them. Whosoever disturbs our sleep, we will crucify him. He doesn't look good to us. We may have been dreaming beautiful dreams and he comes and disturbs our sleep. You want to kill him. The dream was "so beautiful".

The dream may be beautiful and I may not be beautiful, but one thing is certain: IT IS A DREAM, and futile, useless! And if beautiful, then more dangerous because it can attract you more, it can become a drug.

We have been using music as a drug, dancing as a drug. And if you want to use music and dancing as drugs, then they will become not only drugs for your sleep: they will become drugs for sexuality also. So remember this point: sexuality and sleep go together. The more sleepy the person, the more sexual; the more awake, the less sexual. Sex is basically rooted in sleep. When you awake, you will be more loving. The whole energy of sex will have transformed to love.

This sutra says while listening to stringed instruments, hear their complete central sound, their composite central sound; "thus omnipresence." And then you will know what IS to be known or what is worth knowing. You will become omnipresent. With that music, finding the composite central core, you will become awake, and with that awakening you will be everywhere.

Right now, you are "somewhere" — a point which we call "ego — the ego". That is the point where you are. If you can become awake, this point will disappear. You will not be anywhere then: you will be EVERYWHERE — as if you have become the All. You will have become the Ocean, you will have become the Infinite.

The finiteness is with the mind; the Infiniteness enters with meditation.

12
Meditation: An Unburdening
Of Repressions

January 25, 1974, Bombay, India

QUESTIONS:

1.   As repression works automatically in us, how to tell apart the false and real in ourselves?

2.   Would you explain the process of mantra initiation and the reasons for secrecy of the mantra?

3.   Can you compare the chaotic music used in your dynamic meditation and rock music in the West?

The first question: *"Repression has become an automatic reaction in our bodies and minds which we do not even recognize or want to change any more. How can we learn to tell between a false image and a real one in ourselves?"*

Many things have to be understood. One: all your faces are false; you do not have any real face. That is why the question arises over which is false and which is real. If you have the real, you know. Then the question never arises. All the faces are unreal, false, so you do not have any comparisons to make. You do not know the real: that is the difficulty. You have not seen the real and the real is not seen naturally. Much effort is needed to find it.

In Zen they say the real is the original face — the face you had before your birth and the face you will have after your death. That means that all the faces in life, so-called life, are false. How to find out what is the real face? You will have to go back before your birth. That is the only way to find the real face, because the moment you are born you have started being false. You have started being false because it pays to be false.

The child is born, and he has started to be a politician. The moment he is related to the world, to the parents, to the family, he is in politics. Now he has to take care about his faces. He will smile as a bribery. He will try to find out in what ways he should behave so that he is accepted more, loved more, appreciated more. And sooner or later the child will find out what is condemned by the parents, by the family, and he will start repressing it. Then the false has entered.

So all the faces you have are false. Do not try to find out the real one among your present faces. They are all false, similarly false. They are useful: that is why they have been adopted — utilitarian, but not true. And the deepest deception is that whenever you become aware your faces are false, you will create another face which you will think is the real.

For example, a person who lives an ordinary life, in an ordinary world, in a business family, comes to realize the whole of his falseness, the whole inauthenticity of his life, so he renounces it. He becomes a sannyasin and leaves the world, and he may be thinking that now the face is real. It is again a false face. It has been adopted as a reaction to other faces, and with a reaction you can never get to the real. By reacting to a false face you will create another false face. So what is to be done?

The real is not something which has to be achieved. The FALSE is your achievement. The real is not something to be achieved, it is not something to be cultivated. It is something to be discovered! It is already there! You need not try to attain it because any effort will only lead to some other false face. For a false face effort is needed: it has to be cultivated. For the real face you have not to do anything. It is already there. If you simply leave your clinging to the false faces, the false will drop and that which is real will remain. When you have nothing to drop and only that which cannot be dropped is there, you will come to realize what is real.

Meditation is the way to drop the false faces. That is why there is so much insistence on being thoughtless — because without thought you cannot create a false face. In a thoughtless state of awareness, you will be real — because it is basically thought which creates false faces and masks. When there is no thought there can be no face. You will be faceless, or with the real face — and both mean the same.

So be aware of your thought process. Do not fight with it, do not repress it. Simply have awareness: the thoughts are there just like clouds in the sky, and you are looking at them without any prejudice either for or against. If you are against, you will be fighting — and that very fight will create a new thought process. If you are for them, you will forget yourself and you will float in the current of the thought process. You will not be there as a conscious witness. If you are for, you will be in the process. If you are against, you will create another process in reaction.

So do not be for and do not be against. Allow the thoughts to move, let them go wherever they are going, be in a deep let-go, and simply witness. Whatsoever is passing, witness. Do not judge; do not say this is good, this is bad. If the thought of a Divine being comes, do not say, "Beautiful!" The moment you say this you are identified with it, and you are cooperating with the thought process. You are helping it, you are giving energy to it, you are feeding it. And if you are feeding it, it can never drop.

Or, if there is a thought, a sexual thought, do not say, "This is bad; this is sin": because when you say "This is sin", you have created another series of thoughts. Sex is a thought, sin is a thought, God is a thought. Be neither for nor against. Simply look with unprejudiced eyes, just watching indifferently.

This will take time. Because your mind is so occupied with notions, it is very difficult. The moment we see something we have judged it. We do not wait; there is not even a single moment's gap. You see a flower, and you have already said, "It is beautiful." In the very seeing the interpretation comes in.

You will have to be constantly aware to drop this mechanical habit of judging. You see a face and you have already judged — ugly, good, bad or anything else. This judgement has become so deep-rooted that we cannot see anything simply. The mind enters immediately. It becomes an interpretation; it is not a simple vision. It becomes an interpretation! Do not interpret. Simply SEE.

Sit down in a relaxed posture or lie down. Close your eyes and allow your thoughts to move. If you say, "Bad!" if you condemn, then you start repressing them. Then you are not allowing them to move independently. That is why there is so much need for dreams: because whatsoever you are repressing during the day you will have to release in the night. That which is repressed goes on forcing expression: it needs expression. So whatsoever you repress you dream. Dreams are cathartic.

Now modern sleep research says that you can be deprived of sleep and not much harm will result, but you cannot be deprived of your dreams. The old idea that sleep is very necessary has been found to be false. Instead of sleep dreams are very necessary, and sleep is necessary only because you cannot dream without sleep.

Researchers have developed techniques with which it can now be judged from the outside whether you are dreaming or whether you are simply asleep. If you are simply asleep, they will disturb the sleep — the whole night long. When you are dreaming, they will allow it. When you are not dreaming, they will disturb the sleep. No bad result comes out of it, but if they should disturb you when you are dreaming and allow you to sleep when you are not dreaming, within three days you will begin to feel dizzy and within seven days you will feel a deep uneasiness. Your body and mind both will feel ill. Within three weeks you will feel a certain type of insanity.

What happens ? It is because dreams are cathartic. If you go on repressing during the day and if they are not allowed to be expressed, they are accumulated in you, and that accumulation of repression is insanity.

In meditation you are not to repress any thought. But it is difficult because your whole mind consists of judgements, theories, isms, religions, cults. So one who is very deeply obsessed with any idea, a philosophy or a religion, cannot really enter into meditation. It is difficult because his obsession will become the barrier. So if you are a Christian or a Hindu or a Jain, it will be difficult for you to enter meditation because your philosophy gives you judgements: "this" is good and "that" is not good; "this" has to be repressed; "this" is not to be allowed.

All philosophies are repressive and all religions, all ideologies, are repressive because they give you interpretations. They do not allow you to see life as it is. They force interpretations on it.

One who wants to go deep in meditation has to be aware of this nonsense of ideology. Just be a simple man without any philosophy, with no attitude toward life. Just be a seeker — one who is in an inquiry, in a deep inquiry to know what life is. Do not force any ideology over and above it. Then it will be very easy to move into meditation.

Because of this, the greatest meditator the world has ever known, Gautam Buddha, insisted that no ideology is needed, no philosophy is needed, no concepts about life are needed. Whether God is, or is not, is meaningless, irrelevant. Whether *Moksha* (Liberation) exists or not is meaningless. Whether your soul is immortal or not is meaningless.

Buddha was so much anti-philosophy — not because HE was anti-philosophy, but because anti-philosophy can become the basic ground for a meditator to jump into the unknown. Philosophy means knowing something about the unknown WITHOUT knowing it. It is just preconceptions, hypotheses, man-constructed ideologies.

This is to be remembered as a very foundational fact: do not judge; let the mind flow easily. As the river flows, let the mind flow easily. Just sit on the bank watching, and this watching should be pure — without any interpretations. Sooner or later, when the water has flown, when the repressed ideas have moved, you will find gaps coming. A thought will go, and another thought will not be coming, and there will be a gap — an interval. In that interval, nothingness happens. In that interval, you will have the first glimpse of your real face or the original face.

When there is no thought, there is no society. When there is no thought, there is no "other". When there is no other, no society, you need not have any face. Thoughtlessness is facelessness. In that interval, when one thought has gone and another has not appeared, in that interval, for the first time you will know in reality what is your face — the face you had when you were not born and the face you will have when you die.

All the faces in life are false. And once you know the real face, once you feel this inner nature which Buddhists call *Buddha Swabhawa* — the nature of the inner Buddha, when you come to feel this inner nature even once, even with a single glimpse you will be a different person, because now you will constantly know what is false and what is real. Then you will have the criterion. Then you can compare, and there will be no need to ask what is real and what is unreal. The question comes only because you do not know what is real and whatsoever you know is all unreal.

Only through meditation will you be able to learn what is a false image and what is a real, authentic face. Of course, the mind is automatic, and whatsoever you have done has become mechanical. It is hard to break this mechanicalness.

The first thing to be understood: mechanicalness is a necessity of life — and your body has an inner mechanism. Colin Wilson has called it the inner robot: you have a robot within you. Once trained, once you are trained in anything, that training is passed to the robot. You can call it memory, you can call it mind, anything, but the word "robot" is good because it is absolutely mechanical — automatic. It functions in its own way.

You are learning to drive. When you are learning, while you are learning, you will have to be aware, alert. A danger is there. You do not know how to drive and anything can happen, so you will have to be alert. That is why learning is so painful: one has to be alert constantly. When you have learned driving, the learning has been given to the robot part of your mind. Now you can go on smoking, singing, listening to the radio or talking to the friend or even loving your girl friend. You can go on doing anything and the robot part of your being will drive.

You will not be needed; you are relieved of the burden. The robot will do everything. You will not even have to remember where to turn; you need not. The robot will know where to turn, where to stop, where not to stop, what to do and what not to do. You are not needed; you are relieved of the job. The robot does everything.

If something very sudden happens, some accident or something that the robot cannot tackle because it is not trained in it, only then will you be needed. Suddenly there will be a jerk in your body. The robot will be replaced and you will come in its place. You can feel that jerk. When suddenly you feel that an accident is going to happen, there is a jerk inside. The robot moves away; it gives place to you. Now YOU are driving. But when the accident is avoided, again the robot will take over. You will relax and the robot will drive.

And this is necessary for life because there are so many things to do — so many things! And if there is no robot to do them, you will not be capable of doing them at all. So a robot is needed. It is a necessity.

I am not against the robot. Go and give unto the robot whatsoever you learn, but remain the master. Do not allow the robot to become the master. This is the problem: the robot will try because the robot is more efficient than you. Sooner or later the robot will try to be the master, and he will say to you, "Be completely retired. You are not needed. I can do things more efficiently."

Remain the master. What can be done in order for you to remain the master of the robot? One thing — only one thing is possible, and that is sometimes, without any danger, take the reins into your hands. Sometimes, without any danger, take the reins into your hands! Tell the robot to relax, come into the seat, and drive the car — WITHOUT any danger, because in danger it is again automatic. The jerk, the replacement of the robot by you, is automatic.

You are driving: suddenly, without any necessity, tell the robot to relax. You come into the seat and drive the car. You are walking: suddenly remember and tell the body that "Now I will walk consciously. The robot is not allowed. I am in the seat and I will drive the body consciously." You are hearing me: it is the robot part which is hearing me. Suddenly give a jerk to it; do not allow the mind to come in. Hear me directly, consciously.

What do I mean when I say "Hear consciously"? When you are hearing unconsciously, you are just focused on me and you have forgotten yourself completely. I exist, the speaker exists, but the listener is unconscious. You are not aware of yourself as the listener. When I say, "Take the reins in your hands," I mean be aware of two points — the speaker AND the listener. And if you are aware of the two points, the speaker and the listener, you have become the third — the witness.

This witnessing will help you to remain the master. And if you are the master, your robot cannot disturb your life. It IS disturbing your life. Your total life has become a mess because of this robot. It helps, it is efficient, so it goes on taking everything from you — even those things which should not be given to it.

You have fallen in love: it is beautiful in the beginning because it has not been given to the robot yet. You are learning. You are alive, aware, alert, and love has a beauty. But sooner or later the robot will take it over. You will become a husband or a wife, and you will have given the charge to the robot.

Then you will say to your wife, "I love you," but YOU will not be saying it: the robot will be saying it, the gramophone record. Then it is a recorded thing. You just play it again and again, and your wife will understand it — because whenever your robot says, "I love," it means nothing. And when your wife says, "I love you," you too will know it is nothing, because a sentence given by a gramophone record only creates noise. It makes no sense; there is no sense in it.

Then you will want to do everything, yet YOU are not doing. Then love becomes a burden and one even wants to escape from love. All your feelings, all your relationships, are now directed by the robot. That is why sometimes you insist on not doing a certain thing, but the robot insists that you do it because the robot is trained to do it. And you are always a failure and the robot always succeeds.

You say, "I am not going to be angry again," but your saying is meaningless because the robot is trained. And the training has been long, so just a sentence in the mind that "I am not going to be angry again" will not have any effect. This robot has been long trained.

So next time when someone insults you, your decision not to be angry will be of no help. The robot will take charge immediately and the robot will do whatsoever it is trained to do. And then in the end, when the robot has done it, you will repent.

But the difficulty, the deep difficulty, is this, that even this repentance is done by the robot because you have ALWAYS done that: after the anger you have repented. The robot has learned that trick also: it will repent, and again you will do the same thing.

That is why many times you feel that you have done something, said something, behaved in a certain way, in spite of yourself. What does this expression "in spite of yourself" mean? It means that there is another self within you which can act, which can do something, in spite of you. Who is that self? The robot!

What to do? Do not take vows that "I will not be angry again". They are self-defeating; they will not lead you anywhere. Rather, on the contrary, whatsoever you are doing, do it consciously. Take charge from the robot — with any ordinary thing. When eating, eat consciously. Do not do it mechanically as you have done every day. When smoking, smoke consciously. Do not allow your hand to move to the packet, do not bring the cigarette out unconsciously. Be conscious, alert — and there is a difference.

I can raise my hand mechanically, just without any awareness. Or, I can raise my hand with full awareness flowing in my hand. Try it! You will feel the difference. When you are aware, your hand will be raised very slowly, very silently, and you will feel that the hand is filled with the awareness. And when the hand is filled with the awareness, your mind will be thoughtless, because your whole awareness will have moved to the hand. Now no energy is left to think.

When you raise your hand automatically, mechanically, you go on thinking and your hand goes on moving. Who is moving that hand? Your robot. Move it yourself! Do it in the day at anytime, any moment, while doing anything. Take charge from the robot. Soon you will be able to have a mastery over the robot. But do not try it with difficult situations: that is suicidal. We always try with difficult situations, and because of difficult situations you can never win. Start with simple situations where, even if you are not so efficient, no harm is going to result.

We always try with difficult situations. For example, one man thinks, "I am not going to be angry." Anger is a very difficult situation and the robot will not leave it to you. And it is better that the robot should do it because he knows more than you. You decide about sex — not to do something or to do something — but you cannot follow through. The robot will take over. The situation is very complex, and more efficient handling is needed than you can give it right now.

Unless you become so perfectly aware that you can tackle any complex situation without the help of the robot, the robot will not allow you to do it. And this is a very necessary defense mechanism. If it were otherwise, you would make a greater mess of your life — if you were to go on taking things away from the robot in difficult situations.

Try! Start with simple things such as walking. Try with it; there is no harm. You can say to the robot that "There is not going to be any harm. I am just walking — taking a walk — and I am not going anywhere: just walking. So there is no need of you; I CAN BE non-efficient."

And then be aware and walk slowly. Be filled with awareness throughout your whole body. When one foot moves, move with it. When one foot leaves the ground, leave the ground with it. When the other foot touches the ground, touch the ground with it. Be perfectly aware. Do not do anything else with the mind; just turn the whole mind into awareness.

It will be difficult because the robot will interfere continuously. Every moment the robot will try and will say, "What are you doing? I can do it better than you." And he CAN do it better. So try it with non-serious things, with non-complex things, simple things.

Buddha has told his disciples to walk, eat and sleep with awareness. If you can do these simple things, then you will also know how to enter into difficult things with awareness. Then you can try.

But we always try with difficult things; then we are defeated. Then the defeated feeling gives you a deep pessimism about yourself. You start thinking that you cannot do anything. That is very helpful for the robot. The robot will always help you to do something when you are in difficulty because then you are defeated. Then the robot can say to you, "Leave it to me. I can always do it better than you can do it."

Start with simple things. Zen Buddhists, Zen monks, have been so many times reported to have been doing this. When Bosho was asked, "What is your meditation? What is your *sadhana* (spiritual practice)?" He said, "When I feel hungry I eat and when I feel sleepy I go to sleep. This is all."

The man who was asking, he said, "But this we all do. What is special about it?" Bosho repeated again. He said, "When I am hungry 'I' eat and when I feel sleepy 'I' sleep." And that is the difference. When YOU feel hungry your robot eats, when YOU feel sleepy your robot sleeps. Bosho said "I", and that is the difference.

If you become more aware in your day-to-day work, in your ordinary life, the awareness will grow. And with that awareness you will not be just a mechanical thing. For the first time you become a person. Now you are not one. And a person has a face and a mechanical thing has many masks — no face.

If you are a person — alive, alert, aware — you can have an authentic existence. If you are just a mechanical device, you cannot have any authentic existence. Each moment will change you; each situation will change you. You will be just a floating thing with no inner core, with no inner being. Awareness gives you the inner presence. Without it you feel that you are, but you are not.

Someone asked Buddha, "I want to serve humanity. Tell me how I can serve." Buddha looked at the man very deeply, penetratingly, with deep compassion, and then he said, "But where are YOU? WHO will serve humanity? You are not yet. First be, and when you are you need not ask me. When you are, you will do something which just happens to you — which is worth doing."

Gurdjieff noted that everyone comes with the notion that he is, that he already is. Someone came to Gurdjieff and asked, "I am very insane inside. My mind goes on in conflicts, in contradictions, so tell me what I can do to dissolve this mind, to have mental peace, inner calm." Gurdjieff said, "Do not think about the mind; you cannot do anything about it. The first thing is to be present. First YOU have to be. Then you can do something. YOU are not."

What is meant by this "You are not"? It means that you are a robot, a mechanical thing, working according to mechanical laws. Start being alert. Join awareness with anything you are doing — and start with simple things.

The second question: *"Explain the meaning, preparation and process of mantra deeksha — mantra initiation. And what are the reasons why individuals must keep the mantra secret?"*

First try to understand what initiation is — what is *deeksha*. It is a deep communion, a deep transfer of energy from the Master to the disciple. Energy always flows downwards. Every energy flows downwards just like water flows downwards. The Master — one who has attained, one who has known, one who has become — is the highest peak of energy possible, of purest energy — the Everest of energy. This energy can flow downwards to anyone who is receptive, humble, surrendered. This surrendered attitude, the receptive attitude, a deep humbleness will be needed to receive. Otherwise you yourself are a peak; you are not a valley. Then the energy cannot flow downwards to you.

You are a different sort of peak, the peak of ego — not of energy, not of Being, not of bliss, not of consciousness. You are a density of ego, of "I-ness". You are a peak, and with this peak no initiation is possible. Ego is the barrier because ego closes you and you cannot surrender.

To be a disciple, to be initiated, one has to surrender himself totally. And there is no partial surrender. Surrender means "total". You cannot say, "I partially surrender." It makes no sense. Then you are still there with your ego. Ego HAS to be surrendered, and when you surrender the ego you become receptive, open. You become like a valley, and then the peak can flow downwards to you. And I am not talking symbolically. It is so actually.

Have you ever been in love ? Then you can feel that love actually flows between two bodies. It is an actual flow. Energy is being transmitted, transferred, received, given. But love is on the same level. You both can remain peaks of ego, and still love can be.

But with a Master you are not on the same level. And if you try to be on the same level, initiation becomes impossible. Love is possible; initiation becomes impossible. Initiation is possible only when you are on a low level — just humble, surrendered, open to receive. The disciple is feminine, just womb-like, passive to receive. The Master is the male factor in initiation.

This secret of initiation is now completely lost because the more we are educated, the more civilized, the more cultured, then the more egoist we become. And, now, to surrender has become very, very impossible. It has always been difficult, but now it is impossible.

Initiation is a transfer of inner energy, actual energy, and the Master can enter in you and can transform you if you are ready and receptive. But then deep trust is needed — more trust than is needed in love — because you do not know what is going to happen. You are completely in the dark.

Only the Master knows what is going to happen and what he is doing. He knows; you cannot know. And there are things that cannot be said about what is going to happen because with the human mind there are many problems. One problem is this: that if something is said before it happens, it will change the happening. It cannot be said.

So there are many things which the Master cannot say to you. He can do them to you, but he cannot say them to you. That doing is initiation. He actually moves in you — in your body, in your mind. He cleanses you, changes you. The only thing required is your total trust, because without it there is no opening and he cannot enter you: your doors are closed.

You are always defending yourself. Life is a struggle — a struggle for survival, to survive. This struggle gives you a closing. You are closed, afraid. You are afraid to be vulnerable. Someone may enter; someone may do something within you. So you shrink yourself. You remain closed — just hiding behind, constantly defending.

In initiation you have to lose this defense; this armour of defense has to be thrown. You become vulnerable, and then the Master can enter you.

For example, it is just like a deep love act. You can rape a woman, but you cannot rape a disciple. You can rape a woman because it is a bodily rape, and the body can be raped and entered without any consent. Without the will of the woman you can rape. It is a forced thing. The body is material; things can be forced on it.

Something just like this happens in initiation. The Master enters your spirit, not your body. Unless you are ready and receiving, the entrance is not possible. A disciple cannot be raped because it is not a bodily question. It is a question of spirit, and you cannot force entry into a spirit. No violence is possible with it.

So when the disciple is ready and open, just like a loving woman inviting and receptive, ready, in a deep let-go, only then can the Master enter and work. And centuries of work can be done in moments. You may not be able to do in many lives certain things which can be done in a moment. But then you have to be vulnerable, totally trusting. You do not know what is going to happen and what he will do inside you.

A woman is afraid because the sexual act is a journey into the unknown for her. Unless she loves the man, unless she is ready to suffer, to carry the burden of a child, to carry the child for nine months and then make a life commitment to it, unless she is deeply in love, she will not allow the man to enter her body — because it is not simply her body: it is her whole life. When she is in deep love, then she is ready to suffer, to sacrifice. And to sacrifice and suffer in deep love is blissful.

But deeper is the problem with the disciple. It is not a question only of a physical birth, of a new child. It is HIS rebirth. He himself is going to be reborn. He will die in a certain sense and he will be born in a certain different sense. And this is possible if the Master enters him, but the Master cannot force it. No force is possible: the disciple can only invite it.

And that is the problem — a very great problem in spiritual discipleship, because the disciple goes on defending himself or herself, goes on creating more and more armour around him. He behaves with his Master in the same way he would behave with anyone in the world; the same defense mechanisms go on working. And then time is wasted unnecessarily, energy is wasted, and the moment is delayed which can happen right now. But this is natural, and sometimes, even with great Masters, disciples have missed the chance.

Ananda, one of the great disciples of Buddha and the nearest, couldn't attain Liberation while Buddha was alive. Buddha was with Ananda for forty years, and Ananda couldn't attain. But many who came after Ananda attained, and then it became a problem. And Ananda was one of the nearest — the closest. He was sleeping with Buddha, he was moving with Buddha, for forty years continuously. He was like a shadow with Buddha. As much as he knew about Buddha even Buddha might not have known.

But he couldn't attain; he remained the same. And a very ordinary thing was the only barrier: he was an elder cousin-brother of Buddha — an ELDER cousin-brother. This created the ego.

Buddha died. A great council met to write down whatsoever Buddha had said. It had to be written then. Soon those who lived with Buddha would be no more, so everything had to be recorded. But the council would not allow Ananda, and only he knew the greater experiences, the statements of Buddha, his life, his biography. This was all known to Ananda; no one knew so much.

But the council decided that Ananda could not be allowed because he was still unenlightened. He could not record Buddha's sayings because an ignorant man cannot be believed. He would not deceive, but with an ignorant man nothing is reliable. He may think that "this" happened and he may relate it authentically as far as he knows, but he is a man who is not yet Awakened. Whatsoever he has seen and heard in sleep could not be believed, so only those would record who had become Awakened, they decided.

Ananda was weeping just outside the door. The door was closed, and he remained just by the door for twenty-four hours, weeping, crying and screaming. But they would not allow him. For these twenty-four hours he was weeping, weeping, and then suddenly he became aware what had been the barrier — why he hadn't been able to attain while Buddha was alive, what had been the barrier.

Then he went back into his memories. A forty-year-long life with Buddha! He remembered the first day when he came to him for initiation. But he had one condition, and that was why he missed the whole initiation. He had never really been initiated. He could not be initiated because he made a condition.

He came to Buddha and he said, "I have come to be a disciple of yours. Once I become your disciple, you will be the Master and I will have to follow whatsoever you say. I will have to obey. But right now I am your elder brother, and I can order you and you will have to obey. You are not the Master, I am not the disciple. Once I am initiated, you will be the Master and

I will be the disciple. Then I will not be able to say anything, so before I become a disciple these are my three conditions. Say yes to these three conditions; then initiate me."

The conditions were not very big, but a condition is a condition and then your surrender is not total. They were very small conditions, very loving conditions. He said, "One, I will always be with you. You cannot tell me to move anywhere else. While I am alive I will be your shadow; you cannot order me away. Give me the promise — because later on I will be just a disciple, and if you order me away I will have to follow. This will be a promise given to an elder brother — that I will be with you. You cannot tell me to move anywhere else. I will just be your shadow; I will sleep in the room where you sleep.

"Secondly, whenever I will say, 'Meet this man,' you will have to meet him. Whatsoever your reason for not meeting, you will have to agree. If I want that someone should be given your *darshan* (spiritual presence), you will have to give it.

"And thirdly, if I say that someone has to be initiated, you cannot refuse. Grant me these three conditions. Promise me and then initiate me. I will not ask anything again because then I shall be just a disciple."

When he remembered this, while he was weeping, crying before the door of the council, after he went back into his memories, he suddenly became aware that the initiation was not there because he had not been receptive. Buddha had agreed. He said, "Okay!" and he followed the three conditions his whole life. But Ananda missed: the nearest one missed.

And the moment he realized this he became Enlightened. That which couldn't happen with Buddha happened when he was no more: he surrendered.

If there is surrender, even an absent Master can help you. If there is no surrender, even an alive Master who is present cannot help you. So in initiation, in any initiation, surrender is needed.

Mantra initiation means that when you have surrendered, the Master will enter you — your body, your mind, your spirit. He will move in you to find a sound for you so that whenever you chant that sound you will be a different man in a different dimension.

Mantra cannot be given unless you have surrendered totally because mantra-giving means the Master has entered you and felt the deep harmony, the inner music of your being. And then he gives a symbolic sound which is in harmony with your inner music. The moment you chant that sound you enter the world of your inner music: the inner harmony is entered.

That sound is just a key, and a key cannot be given unless the lock is known. So I cannot give you a key unless I know your lock, because a key is meaningful only when it can UNLOCK. Any key will not do, and everyone is a particular lock. You need a particular key. That is why mantras are to be kept secret.

If you give your mantra to someone he may experiment with it, but that key will not suit that lock. And sometimes, when you force a wrong key into a lock, you can destroy the lock, you can disturb the lock. You can so much disturb it that even when a right key is found it may not work. That is why mantras are to be kept absolutely secret. They are not told to anyone. That is a promise you make. The Master gives you a key: it is a key only for you. You cannot go on distributing it, and for many that will be harmful.

You will be allowed to give keys only when YOUR lock is totally opened. But then you will not give THIS key to anyone. Then you will have become capable of entering into the other. Then you will be able to feel the lock and devise a key for it.

The key is always devised by the Master. If there is a heap of keys, one who doesn't know may think all keys are the same. There may be only very small differences, minute differences, and even the same word can be used differently. For example, Aum: this has three sounds — "A-U-M." If emphasis is given on the "U", the mid-sound, it is one key. If emphasis is given on the "A", it is a different key. If the emphasis is given on the "M", it is still a different key: it will open different locks.

That is why there is so much emphasis on the exact use of the mantra — on the EXACT use of the mantra as it is given by the Teacher.

So the Teacher gives the mantra in your ear; he chants it exactly as it should be used. He chants it in your ear, and you have to become so alert that your whole consciousness comes to the ear. He chants it, and then it enters into you. You have to remember it now — the exact use of it.

That is why individuals must keep their mantras secret. They should not be made public. They are dangerous, and if you are initiated you know it. If a Master has really given you a key, you know it. You treasure it like anything; you cannot go on distributing it. It can be harmful for others and it can be harmful for you also — for many reasons.

Firstly, you are breaking a promise, and the moment the promise is broken, your contact with the Master is broken. You will not be in contact with him again. If the promise is kept, there is a constant contact.

Secondly, if you give the mantra to anyone and talk about it, it comes to the surface of the mind. The deeper roots are broken; it becomes a gossip.

Thirdly, if you can keep anything secret, the more you keep it secret, the deeper it goes: it is bound to go deeper.

It is said of Marpa that when he was given the secret mantra by his Guru, the promise was there that the mantra would be kept absolutely secret. "You are not to talk about it," he was told.

Then Marpa's Guru appeared in his dream and he said, "What is your mantra?" Even in dream Marpa kept his promise. He refused to tell it. And it is said that because of the fear that someday in a dream the Master may come or send someone, and he may be so asleep that he would break the secret and the promise would be broken, he stopped sleeping altogether. He would not sleep!

He had not been sleeping for seven or eight days, and his Master asked Marpa, "Why are you not sleeping? I see you do not go to sleep at all, so what is the matter?" Marpa said, "You are playing tricks with me. You came in a dream and you were asking for the mantra. I cannot tell even you. Once the promise is there, it will not come out of my mouth even in a dream. But then I became fearful. In sleep, who knows! Someday I may forget."

If you are so aware of keeping the promise that even in dream you remember it, then it is going deep. It is going deep; it is entering inner realms. And the deeper it moves, the more it will be a key to you — because the lock is at the deepest layer. Try with anything. If you can keep it a secret, it will move deep. If you cannot keep it a secret, it will move out.

Why do you want to say something to someone? Why do you chatter? Really, anything that you chatter about you are relieved of. Once you tell it you are relieved of it; it has moved out.

The whole psychoanalysis is nothing but this. The psychoanalyst is just listening and the patient goes on talking. It helps the patient — because the more he talks about his problems, inner conflicts and associated ideas, the more he is relieved of them. The reverse happens when you can keep a secret. At no moment are you allowed to talk about it — at NO moment! It will enter deep, deep, and one day it will hit the exact lock.

One question more: *"In reference to the meditation techniques based on sounds, please explain the difference between the chaotic music played in your dynamic meditation and the shake or rock music of the West."*

Your mind is in chaos. That chaos has to be brought out, acted out. Chaotic music can be helpful, so if you are meditating and chaotic music is played or chaotic dancing is there around you, it will help to bring out your chaos. You will flow in it, you will become unafraid of expression. And this chaotic music will hit your chaotic mind within and will bring it out. It helps.

Rock, jazz, or other musics which are chaotic in a way also help something to come out, and that something is repressed sexuality. I am concerned with ALL your repressions. Modern music is more concerned just with your repressed sex. But there is a similarity. However, I am not concerned ONLY with your repressed sex. I am concerned with ALL your repressions — sexual or not sexual.

Rock music or other musics like that are so influential in the West because of Christianity. Christianity has been repressing sex for twenty centuries. They have forced sex to go so deep down inside that every man has become a pervert deep down. So the West has to relieve itself of the sin that Christianity has done with man, with his mind, through music, through dance, through chaotic painting, chaotic poetry — in every dimension.

In the West mind has to be completely freed somehow from the whole long past of repressive centuries. In every way they are doing it. All that is influential today is chaotic. But sex is not the ONLY thing. There are many other things also. Sex is the basic thing; it is very important: But there are other things also. Your anger is repressed, your sadness is repressed, even your happiness is repressed.

Man as he is is a repressed being. He is not allowed ... really, he is not allowed to do anything. He has just to follow rules. He is not a free agent, but just a kept slave — and the whole sociey is a big prison. The walls are very subtle: they are glass walls, transparent. You cannot see them, but they are — and everywhere they are ! Your morality, your culture, your religion, they are all walls. They are transparent; you cannot see them. But whenever you want to cross them you are thrown back.

This state of mind is neurotic. The whole society is ill ! That is why I so much insist on chaotic meditation. Relieve yourself, act out whatsoever society has forced on you — whatsoever situations have forced on you. Act them out, relieve yourself of them, go through a catharsis. The music helps.

Once you can throw out everything that has been repressed in you, you will become natural again, you will be a child again. And with that child many possibilities open. With you everything is closed. When you become again a child, then only can your energies be transformed. Then you are pure, innocent, and with that innocence and purity transformation is possible.

Perverted energies cannot be transformed. Natural, spontaneous energy is needed. That is why I insist so much on acting out things: so that you can throw the society out. The society has entered you very deeply. It has not left YOU anywhere; it has entered from everywhere. You are a citadel, and the society has entered from everywhere. Its police, its priests, they have done much to make you a slave. You are not free, and man can attain to bliss only when he becomes a total freedom.

For you to be made a total freedom the whole society has to be thrown out of you, but that doesn't mean that you are going to become anti-social. Once you throw the society out, once you become aware of your pure freedom inside, you can live with the society; no need to be "anti". But then the society cannot enter into you. You can move in it, you can act in it, but then the whole thing becomes just a psychodrama: you are acting. Now the society cannot kill you, cannot make a slave of you: you are acting knowingly.

Those who become anti-social simply show that they are still bound to the same society. All the anti-social movements in the West are reactionary, not revolutionary. You are reacting to the same society, you are related to the same society in a reverse manner. You are standing on your head: that is all. You are doing *shirshasana* (the headstand posture), but you are the same person. Whatsoever the society is insisting upon, you are doing quite the contrary — but you are still following the society. This will not help.

If you are "anti", you will never be beyond the society. You are part of it. If the society dies, you will die. Think of what in the West they now call the establishment — the society that is established — and the alternate societies of hippies, yippies, or others: they exist as a PART OF this establishment. If the establishment is dissolved, they will be nowhere. They cannot exist by themselves; they are just a reaction.

You cannot create a society of hippies by itself. Hippies can exist only as an alternate society WITH an establishment — just as a reaction. They cannot exist independently. So howsoever they may think that they are independent, they are not independent. They exist against the establishment. The establishment is their source, their life. Once the establishment is not there, they will be at a loss where to move and what to do. Whatsoever they are doing is dictated by the establishment. They go against it, but the directions, the instructions, are given by the establishment.

If the establishment says short hair, you can be long-haired. But if there is no establishment, then what to do ? If the establishment says cleanliness, you can be dirty. But if there is no establishment and no fuss about cleanliness, you are nowhere. If the establishment says "this", you can do "that" — quite the reverse — but you follow the establishment.

So anti-socials are not revolutionaries. They are reactionaries, a part and a product of the same society — those who have moved against it in bitterness.

A meditator, a sannyasin, is not anti-society: he is BEYOND society. He is not against the establishment, neither is he for it, but he takes it non-seriously. He knows it is just a play; he moves in it like an actor. And if you can move in the society like an actor on the stage, it never touches you: you remain beyond it. So do not be for it, do not be against it.

But how can you do it ? You can do it only when you have thrown the society out of YOU. If it is there, then there are two paths open to you: follow it or go against it. But you are bound to it; you are in bondage. First one has to clean oneself of society. Then, for the first time, you become an individual. Right now you are not: you are just a social unit.

When the society is thrown out, when its entire presence is thrown out, you are again back to your childhood: you have become innocent. And this innocence is deeper than that which any child can have because you know the fall as well and now you have risen. It is a resurrection. You have experienced, you have known the whole nonsense. Now you are again pure. This purity becomes the temple for the Divine.

Once you can throw the society out of you, without any bitterness, without going against it or being involved in any reaction, if you can simply throw society out of you, the Divine can enter into you.

With society in the Divine will remain out; with society out the Divine can enter: because the Divine means "Existence". Society is a human, local phenomenon. Existence is greater — infinite. It is not concerned with man, morals, traditions. It is concerned with the very roots of Being.

One has to be beyond society, not against it, remember. And this chaotic method helps you; it is a catharsis.

13
Sound Methods For The Dropping Of Mind

January 26, 1973, Bombay, India

SUTRAS:

18. Intone a sound audibly, then less and less audibly as feeling deepens into this silent harmony.

19. With mouth slightly open, keep mind in the middle of the tongue. Or, as breath comes silently in, feel the sound "HH".

20. Center on the sound "AUM" without any "A" or "M".

Tantra divides life into two dimensions: one is the *sansar* — that which is, the world — and the other is *Moksha* — that which can be, the Ultimate, the hidden which can become manifest. But there is no contradiction between these two. The hidden is just here and now, in the world — of course, unknown to you, but not non-existent. It is there! The Ultimate and the immediate are not two things, but just two dimensions of one Existence. So for tantra there is no contradiction, there is no duality. The One appears as two because of our limitations: because we cannot see the whole. The moment we can see the whole, one appears as one. The division is not in reality, but in our limited knowledge. That which we know is *Sansar* — the world — and that which is unknown but which can be known is *Moksha* — the Transcendental, the Ultimate, the Absolute.

For other traditions, there is a conflict between the two; for tantra there is no conflict. This has to be understood very deeply in the mind and in the heart. Unless this is understood deeply, you will never be able to understand the viewpoint of tantra. And whatsoever is your belief, the belief is of duality. Whether you are a Christian or a Mohammedan or a Hindu or a Jain, your belief is of duality, of conflict. The world appears to be something which is against the Divine, and you have to fight the world to reach the Divine. This is the common belief of all so-called religions, particularly organized religions.

Mind can understand duality very easily. Rather, it can understand ONLY duality because the very function of the mind is to divide, the very function of the mind is to cut the whole into fragments.

The mind works like a prism, and when a ray of light enters the prism, it is divided into seven colours. Mind is a prism and reality is divided through it. That is why mind revels in analysis. It goes on dividing into fragments, and it cannot prevent itself unless there is nothing to be divided anymore. So mind has a tendency to reach to the atomic, the lowest division. It goes on dividing, dividing, until a moment comes when no division is possible. If division is still possible, it will divide still further.

Mind goes to the fragment, to the minutest fragment, and reality is a whole, not the fragment. So a completely reverse process is needed to know the real: a process which is of synthesis — not of analysis, a process which crystallizes — not one which divides. A no-mind process is needed.

Tantra denies dividings and tantra says that the whole is whole. The part that we know is the world, the part that is hidden is the Divine, or God, or whatsoever you name it. But the hidden is just here and now. You are not aware of it, but it is here and now. It is already! For you it will be in the future, but in the Existence it is here and now. You may have to travel to it; you may have to attain a no-mind attitude of looking at things: then it will be revealed. You are just standing and the morning sun is rising, but you are standing with closed eyes. The morning is here and now, but for you it is not here and now. When you will open your eyes, only then will it become a fact for you.

In the Existence the morning exists, but not for you. You are closed to it; it is hidden for you. Only darkness is for you and the light is hidden. But if you open your eyes, any moment the morning will become a fact to you. It was already a fact; only you were blind.

Tantra says that the world is already the Divine, but YOU are blind. So whatsoever you know in your blindness is to be called the world and whatsoever is hidden because of your blindness is the Divine. This is one of the basic tenets — that this *sansar* is the *Moksha,* this very world is Divine, this very world is the Ultimate. The immediate and the Ultimate are not two, but one. The here and there are not two, but one. Because of this insistence, many things become possible for tantra. One, tantra can accept everything, and the deep acceptance relaxes you completely. Nothing else can relax you!

If there is no division between this world and that, if the transcendental is imminent here and now, if matter is just the body of the Divine, then nothing is denied, nothing is condemned and you need not be tense. Even if it may take ages for you to come to Realize the Divine, there is no hurry for tantra. It is already there, and time is not lacking. It is eternally here. Whenever you will open your eyes you will find it. And whatsoever you are already getting is the hidden Divine.

So the Christian attitude of condemnation, of sin or other such religious attitudes is totally a lie to tantra — and absurd, because if you condemn something you also become divided inwardly. You cannot divide things only outwardly. If you divide, you also will be divided — parallelly. If you say that this world is wrong, then your body will become wrong because your body is part of this world. If you say that this world is something which is a hindrance to reaching the Ultimate, then your whole life will be condemned, and you will feel guilty. Then you cannot enjoy. Then you cannot live. Then you cannot laugh. Then seriousness will become your face.

You can be only serious. You cannot be non-serious, you cannot be playful. That has happened to all the minds all over the world. They become dead, serious. Through seriousness they become dead because they cannot accept life as it is. They deny it, and they feel unless they deny they cannot reach the other world.

So the other world becomes the ideal, the future, the desire, the vision, and this world becomes a sin. Then one feels guilty with it. And any religion that makes you guilty, makes you neurotic. It drives you crazy! In this sense, tantra is the only healthy religion. And whenever any religion becomes healthy, it becomes tantra: it becomes tantric. So every religion has two aspects. One is the outer aspect: the church, the organization, the publicized, the public face, the exoteric. This aspect is aways life denying. The other aspect is the inner core; every religion has that too: the esoteric. It is always tantric — totally accepting.

Unless you accept the world totally, you cannot be at ease within. Non-acceptance creates a tension. Once you accept everything as it is, you are at home in the world. Tantra says this is a basic thing: you must be at home! Only then does something more become possible. If you are tense, divided, in conflict, in anguish, in guilt, how can you transcend? You are so much mad inside, you cannot travel further. You are so much engaged here, so much possessed by the here, you cannot go beyond.

This seems paradoxical. Those who are too much against the world are too much in it; they have to be. You cannot go away from your enemy. You are possessed by the enemy. If the world is your enemy, no matter what you do or pretend to do you will remain worldly. You may even go against it; you may renounce it: but your very approach will be worldly.

I have seen one saint — a very renowned one. He will not touch money. And if you put some coins before him, he will close his eyes. This is neurotic! This man is ill! What is he doing! But people worship him because of this. They think he is too "otherworldly". He is not! He is too much in the world. Even you are not so much in the world. What is he doing? He has just reversed the process. Now he is "standing on his head". He is the same man — the same man who was greedy for money. Constantly he must have been thinking of money, accumulating possessions. Now he has become quite the opposite, but he remains the same within. Now he is against money. Now he cannot touch it.

Why this fear? Why this hatred? Remember, whenever there is hatred it is love gone reverse. You cannot hate a thing unless you are deeply in love with it. You can hate it only if you have been in love with it. Hate is always possible only through love. You can be against something only if you have been too much for it, but the basic attitude remains the same. This man is greedy.

I asked this man, "Why are you so much afraid?" He said, "Money is the hindrance. Unless I use will against my greed toward money, I cannot reach the Divine." So now it is only a new sort of greed. He is in a bargain. If he touches money he loses the Divine — and he wants to get the Divine, he wants to possess the Divine, so he is against the money.

Tantra says do not be for the world, do not be against the world. Just accept it as it is. Do not create any problem out of it. How is this going to help you? If you do not create any problem out of it, if you do not grow neurotic over it — this way or that, if you remain simply in it and accept it as it is, your whole energy is relieved from it and can move to the hidden realm, to the hidden dimension.

Acceptance in this world becomes transcendence for that. Total acceptance here will lead you, will transform you, to the other dimension, the hidden dimension, because all your energy is relieved. It is not engaged here. Tantra believes deeply in the concept of *niyati* — fate. Tantra says take this world as your fate and do not be worried about it. Once you take it as your *niyati*, as your fate, you accept it, whatsoever it is. You are not worried about changing it, about making it different, about making it according to your desire. Once you accept it as it is and you are not bothered by it, your total energy is relieved, and then this energy can penetrate inwards.

These techniques can be helpful only if you take this attitude; otherwise they will not be helpful. And they look so simple. If you start them directly as you are, they will seem simple, but you will not succeed in them. The basic framework is lacking.

Acceptance is the basic framework. Once the acceptance is there in the background, these very simple methods will work wonders.

The sixth method (concerning sound): *"Intone a sound audibly, then less and less audibly as feeling deepens into this silent harmony."*

"Intone a sound audibly, then less and less audibly as feeling deepens into this silent harmony." Any sound will do, but if you love a certain sound it will be better: because if you love a certain sound, then the sound is not just sound. When you intone the sound, then you are also intoning a hidden feeling with it, and by and by the sound will be dropped and only feeling will remain.

The sound has to used as a passage toward feeling. Sound is mind and feeling is heart. Mind has to use a passage toward the heart. It is difficult to enter the heart directly. Because we have been missing it so much and for so many lives, we do not know from where to move to the heart. How to enter it? The door seems closed.

We go on talking about the heart, but that talk also is just in the mind. We say that we love through the heart, but this too is cerebral. This too is cerebral — in the head. Even the talk of the heart is in the head and we do not know where the heart is. I do not mean the physical part of it: we know about that. But then physicians will say, medical science will say, that there is no possibility of love in it. It is just a pumping system. Nothing else is in it, and all else is just myth and poetry and dreaming.

But tantra knows a deep center hidden behind your physical heart. That deep center can only be reached through the mind because we are standing in the mind. We are there in the head, and any travel inwards has to begin from there. Mind is sound. If all sound stops, you won't have any mind. In silence there is no mind: that is why so much insistence on silence. Silence is a no-mind state.

Ordinarily we say, "My mind is silent." This is absurd, meaningless, because mind means absence of silence. So you cannot say that the mind is silent. If mind is, there cannot be any silence, and when silence is, there is no mind. So there is no such thing as a silent mind. There cannot be. It is just saying that someone is alive-dead. It makes no sense. If he is dead, then he is not alive. If he is alive, then he is not dead. You cannot be alive-dead.

So there is nothing like a silent mind. When silence comes, mind is not there. Really, mind goes out and silence comes in; silence comes in and mind goes out. Both cannot be there. Mind is sound. If the sound is systematic, you are sane. If the sound has gone chaotic, you are insane. But in both the cases sound is there, and we exist at the point of mind.

So how to drop from that point to the inner point of the heart ? Use sound, intone sound. One sound will be helpful. If there are many sounds in the mind, it is difficult to leave them. If there is only one sound, it can be left easily. So first many sounds are to be sacrificed for one sound. That is the use of concentration.

Intone one sound. Go on intoning it, first audibly so that you can hear it, and then by and by, slowly, inaudibly. No one else can hear it then, but you can hear it inside. Go on slowing it, make it less and less audible, and then suddenly drop it. There will be silence — an explosion of silence, but feeling will be there. Now there will be no thought, but feeling will be there.

That is why it is good to use a sound, a name, a mantra, for which you have some feeling. If a Hindu uses "Ram", he has some feeling for it. It is not simply a word for him. It is not only in his head. The vibrations reach to his heart also. He may not be aware, but it is deep-rooted in his bones, in his very blood. There has been a long tradition, a long conditioning, for many lives. So if you have been attached to one sound continuously, it is very deep-rooted. Use it! It can be used.

If a Christian uses "Ram" he can use it, but it will remain in the mind: it will not go deep. It is better that he uses "Jesus" or "Maria" or something else. It is very easy to be influenced by a new idea, but it is difficult to use it. You do not have any feeling for it. Even if you are convinced in the mind that this will be better, this conviction is on the surface.

One of my friends was ill in Germany. He was there for thirty years and he completely forgot his mother tongue. He was a Maharashtrian and his mother tongue was Marathi. Marathi was his mother tongue, and he forgot it. For thirty years he was using German. German became just like his mother tongue. I say "just like" because no other tongue can become your mother tongue. There is no possibility because the mother tongue remains deep down inside of you. He consciously forgot it, and he was not able to speak or understand it.

Then he fell ill — and he was so ill that his whole family had to go there to see him. He was unconscious. Sometimes consciousness would come, but whenever he would become conscious he would speak German and whenever he would become unconscious he would mutter in Marathi. When he was unconscious, he would speak Marathi in his unconsciousness. When he was conscious, he would speak German. Consciously he couldn't understand anything of Marathi; unconsciously he couldn't understand anything of German.

Deep in the unconscious Marathi remained. It was the mother tongue, and you cannot replace it. You can put other things over and above it; you can overimpose other things. But you cannot replace it. Deep down, it will remain.

So if you have a feeling for a certain sound, it is better to use it. Do not use an intellectual sound. It will be of no help because the sound has to be used to make a passage from the mind to the heart. So use some sound for which you have a deep love, a certain feeling.

If a Mohammedan uses "Ram", it is very difficult: the word means nothing to him. That is why the two oldest religions never believe in conversion — Hinduism and Judaism. They are the two oldest religions, the two original religions, because all other religions are just offshoots of these two religions. Christianity and Islam are offshoots of the Jewish tradition; Buddhism, Jainism, Sikhism are offshoots of Hinduism. These two original religions never believed in conversion, and the reason was this: that you can convert a man intellectually, but you cannot convert a man from his heart. You can convert a Hindu into a Christian, you can convert a Christian into a Hindu, but the conversion will remain of the mind. Deep down a converted Hindu remains a Hindu.

He may go to a church and he may pray to Mary or to Jesus, but his prayer remains of the head. You cannot change the unconscious. And if you hypnotize him, you will find he is a Hindu. If you hypnotize him and let him reveal his unconscious, you will find he is a Hindu.

Hindus and Jews never believed in conversion because of this basic fact. You cannot change a man's religion because you cannot change his heart and unconscious feelings. And if you try, then you disturb him, because you give him something which will remain on the surface and you divide him. Then he becomes a split personality. Deep down he is a Hindu; on the surface he is a Christian. He will use Christian sounds, mantras, which will not go deep, and he cannot use Hindu sounds which can go deep. You have disturbed his life.

So find a certain sound for which you have some feeling. Even your own name may be helpful — even your own name! If you do not have any feeling for anything else, then your own name will be helpful. There are many cases on record: One very famous mystic, Bukkh, used his own name, because he said, "I do not believe in any God. I do not know about Him, I do not know what His name is. There are names I have heard, but there is no proof that they are His name. And I am in search of myself, so why not use my own name?" So he would use his own name, and just by using his own name he would drop down into silence.

If you do not have any love, use your own name. But it is very difficult because you are so condemning toward yourself that you do not have any feeling, you do not have any respect toward yourself. Others may be respectful toward you, but you are not respectful toward yourself.

So the first thing is to find any sound that will be helpful: for example, your lover's name, your beloved's name. If you love a flower, then "rose" will do, or anything — or any sound that you feel good using, uttering, listening to, from which you feel a certain well being coming to you. Use it! If you cannot find one, then there are some suggestions from traditional sources. "Aum" can be used, "Amen" can be used, "Maria" can be used, "Ram" can be used, or Buddha's name, or Mahavir's name, or any name that you have a love for. But a feeling must be there. That is why the Guru's name can be helpful, if you have the feeling. But feeling is essential!

"Intone a sound audibly, then less and less audibly as feeling deepens into this silent harmony": And go on reducing the sound. Intone it more slowly, more inaudibly so that even you have to make an effort to hear it inside. Go on dropping, go on dropping, and you will feel the change. The more sound will drop, the more you will be filled with feeling. When sound disappears, only feeling remains. This feeling cannot be named. It is a love, a deep love, but not toward anyone; this is the difference.

When you use a sound or a word, the love is attached to a label. You say, "Ram-Ram-Ram": you have a deep feeling for this word, but the feeling is addressed to Ram, narrowed to Ram. When you go on reducing the "Ram", a moment will come when "Ram" disappears, the sound disappears. Now only the feeling remains, the feeling of love — not toward Ram: it is now not addressed. There is simply a feeling of love — not toward anyone, not even "toward": there is simply a feeling of love, as if you are in an ocean of love.

When it is not addressed, then it is of the heart. When it is addressed, it is of the head. Love toward someone is through the head; simple love is of the heart. And when love is simple, unaddressed, it becomes prayer. If it is addressed, it is not yet prayer; you are just on the way. That is why I say if you are a Christian you cannot start as a Hindu. You should start as a Christian. If you are a Mohammedan, you cannot start as a Christian. You should start as a Mohammedan. But the deeper you go, the less you will be a Mohammedan or a Christian or a Hindu.

Only the start will be Hindu, Mohammedan or Christian. The more you will proceed toward the heart, as the sound will be less and less and feeling more and more, you will be less a Hindu, less a Mohammedan. When the sound disappears, you will simply be a human being — no Hindu, no Mohammedan, no Christian.

That is what is the meaning of sects or religion. Religion is one, sects are many. Sects help you to begin. And if you think that they are the end, then you are finished. They are just the beginning. You have to leave them and go beyond because the beginning is not the end. In the end there is religion; in the beginning there is just a sect. Use the sect toward religion; use the limited toward the unlimited; use the finite toward the Infinite.

Any sound will do. Find your own sound. And when you intone it, you will feel whether you have a loving relationship with it, because the heart will start vibrating. Your whole body will begin to be more sensitive. You will feel as if you are falling into something warm just like your beloved's lap: something warm begins enveloping you. And this is a physical feeling also, not simply a mental feeling. If you intone a sound which you love, you will feel a certain warmth around you, inside you. Then the world is not a cold world. It is warm!

If you have gone to a Hindu temple, then you must have heard the *"garbhagriha"* — the womb house. The innermost center of the temple is known as *"garbha"* — the womb. You might not have observed why it is called the womb. If you intone the sound of the temple (and every temple has its own sound, its own mantra, its own *ishta-devata* — its own deity, and the related mantra of the deity), if you intone that sound, the same warmth is created as there is in the womb of the mother. That is why the *garbha*, the womb of the temple, is made just similar to the womb of the mother — round-shaped, closed — almost closed, with only one opening. When Christians came for the first time to India and discovered Hindu temples, they felt that these temples were really unhygienic — not ventilated at all, with only one little door.

But the womb is with only one door and not ventilated at all. That is why the temple was made only with one door, just like a womb, and if you intone that sound, that womb becomes alive. And it is also called the *garbha*, — the womb, because you can get a new birth there. You can become a new man. If you intone a sound that you love, that you have feeling for, you will create a sound-womb around you.

So it is good not to practice this method under the open sky. You are very weak. You cannot fill the whole sky with your sound. It is better to choose a small room, and if the room is such that it vibrates your sound it is good: it will help you. And if you can choose the same place every day, it would be very good. It becomes charged! If the same sound is repeated every day, every atom, the very space, becomes a milieu.

That is why, in temples, followers of other religions were not allowed. There was not anything wrong in Mecca, but no one can enter if he is not a Mohammedan and this is good. Nothing is wrong in it. It is because Mecca belongs to a particular science. One who is not a Mohammedan goes there with a sound which will be disturbing to the whole milieu. If a Mohammedan is not allowed into a Hindu temple, there is no insult in it. And all those social reformers who do not know anything about temples, religion and esoteric science, they go on giving slogans — nonsense slogans, and they are disturbing everything.

A Hindu temple is for Hindus because a Hindu temple is a particular place, a created place. For millennia they have been working on it to make it alive, and anyone can disturb it. That disturbance is very dangerous. A temple is not a public place. It is for a particular purpose and for particular people. It is not for visitors. That is why visitors were not allowed in the old days. Now they are allowed because we do not know what we are doing. A visitor should not be allowed! It is not a place to see — to go to for sightseeing. It is a created space filled with particular vibrations.

If it is a Ram temple and you were born in a family where Ram's name has been sacred — loved, then when you enter an alive space which is always filled with Ram's name, even if you do not want to chant, even if you are not using the Ram mantra, you will start chanting. The space all around will press you. Those vibrations all around will hit you, and you will start chanting from deep down. So use a place: a temple is good.

These methods are temple methods. A temple is good or a mosque or a church. Your own house is not good for these methods, because with so many sounds you have a chaotic space around you and you are not so strong that just by your sound you can change the space. You are NOT so strong! So it is better to go to a certain place which belongs to a certain sound, and then use it. And it is good to go to the same place every day.

By and by you will become powerful. By and by you will drop down from the mind to the heart. Then you can do this method anywhere and the whole cosmos becomes your temple. Then there is no problem. But in the beginning it is good to choose the place, and if you can even choose the time, the exact time every day, it is good because then the temple waits for you. Right at that exact time, the temple waits for you. It is more receptive; it is happy that you have come — the whole space. And I mean physically: this is not a symbolic thing, but a physical one.

It is just as if you take your meals every day at a particular time: at that particular time your whole body feels the hunger. The body has its own inner clock. It feels the hunger exactly at that time. If you go to sleep every day at a particular time, your whole body gets ready at that particular period. If you change every day your sleeping time and your food time, you are disturbing your body.

Now they say your age will be affected by it. If you go on daily changing your body routine, then if you were going to be alive for eighty years you will be alive only for seventy years. Ten years will be lost. And if you go regularly with the body clock, then if you were going to live for eighty years you will live for ninety very easily. Ten years can be added.

Exactly like this, everything all around you has its own clock, and the world moves in cosmic time. If you enter the temple at exactly the same time every day, the temple is ready for you and you are ready for the temple. These two readinesses meet, and the results are magnified a thousandfold.

Or, you can create a small corner in your house. But then do not use that corner for any other purpose, because every purpose has its own vibrations. If you use that corner for a business purpose or you play cards there, that space becomes confused. And now these confusions can even be recorded on mechanical devices; it can be known if the space is confused.

If you can create a corner in your house, a small temple, it is very good. If you can afford a small temple, that is the first thing to be tried. But do not use it for any other purpose. Let it be absolutely private for you, and results come very soon then.

The seventh sound technique: *"With mouth slightly open, keep mind in the middle of the tongue. Or, as breath comes silently in, feel the sound 'HH'."*

With mouth slightly open, keep mind in the middle of the tongue. Or, as breath comes silently in, feel the sound 'HH'." Mind can be focused anywhere in the body. Ordinarily, we have focused it in the head, but it can be focused anywhere. And with the change of the focus, your qualities change. For example, in many Eastern countries; Japan, China, Korea, traditionally it has been taught that mind is in the belly, not in the head. And because of this, those who thought that mind is in the belly had different qualities of mind. You cannot have those qualities because you think mind is in the head.

The mind is nowhere! The brain is in the head; the mind is not there. "Mind" means your focusing. You can focus it anywhere, and once focused it is very difficult to remove it from that point.

For example, now psychologists and workers who are doing research in human depth say, now they say, that when you are making love your mind must move from the head to the genital area; otherwise your sex will be a frustration. If it remains in the head, you cannot go deep into sex. No orgasm will result, and the experience will not be orgasmic. It will not give you a peak. You may produce children, but you will not have known what is the highest peak of love.

You have not known that about which tantra talks or Khajuraho depicts. You cannot! Have you seen Khajuraho? Or if you have not seen Khajuraho, you might have seen pictures of the Khajuraho temple. Then look at the faces, at couples making love. Look at the faces! The faces look Divine! They are in the act of sex, but the faces are as ecstatic as any Buddha's face. What is happening to them? This sex is not cerebral. They are not making love through the head; they are not thinking about it. They have dropped down from the head. Their focusing has changed.

Because of this dropping from the head, the consciousness has moved to the genital area. The mind is no more. The mind has become no-mind. Their faces have the same ecstasy as a Buddha has. This sex has become a meditation. Why? Because the focus has changed. If once you can change the focus of your mind, if you can remove it from the head, the head is relaxed, the face is relaxed. Then all tensions have dissolved. You are not there: the ego is not there.

That is why, the more mind becomes intellectual, rational, the less capable it becomes of love, because love needs a different focusing. In love you need a focusing near the heart; in sex you need a focusing near the genital center. If you are doing mathematics, the head is okay. But love is not mathematics and sex is absolutely not. And if the mathematics continues in the head and you are making love, you are simply wasting energy. Then this whole effort will be disgusting.

But mind can be changed. Tantra says there are seven centers, and mind can be changed to any center. Each center has a different functioning. If you concentrate on a particular center, you become a different man.

In Japan there has been a military group that is just like the Kshatriyas in India, known as "Samurai". They are trained to be soldiers, and their first training is to bring the mind down to just two inches below the navel. In Japan, this center is called the *"hara"*: the Samurai are trained to bring the mind to the *hara*. Unless a soldier can bring his mind's focusing to the *hara*, he is not allowed to go to fight, and this is right. The Samurai are the greatest fighters the world has ever known, the greatest warriors. In the world there is no comparison with a Samurai. He is a different man, a different being, because his focusing is different.

They say that when you are fighting there is no time. Mind needs time to function; it calculates. If you are attacked and your mind thinks about how to protect, you have missed the point already; you have lost. There is no time. You must function timelessly, and mind cannot function timelessly. Mind needs time! Howsoever short, mind needs time!

Below the navel there is a center, the *hara*, which functions timelessly. If the focusing is at the *hara* and the fighter is fighting, then his fight is intuitive, not intellectual. Before you attack him, he knows. It is a subtle feeling in the *hara*, not in the head. It is not an inference: it is a psychic telepathy. Before you attack him, before you think of attacking him, the thought has reached him. His *hara* is hit and he is ready to protect himself. Even before you have attacked, he is in defense. He has protected himself.

Sometimes, if two persons are fighting and both are Samurai, defeating the other is a problem. Neither can defeat the other; it is a problem. No one can be declared the winner. In a way it is impossible because you cannot attack the man. Before you attack, he knows.

There was one Indian mathematician. The whole world was wonderstruck because he would not calculate. Ramanujam was his name. You would give him the problem and he would give you the answer immediately. One of England's best mathematicians, Hardy, was mad after Ramanujam. Hardy was one of the best mathematicians ever born, and he had to work with a particular problem for six hours. But with Ramanujam, you would give him the problem and he would answer you immediately. There was no possibility for the mind to function in this way as the mind needs time.

Ramanujam was asked again and again, "How do you do it ?" He would say, "I don't know. You give me the problem, and the answer comes to me. It comes from somewhere below. It is not from my head." It was coming from the *hara*. He was not aware, he was not trained, but this is my feeling: he must have been a Japanese in his previous birth because in India we have not worked much upon the *hara*.

Tantra says focus your mind on different centers, and different will be the result. This technique is concerned with focusing on the tongue, in the middle of the tongue. Why ? "With mouth slightly open" — as if you are going to speak: not closed, but slightly open as if you are going to speak — not like when speaking, but like when you are just going to speak. The mouth is open like when you are expecting to speak.

Then keep the mind in the middle of the tongue. You will have a very strange feeling because the tongue has a center just in the middle which controls your thoughts. If you suddenly become aware and you focus on that, your thoughts will stop. Just in the middle, focus as if your whole mind has come to the tongue: just in the middle ! Let the mouth be slightly open as if you were going to speak, and then focus the mind as if it is not in the head. Feel it as if it is in the tongue, just in the middle.

The tongue has the center of speech, and thought is speech. What are you doing when you are thinking ? Talking within. Can you think anything without talking within ? You are alone; you are not talking to anyone. You are thinking. What are you doing while you are thinking ? Talking within — talking to yourself. Your tongue is involved. Next time, while you are thinking, be aware. Feel your tongue. It is vibrating as if you are talking to someone else. And then feel it — and you can feel that the vibrations are centered in the middle. They arise from the middle and then they spread all over the tongue.

Thinking is talking within. If you can bring your total consciousness, your mind, to the center of the tongue, thinking stops. So those who have been practising silence, they are simply practising not to talk. If you stop talking outwardly, then you will become very deeply aware of talking inside. And if you remain completely silent for one month or two months or one year, not talking, you will feel your tongue vibrating violently. You are not feeling it because you go on talking and the vibrations are released. But even now, if you stop and become conscious while thinking, you will feel your tongue vibrating a little. Stop your tongue completely and then try to think: you cannot think. Stop your tongue completely as if frozen; do not allow it to move. You cannot think then.

The center is just in the middle, so bring your mind there. "With mouth slightly open, keep mind in the middle of the tongue. Or, as breath comes silently in, feel the sound 'HH'." This is the second technique. It is just similar. "Or, as breath comes silently in, feel the sound 'HH'."

With the first technique, your thinking will stop. You will feel a solidity within — as if you have become solid. When thoughts are not there you become immovable. Thoughts are the inner movement. And when thoughts are not there and you have become immovable, you have become part of the Eternal which only appears to move, but which is immovable, which remains unmoved.

In thoughtlessness, you become part of the Eternal, the unmoved. With thought, you are part of the movement because the nature is movement, the world is movement. That is why we have called it the *sansar*. The *sansar* means the wheel: it is moving and moving and moving. The world is movement and the hidden, the Ultimate, is unmoved, unmoving, immovable. It is just like a wheel that is moving, but a wheel is moving on something which never moves. A wheel can move only because in the center there is something which never moves, which remains unmoved. The world moves and the Transcendental remains unmoved. If your thoughts stop, suddenly you drop from this world to the other. With the movement stopped inside, you become part of the Eternal — that which never changes.

"Or, as breath comes silently in, feel the sound 'HH'." Open your mouth slightly, as if you are going to speak. Then inhale, and be aware of the sound which is created by inhaling. It is just "HH" — whether you are exhaling or inhaling. You are not to make the sound. You are just to feel the incoming breath on your tongue. It is very silent. It is ! You will feel "HH". It will be very silent, very slightly audible. You have to be very alert to be aware of it. But do not try to create it. If you create it, you have missed the point. Your created sound will be of no help. It is the natural sound that happens when you inhale or exhale.

But the technique says while inhaling, not exhaling, because while exhaling, you will go out and with the sound YOU will go out, while the effort is to go in. So while inhaling, hear the sound "HH". Go on inhaling and go on feeling the sound "HH". Sooner or later you will feel that the sound is not being created only at the tongue: it is being created in the throat also. But then it is very very inaudible. With very deep alertness you can become aware of it.

Start from the tongue, then by and by be alert: go on feeling it. You will hear it in the throat, then you will start hearing it in the heart. And when it reaches the heart, you have gone beyond mind. All these techniques are just to give you a bridge from where you can move from thought to no-thought, from mind to no-mind, from the surface to the center.

The eighth sound technique: *"Center on the sound 'AUM' without any 'A' or 'M'."*

"Center on the sound 'AUM' " — A-U-M, Aum — without any "A" or "M". Just the "U" remains. This is a difficult technique, but for some it may be suitable, particularly for those who work with sound: musicians, poets, those who have a very sensitive ear, for them this technique can be helpful. For others, those who have no sensitive ear, this is very difficult because it is very delicate.

You have to intone "Aum" and you have to feel in this Aum three sounds separately: A-U-M. Intone Aum, and in the sound you have to feel three sounds — A-U-M. They are there, infused together. A very delicate ear can be aware, can hear A-U-M separately while intoning. They are separate — very close, but separate. If you cannot hear them separately, then this technique cannot be done. Your ears will have to be trained for it.

In Japan, particularly in Zen, they train the ears first. They have a method of training the ears. The wind is blowing outside: it has a sound. The Master will say, "Concentrate on it. Feel all the nuances, the changes: when the sound is angry, when the sound is furious, when the sound is compassionate, when the sound is loving, when the sound is strong, when the sound is delicate. Feel the nuances of the sound. The wind is blowing through trees: feel it. The river is running: feel the nuances."

For months together the seeker, the meditator, will be sitting by the side of the bank of the river, listening to it. It has different sounds. Everything is changing. In the rain it will be flooded. It will be very much alive — overflowing. The sounds will be different. In the summer it will be reduced to nothingness. Sounds will cease. But there will be inaudible sounds if one is listening, if you listen. The year round the river will be changing, and one has to be aware.

In Herman Hesse's book *Siddhartha*, Siddhartha lives with a boatman. And there is no one, just the river, the boatman and Siddhartha. And the boatman is a very silent man. He has lived all his life with the river. He has become silent, so he rarely speaks. Whenever Siddhartha feels lonely, he tells Siddhartha to go to the river, to listen to the river. It is better than listening to human words.

And then, by and by, Siddhartha is attuned to the river. Then he begins to feel its moods: the river changes moods. Sometimes it is friendly and sometimes it is not; and sometimes it is singing and sometimes it is weeping and crying; and sometimes there

317

is laughter and sometimes there is sadness. And then he begins to feel the slight delicate differences. His ear becomes attuned.

So in the beginning you may feel it difficult, but try. Intone Aum, go on intoning it, feeling A-U-M. Three sounds are combined together in it: A-U-M is a synthesis of three sounds. Once you start feeling them differently, then drop "A" and "M". Then you cannot say AUM: "A" will be dropped, "M" will be dropped. Then "U" will remain. Why? What will happen? The real thing is not the mantra. It is not A-U-M or the dropping. The real thing is your sensitivity.

First you become sensitive of three sounds, which is very difficult. And when you become so sensitive that you can drop the "A" and "M" and only the middle sound remains, in this effort you will lose your mind. You will be so much engrossed in it, so deeply attentive to it, so sensitive to it, that you will forget to think. And if you think, you cannot do this. This is just an indirect way to bring you out of your head. And so many ways have been tried, and they look very simple. You wonder, "What can happen? Nothing will happen by such simple methods."

But miracles happen because they are just indirect. Your mind is being focused to something very subtle. If you focus, you cannot go on thinking; mind will drop. Suddenly one day you will become aware, and you will wonder what has happened.

In Zen they use koans. One of the famous koans they tell to the beginner is, "Go and try to hear the sound of one hand. You can create a sound with two hands. If one hand can create a sound, hear it."

One small boy was serving a Zen Master. He would see many people coming. They would come to the Master, put their heads at his feet, and then they would ask the Master to tell them something to meditate on. He would give them a koan. The boy was just doing some work for the Master; he was serving him. He was just nine or ten years of age.

Seeing every day many people coming and going, one day he also came very seriously, put his head at the Master's feet, and then asked him, "Give me some koan, some object for meditation." The Master laughed, but the boy was very serious, so the Master said, "Okay! Try to hear the sound of one hand. And when you have heard it, then come to me and tell me."

The boy tried and tried. He couldn't sleep the whole night. In the morning he came and he said, "I have heard. It is the sound of the wind blowing through the trees." The Master said, "But where is the hand involved in it? Go again and try." So he would come every day. He would find some sound and then he would come, and the Master would say, "This is also not that. Go on trying, go on trying!"

Then one day the boy didn't come. The Master waited and waited, and then he told his other disciples to go and find out what had happened. It seemed the boy had heard. So they went around. He was sitting under a tree, absorbed — just a newborn Buddha. They came back and they said, "But we are afraid to disturb the boy. He is looking just like a newborn Buddha. It seems he has heard the sound." So the Master came, put his head at the boy's feet and asked him, "Have you heard? It seems you have heard." The boy said, "Yes, but it is soundlessness."

How did this boy develop? His sensitivity developed. He tried every sound, he listened attentively. Attention developed. He would not sleep. The whole night he would listen for what is the sound of one hand. He was not so intellectual as you are, so he never thought that there cannot be any sound of one hand. If the koan is given to you, you are not going to try. You will say, "What nonsense! There cannot be any sound with one hand."

But the boy tried. The Master had said there must be something in it, so he tried. He was a simple boy, so whenever he would hear something, whenever he would feel this was something new, he would come again. But by this process his sensitivity developed. He became attentive, alert, aware. He became one-pointed. He was in search, and the mind dropped because the Master said, "If you go on thinking you may miss. Sometimes there is the sound which is of one hand. Be so alert that you do not miss it."

He tried and tried. There is no sound of one hand, but that was just an indirect method to create sensitivity, awareness. And one day, suddenly, everything disappeared. He was so attentive that only attention was there, so sensitive that only sensitivity was there, so aware — not aware of something, but simply aware ! And then he said, "I have heard it, but it is soundlessness, it is soundlessness !" But you have to be trained to be attentive, to be alert.

Center on the sound "AUM" without any "A" or "M". And this is just a method to make you very delicately aware of the subtle nuances of sound. Just doing this, you will forget AUM. Not only will "A" drop, not only will "M" drop, but one day suddenly you will also drop, and there will be soundlessness, and you will be a newborn Buddha sitting under a tree.

14
Surrendering In Sex And Surrendering To A Master

January 27, 1973, Bombay, India

QUESTIONS:

1. If tantra teaches to be in the middle, how can one understand the difference between indulgence and repression?

2. Is there any connection between opening up to a Master and opening up in sex?

The first question: *"Last night you discussed the attitude of total acceptance as the basic ground for all tantric "sadhana" (spiritual practice). If I remember correctly, on another day you said that the science of tantra teaches to be in the middle in everything, being free from the extremes in life. In this reference, explain how one can come to understand the difference between indulgence and repression in sex life."*

Accepting the total life means the middle path. If you deny, you move to the opposite extreme. Denial is extreme. If you deny anything, you deny it for something. Then you move to one extreme. If one denies sex, he will move to *brahmacharya* — celibacy — to the other extreme. If you deny *brahmacharya*, you will move to indulgence — to the other extreme. The moment you deny, you have accepted the extreme path.

Acceptance of totality is automatically to be in the middle. You are neither for something nor against something. You have not chosen: you are just floating in the stream. You are not moving toward a goal: you have no choice. You are in a let-go.

Tantra believes in a deep let-go. When you choose, your ego comes in. When you choose, your will comes in. When you choose, you are moving against the whole universe. You have your own choice. When you choose, you are not choosing the universal flow: you are standing aloof, isolated; you are like an island. You are trying to be yourself against the whole flux of life.

Non-choosing means you are not to decide where life goes. You allow the life to move, to take you with it, and you have no fixed goal. If you have a fixed goal, you are bound to choose. Life's goal is your goal. You are not moving against life; you have no ideas of your own against life. You leave yourself, you surrender yourself, to the life force itself. This is what tantra means by total acceptance.

And once you accept life in its totality things start happening, because this total acceptance frees you from your ego point. Your ego point is the problem: because of it you create problems. There are no problems in life itself; Existence is "problemless". You are the problem and you are the creator of the problem, and you create problems out of everything. Even if you meet God, you will create problems out of Him. Even if you reach Paradise, you will create problems out of Paradise — because you are the original source of the problems. You are not going to surrender. This non-surrendering ego is the source of all problems.

Tantra says that it is not a question of achieving something; it is not a question of achieving *brahmacharya*. If you achieve *brahmacharya* — celibacy, against sex, your *brahmacharya* will remain basically sexual. Two extremes, howsoever opposite, are parts of one whole — two aspects of one thing. If you choose one, you have chosen the other also. The other will be hidden now, repressed. What does repression mean? Choosing one extreme against the other which is a basic part of it.

You choose *brahmacharya* against sex, but what is *brahmacharya*? It is just the reversal of sex energy. You have chosen *brahmacharya*, but you have also chosen sex with it. Now *brahmacharya* will be on the surface, and deep down there will be sex. You will be disturbed because your choice will create the disturbance. You can choose only one pole, and the other pole follows automatically. And you are against the other pole, so now you will be disturbed.

Tantra says do not choose: be choiceless. Once you understand this, the question will never arise of what is indulgence and what is repression. Then there is no repression and no indulgence. The question arises only because you are still choosing. There are people who come to me, and they say, "We will accept life, but if we accept life when will *brahmacharya* happen?" They are ready to be in total acceptance, but the readiness is false — just superficial. Deep down they are still clinging to the extremes.

They want *brahmacharya* — celibacy. They have not achieved it fighting with sex, so when they hear me they think, "As we have not been able to achieve it through fighting, now we should achieve it through acceptance." But the achieving mind, the motivated mind, the greedy mind, is there — and the goal is there, the choice is there.

If you have something to achieve, you cannot accept the totality. The acceptance is not total. Then you are also trying acceptance as a technique to achieve something. Acceptance means now you leave that achieving mind, that motivated mind that is always for something — hankering for something: you leave it! You allow life to flow freely, just as the wind is flowing through the trees. You allow life to be free, to move freely through you: you have no resistance. Wherever it leads, you are ready to move. You have no goal. If you have any goal, then you will have to resist life, then you will have to fight it.

If the tree has some goal, some leaning, some idea, then it cannot allow the wind to move freely through it. If it wants to go south, then the wind which is forcing it north will be the enemy. If you have some goal, you cannot accept life as a friend. Your goal creates the enmity. If you expect something out of life, you are forcing yourself on life, you are not allowing life to happen to you. Tantra says things happen when you do not expect them, things happen when you do not force them, things happen when you are not hankering after them.

But this is a consequence, not a result. And be clearly aware of the difference between "consequence" and "result". A result is consciously desired; a consequence is a by-product. For example, if I say to you that if you are playing happiness will be the consequence, any play, you will try it for a result. You go and you play, and you are waiting for the result of happiness, but I told you it will be the consequence, not the result.

"Consequence" means that if you are really in the play, happiness will happen. If you constantly think about happiness, then it is going to be a result; it will never happen. A result is a conscious effort; a consequence is just a by-product. If you are deep in play, you will be happy. But the very expectation, the conscious longing for happiness, will not allow you to be deep in play, and the longing for the result will become the barrier and you will not be happy.

Happiness is not a result: it is a consequence. If I tell you that if you love you will be happy, happiness will be a consequence, not a result. If you think that because you want to be happy you must love, nothing will come out of it. The whole thing will be bogus because one cannot love for any result. Love happens! There is no motivation behind it!

If there is motivation, it is not love. It may be anything else. If I am motivated and I think that because I long for happiness I will love you, this love will be false. And because it will be false, happiness will not result out of it. It will not come; that is impossible. But if I love you without any motivation, happiness follows like a shadow.

Tantra says acceptance will be followed by transformation, but do not make acceptance a technique for transformation: it is not! Do not long for transformation. Only then does transformation happen. If you desire it, your very desire is the hindrance. Then there is no question of what indulgence is and what repression is.

This question comes only to the mind because you are not ready to accept the whole. Accept it! Let it be indulgence and accept it! If you accept it, you will be thrown to the middle. Or let it be repression and accept it! If there is acceptance, you will be thrown to the middle. Through acceptance you cannot remain with the extreme. "Extreme" means denial of something — accepting something and denying something. "Extreme" means being for something and against something. The moment you accept whatsoever is the case, you will be thrown to the middle: you will not remain with the extreme.

So forget any intellectual understanding of what repression is and what indulgence is. It is nonsense and it will not lead you anywhere. Just accept, wherever you are. If you are in indulgence, accept it. Why be afraid of it?

But there is a problem. If you are in indulgence, you can remain in indulgence only if you are simultaneously trying to transcend it. That gives a good feeling to the ego: you can feel good and you can postpone. You know this is not going to be forever. You feel, "Today I am indulgent, but tomorrow I will be beyond it." The tomorrow helps you to be in indulgence today. You know that "Today I am drinking alchohol or smoking, but this is not going to be for all my life. I know this is bad, and tomorrow I am going to leave it."

That hope for tomorrow helps you to indulge today, and that is a good trick. Those who want to indulge, they must have great ideals. Those ideals give you opportunity. Then you need not feel very guilty about whatsoever·you are doing because in the future everything is going to be okay. This is just for the moment. This is a trick of the mind. So those who indulge, they always talk of non-indulgence. Those who indulge, they go to the Masters, to the Gurus who are against it, and you can see a deep relationship.

If you are after riches, money, power, you will always worship someone who is against riches — the ascetic. One who has renounced will be your ideal. A rich society can worship and respect only one who has renounced riches. Look around and you will see. If you are indulging in sex, you must respect a person who has gone beyond it, who has become a *brahmachari* — a celibate. You will worship him. He is the ideal; he is your future. You are thinking that someday you are going to be like this man. You worship him.

And if one day some rumor comes to you that he is indulging in sex, the respect is gone because you cannot respect yourself.

You are so self-condemning of whatsoever you are, that if you find that your Guru is just like you, the respect is gone. He must be just the opposite. Then he gives you hope. Then he can lead you to the opposite end. Then you can follow him.

So there is always a very deep relationship between followers and the Master. You will always see them on opposite poles: the follower will be just on the opposite pole, and he is a follower only because of this. If you are obsessed with food, then you can respect only a person who goes for long fasting. He is "the miracle". You hope someday to attain the same. He is your future. You can worship him and respect him. He is the image, but this image helps you to be whatsoever you are. It is not going to change you. The very effort to change, the very idea to change, is the hindrance. This is the insight of tantra.

Tantra says whatsoever you are, accept it. Do not create any ideals. They are dreams — and false. Accept whatsoever is: do not call it good or bad; do not try to justify it or rationalize it. Live in the moment and see that this is the case. Remain with the fact and accept it. This is difficult — very difficult, arduous. Why is it so difficult ? Because then your ego is shattered. Then you know that you are a sexual animal. Then the high ideal of *brahmacharya* cannot help your ego at all. Then you know that you are ninety-nine per cent an animal, and that one per cent I leave you just not to shock you too much.

With the ideals of Mahavir, Buddha, Krishna, Christ, you feel you are ninety-nine per cent Divine and only one per cent is lacking. So sooner or later, by the grace of God, you will attain it. You feel happy as you are. That will not help. That will not help at all ! That can help only to postpone the real problem, the real crisis, and unless you face that crisis, you will never be transformed. One has to pass through it; one has to suffer it. But only the "facticity" of life leads you toward the truth. Fictions will not help.

So remain with the fact. Whatsoever you are — animal or whatever — is okay. Sex is there, anger is there, greed is there: okay, so it is there. It is so; such is the case. The universe happens to you in this way; you have found yourself in this way. It is how life has made you, it is how life is forcing you, leading you to somewhere.

Relax and allow the life to lead you. What is the difficulty in relaxing? The difficulty is that if you relax, you cannot maintain the ego. Ego can be maintained only in resistance. When you say no, ego is strengthened. When you say yes, ego simply disappears.

That is why it is so difficult to say yes to anything. Even in ordinary things it is so difficult to say yes. We want to say no. The ego, the "I", feels good only when it is fighting. If you are fighting with someone else, it is "good": the ego feels good. If you are fighting with yourself the ego feels even more good, because to fight with someone else creates more problems around you. When you are fighting with yourself, there is no problem around you. When you are fighting with someone else, the society will create problems for you. When you are fighting with yourself, the whole society will worship you. It is good because you are not harming anyone.

And, really, if you are someone who is harming yourself, if you are not allowed to harm yourself you will harm others. Otherwise, where will that energy move? So society is always happy with those idiots who are harming themselves. The society feels good because the violence is redirected back. They will not do any harm.

That is why we call them "sadhus" — the good ones. They are good ones because they can do much harm. They ARE doing it, but they are doing it to themselves. They are suicidal. A killer, a murderer, can become suicidal if he turns against himself, so the society feels good, unburdened of a murderer if he becomes suicidal. The society pays respect, appreciates him. But the person remains the same: he remains violent. Now he is violent with himself. Or, he remains greedy, but he talks of non-greed.

But look! Try to understand the talk of non-greed. The base is always greed. They say that if you are non-greedy, only then will you achieve Paradise. And what is to be gained in Paradise? Everything that greed would like.

So be non-greedy "to achieve Paradise". If you are not a celibate, you will not go to heaven. And what are you going to achieve in heaven? All that you condemn here on earth. Then beautiful women are allowed, and there is no comparison — because anyone who is beautiful on earth will become ugly: this is what *shastras* (scriptures) say. And the women that are in heaven never become old: they remain fixed at the age of sixteen. So be celibate here so that you can indulge there.

But what type of logic is this? The motivation remains the same. The motivation remains exactly the same! Only the objects change, the time sequence changes. You are postponing your desires for the future. This is a bargain.

Tantra says try to understand this whole working of the mind, and then it is good not to fight, then it is good to flow as you are and accept it. We are afraid because if we accept, then how will we change? And tantra says acceptance is transcendence. You have tried fighting and you have not changed. Look at your whole life; analyze it. And if you are honest you will find that you have not changed a single bit, not an inch. Move back toward your childhood. Analyze your whole life, and no matter what you may be talking and thinking, the exact, actual life has remained the same. And you have been fighting continuously. Nothing happens out of it.

So now try tantra. Tantra says do not fight: no one ever changes with fight. Accept! Then there is no question of what is indulgence and what is repression, and what is *brahmacharya* and what is this and that. There is no question then! Whatsoever is, you accept it and flow with it. You dissolve your ego resistance, you relax into the Existence and go wherever it leads. If the destiny of the Existence is that you are meant to be an animal, then, says tantra, be an animal.

What will happen out of it and how does it happen? Tantra says total transformation happens — because once you accept, the inner division dissolves: you become one. Then there are not two in you — the saint and the animal, the saint repressing the animal and the animal throwing the saint aside every moment. Then there is no two in you. You become one.

And this oneness gives energy. All your energy is wasted in inner fight and conflict. This acceptance makes you one. Now there is no animal who is to be condemned and no saint who is to be appreciated. You are whatsoever you are. You have accepted it, you have relaxed with it, so your energy becomes one. Then you are a whole and not divided against yourself.

This wholeness is an alchemical transformation. With this wholeness you have energy. Now you are not wasting your life. There is no inner conflict; you are at ease within. This energy which you gain through non-conflict becomes your awareness.

Energy can move in two dimensions. If it moves in fight, you are wasting it every day. If it accumulates and there is no fight, a moment comes just like when you go on heating water to a hundred degrees: then the water becomes something else; it evaporates. Then it is no more liquid. It becomes a gas. It will not become transformed at ninety-nine degrees. It will become transformed only at a hundred degrees.

The same happens inwards. You are wasting your energy every day, and the evaporating point never comes. It cannot come because energy is not accumulated at all. Once the inner fight is not there, energy goes on accumulating and you feel more and more strong.

But not the ego: the ego feels strong only when fighting. When there is no fight, the ego becomes impotent. YOU feel strong, and that "you" is a totally different thing. You cannot know about it unless you are whole. Ego exists with fragments, division. This "you", the Self or what we call the *Atman*, exists only when there is no division, no inner fight. "*Atman*" means the whole: "Self" means the undivided energy.

Once this energy is undivided, it goes on accumulating. You are producing it every day. Life energy is produced in you, but you are wasting it in fight. This same energy comes to a point where it becomes awareness. This is automatic. Tantra says this is automatic. Once you know how to be whole, you will become more and more aware, and the day will come when your total energy will be transformed into awareness.

When the energy is transformed into awareness many things happen, because then the energy cannot move to sex. When it can move to a higher dimension, it will not move to a lower dimension. Your energy goes on moving to the lower dimension because there is no higher for you. And you do not have the level of energy where it CAN move into the higher, so it moves into sex. It moves into sex and you become afraid of it, so you create the ideal of *brahmacharya,* and you become divided. Then you become less and less energetic. You are wasting energy !

This is a very potent experience — that when you are weak you feel more sexual. This looks absolutely absurd in biological terms, because biology will say that when you are more potent you will feel more sexual. But this is not the case. When you are weak, ill, you will feel more sexual. When you are healthy and a subtle well-being is there, you will not feel so sexual.

And the quality of sex will also be different. When you are weak, the sexuality will be a sort of disease and a vicious circle will be created. Through sex you will become more weak, and the more weak you become the more sexual you will feel. And the sex will become cerebral: it will move into your head.

When you are healthy, when a well-being is there, when you feel blissful — relaxed, you are not so sexual. Then even if sex happens, it is not a disease. Rather, it is an overflowing. A totally different quality is there. When sex is an overflowing, it is just love expressing itself through bio-energy. It is creating a deep sharing, a deep contact through bio-energy. It is a part of love.

When you are weak and sex is not overflowing it is a violence against yourself, and when it is a violence against yourself it is never love. A weak person can have sex, but his sex is never love. It is more or less rape — and rape to both the parties. To himself also it is a rape, but then a vicious circle is created: the more weak he feels, the more sexual he feels.

But why does this happen ? Biology has no explanation for it, but tantra has an explanation. Tantra says that sex is an antidote against death. Sex is an antidote against death ! Sex means life for society. You may die, but life will continue. So whenever you feel weak, death is near. Tantra says that then sex will become very important because you may die at any moment. Your energy layer has gone down. You may die at any moment, so indulge in sex so someone can live. Life should go on.

For tantra, old men are more sexual than young men. And this is a very deep insight. Young men are more sexually potent, but not so sexual; old men are less sexually potent, but more sexual. So if we can enter an old man's mind, then we can know what is happening.

As far as sex energy is concerned, it is less in old men, more in young men. But as far as sexuality is concerned (sexuality means thinking about sex), it is more in old men than in young men. Death is coming near and sex is the antidote of death, so now the weakening energy would like to produce someone. Life must continue. Life is not concerned with you, life is concerned with itself. This is a vicious circle.

And the same happens in the reverse order also. If you are overflowing with energy, sex becomes less and less important and love becomes more and more important. And then sex can happen just as a part of love, as a deep sharing. The deepest sharing can be of bio-energy because that is the life force. To whomsoever you love you want to give something. Giving is part of love. In love, you give things. The greatest gift can be of the life energy of yourself. In love, sex becomes a deep gift of bio-energy, of life. You are giving a part of yourself.

Really, in every act of sex you are giving yourself totally. Then a different circle is created: the more you feel love, the more you become strong. The more you feel love, the more you share love, then the more strong you become because in love the ego is dissolved. In love you have to flow with life.

You need not flow with life in politics. Rather, you will be a fool if you flow with life in politics, because there you have to force yourself against life: only then can you rise in politics. If you are doing business you will be a fool if you flow with life. You will be nowhere, because you have to fight, you have to compete, you have to be violent. The more violent and the more mad, the more you will succeed there. It is a struggle.

Only in love is there no competition, no fight, no violence. You succeed in love only when you surrender. So love is the only anti-worldly thing in the world, the only non-worldly thing in the world. And if you are in love you will become more a whole — undivided; more energy will be accumulated. The more the energy, the less will be the sexuality. And a moment comes when the energy comes to a point where transformation happens, and energy becomes awareness. Sex disappears, and only a loving kindness, a compassion, remains.

Buddha has a glow of loving compassion. This is sex energy transformed. But you cannot achieve it through fight, because fight creates division and division makes you more sexual. This is the insight of tantra — absolutely different from whatsoever you may have been thinking about sex and *brahmacharya*. Only through tantra does a real *brahmacharya*, a real purity and innocence, happen. But then it is not a result: it is a consequence. It follows total acceptance.

The second question : *"My mind thinks that it is anxious to receive your message, yet toward the end I find myself resisting and getting tired. I suspect that if I were open sexually I would allow myself to receive without any closing. Is there any connection between opening to a Master and opening up in sex? My background gives a negative and passive meaning to surrender. I know I will not go deeper unless I am able to overcome this negativity that seems to be engraved in my psyche. Is surrender possible when the opposite is planted so deeply?"*

Yes, there is a connection between surrender and sex, because sex is the first surrender — a biological surrender — which you can experience easily. What does surrender mean? It means to be open, unafraid, vulnerable. It means allowing the other to enter you. Biologically, naturally, sex is the basic experience where, without any effort, you allow someone to enter you, or someone to be so deeply close to you that you are not armoured against him. You are not resisting, not holding yourself back, but you are flowing: relaxed — not afraid, not thinking of the future, of the result, of the consequences, but just being in the moment. Even if death occurs, you will accept it.

In deep love, lovers have always felt that this is the right moment to die. And if death occurs, then even death can be welcomed in this moment. They are open: even for death they are open. If you are open for life, you will be open for death. If you are closed for life, you will be closed for death.

Those who are afraid of death are basically afraid of life. They have not lived; that is why they are so afraid of death. And the fear is natural. If you have not lived at all you are bound to be afraid of death, because death will deprive you of the opportunity to live and you have not lived yet. So if death comes, then when will you live ?

One who has lived deeply is not afraid of death. He is fulfilled, and if death comes he can welcome it, accept it. Now whatsoever life can give, life HAS given. Whatsoever can be known in life, he has known it. Now he can move into death easily. He would rather like to move into death so that he can know something unknown, something new. In sex, in love, you are fearless. You are not fighting for something in the future. This very moment is paradise; this very moment is eternal.

But when I say this, I do not necessarily mean that you have experienced it through sex. If you are afraid, resisting, then in sex you can have a biological release — a sexual release, but you will not attain to the ecstasy tantra talks about.

Wilhelm Reich says you have not known sex at all unless in sex you can attain a deep orgasm. It is not only a release of sex energy: your whole body must become relaxed. Then the sex experience is not localized at the sex center, but it spreads all over the body. Your every call is bathed in it, and you have a peak — a peak in which you are not a body. If you cannot attain a peak in sex, a peak in which you are not a body, you have not known sex at all. That is why Wilhelm Reich says a very paradoxical thing. He says sex is spiritual.

This is what tantra says, and the meaning is that in deep sex you will not be a body at all: you will become just a spirit that is hovering. Your body will be left far behind; you will have forgotten it completely. It will be no more. You will not be part of the material world: you will have become immaterial. Only then is there orgasm. That is what tantra says about *sambhog* — intercourse.

There comes a total relaxation, a feeling that now you are fulfilled, a feeling that there is no need to desire anything. Unless this feeling happens to you in sex — this feeling of desirelessness, you have not known sex at all. You may have produced children, but that is easy — and a different thing.

Only man can achieve this spirituality in sex. Otherwise sex is just an animal instinct. But when teachers, monks, condemn sex, you nod your head that they are right. When tantra says something, it is difficult to believe in it because it is not your experience. That is why tantra couldn't become a universal message yet. But the future is good — because the more man will become wise and understanding, the more tantra will be felt and understood.

Only within these hundred years has psychology laid foundations for a world which will be tantric. But you nod your head with someone who is condemning sex because you also have the same experience. You know that "nothing happens in it", and after sex you feel depressed. That is why so much condemnation: everytime you move into it you feel depressed. Later on you repent.

Tantra, Wilhelm Reich, Freud and others who know, agree absolutely that if you achieve an orgasm in sex the glow will last for hours afterwards and you will feel absolutely different — without any worries, without any tensions. Euphoria will result, they say; ecstasy will be there. And that ecstasy happens only when there is really a let-go — when you are not holding yourself back, you are not fighting: you are just moving with the life energy.

Life energy has two layers, and it will be good to understand this. I was talking about breath, and I told you that breath was something like a link between your voluntary system and your non-voluntary system. In your body the major part is non-voluntary. The blood circulates, and you are not asked to do anything. You cannot do anything. It just goes on circulating. Only during these last three hundred years could man know that blood circulates. Before that it was thought that blood just filled into the body — not that it was circulating, because you cannot feel its circulation. It goes on working without you, without your knowledge. It is non-voluntary.

You eat food; then the body starts working. Beyond your mouth you are not needed. The moment food goes beyond your mouth, the body takes it: the non-voluntary system goes on working on it. And it is good that it works this way. If it were left to you, you would create a mess. It is such a great work that if you had to do it you would not be able to do anything else. If you had taken a cup of tea, it would be enough to keep you engaged the whole day — to work it out, to transform it into blood. And the work is so much.

The body works non-voluntarily, but there are a few things you can do voluntarily. I can move my hand, but I cannot move the blood that moves the hand. I cannot do anything directly with the bone that moves the hand. I cannot do anything with the system that works, but I can move my hand. I can move my body, but I cannot do whatsoever goes on within it. I cannot interfere. I can jump, I can run, I can sit, I can lie down, but inside I cannot do anything. Just on the surface am I allowed freedom?

Sex is a very mysterious phenomenon. You start it, but a moment comes when you are no more. Sex is started as a voluntary thing; then there is a limit. If you cross that limit you cannot come back; if you do not cross that limit you CAN come back. So sex is both voluntary and non-voluntary. There is a limit to which your mind will be needed. But if you do not lose your mind, your head, your reason, your consciousness, your religion, your philosophy, your way of life, if you do not lose your mind, then the boundary will not be crossed and you will be experiencing sex in the voluntary realm.

This is what is happening. Then after sex you will feel depressed, against it — and you will be thinking of renouncing life and taking a vow against it. Of course, these vows will not go on long. Within twenty-four hours you will be okay and ready to move again into sex. But it becomes a repetition and the whole thing seems futile. You accumulate energy; then you throw it and nothing results out of it. And this is a long boredom, a drab thing. That is why monks and teachers who are against sex appeal to you: they are talking about something you can understand.

But you have not known the non-voluntary sex, — the deepest biological dimension: you have not touched it, and you always come back from the limit because that limit creates fear. Beyond that limit your ego will not be; beyond that limit you will not be. The sex energy will take hold of you: it will possess you. Then you will be doing something which you cannot control.

Unless you can move to this uncontrolled phenomenon, you cannot achieve orgasm. And once you know this uncontrolled life energy, you are no more in it. You have become just a wave in a great ocean, and things are just happening. You are not forcing them to happen.

Really, you are not active: you have become passive. In the beginning, you are active, and then a moment comes when you become passive. And when you become passive, only then does orgasm happen. If you have known it, then you can understand many things. Then you can understand religious surrender also. Then you can understand the surrender of a disciple to a Master. Then you can understand the surrender of someone to the Existence itself. But if you do not know any surrender, it is difficult even to conceive of what it means.

So it is right: sex is deeply related with surrender. If you have known deep sex, you will be more capable of surrendering because you have known a deep pleasure that follows surrender. You have known a bliss that comes as a shadow of surrender. Then you can trust.

Sex is biological surrender, "Samadhi" (Cosmic Consciousness) is existential surrender. Through sex you touch life; through Samadhi — ecstasy, you touch Existence: you move even deeper than life; the basic Existence is touched. Through sex you move from yourself to another person; in Samadhi you move from yourself to the Whole, to the Cosmos.

Tantra is (if you allow me), tantra is "Cosmic sex"! It is a falling in love with the whole Cosmos, it is a surrender toward the whole Cosmos. And you have to be passive. To a limit you have to be active. Beyond that limit you are not needed: you are a hindrance then. Then leave it to the life force; leave it to the Existence.

The second thing: if you go on thinking about surrender as negative and passive, nothing is wrong in it. It is passive and negative, but the negativity and the passivity is nothing condemnable. In our minds, the moment we hear the word "negative" some condemnation enters, the moment we hear "passive" some condemnation enters — because for the ego, both of these are deaths.

Nothing is wrong in being passive. Passivity is a way to be in deep contact with the universe. And you cannot be active with it: that is the difference between religion and science. Science is active with the universe, religion is passive with the universe. Science is just like the male mind — active, violent, forcing; religion is a feminine mind — open, passive, receptive. Receptivity is always passive. And Truth is not to be created: it is to be received.

You are not going to create the Truth. The Truth is already there! You have to receive it! You have to become the host and then the Truth will become your guest. And a host has to be passive. You have to be like a womb to receive it. But your mind is trained for activity — to be active, to do something — and this is the realm where whatsoever you do will become a hindrance. Do not do: just be! This is what passivity means: do not do anything. Just be, and allow that which is already there to happen to you. You are not needed creatively, actively, to do something. You are needed just to receive. Be passive; do not interfere. Nothing is wrong with passivity.

Poetry happens when you are passive. Even the greatest discoveries of science have happened in passivity. But the attitude of science is active. Even the greatest things in science happen only when the scientist is passive, just waiting, not doing anything. And religion is basically passive.

What is Buddha doing when he is meditating? Our language, our terms, give a false impression. When we say Buddha is meditating, it appears, because of the terms used, that he is doing something. But meditation means "not doing". If you are doing something, nothing will happen.

But all doing is just like sex: in the beginning you have to be active; then a moment comes when activity ceases and you have to be passive. When I say "Buddha is meditating", I mean Buddha is no more. He is not doing anything: he is just passive — a host waiting, just waiting. And when you are waiting for the unknown, you cannot even expect anything. You do not really know what is going to happen, because if you know then the waiting becomes impure and the desire enters. You do not know anything!

All that you had known has ceased, all the known has dropped. The mind is not functioning: it is just simply awaiting. And then everything happens to you. The whole universe falls into you; the whole universe enters from all sides into you. All the barriers are withdrawn. You are not withholding yourself.

Nothing is wrong with passivity. Rather, your activity is the problem. But we are trained for activity because we are trained for violence, struggle, conflict. And it is good as far as it goes, because in the world you cannot be passive. In the world you have to be active, fighting, forcing your way. But that which is so helpful in the world is not helpful when you move toward a deeper existence. Then you have to reverse your steps. Be active if you are moving in politics, in society, for riches or for power. Be inactive if you are moving into God, into religion, into meditation. Passivity is the way there.

And nothing is wrong about the negative either — nothing is wrong! "Negative" only means that something has to be dropped. For example, if I want to create space in this room what am I going to do? What is the process to create space? What am I going to do? Can I bring space from outside and fill this room? I cannot bring space from outside. The space is already here; that is why it is a room. But it is filled with people or furniture or things, so I remove things and people out of it. Then the space is discovered, not brought. It was already here, but filled. So I do a negative process: I empty it.

"Negativity" means emptying yourself, not doing something positive, because that which you are trying to discover is already there. Just throw out the furniture. Thoughts are the furniture in the mind. Just throw them out, and the mind becomes a space. And when the mind is a space, it becomes your soul — your *Atman.* But when it is filled with thoughts, desires, it is mind. Vacant, empty, it is not mind. Negation is a process of elimination. Eliminate things.

So do not be afraid of the words "negative" and "passive". If you are afraid, you can never surrender. Surrender IS passive and negative. It is not something you are doing. Rather, you are leaving your doings, you are leaving the very notion that you can do. You cannot do: this is the basic feeling. Only then is there surrender. It is negative because you are moving into the unknown. The known is left.

When you surrender to a Master it is one of the miracles, because you do not know what is going to happen and what this man is going to do to you. And you can never be certain whether he is real or not. You cannot know to whom you are surrendering and where he is going to lead you. You will try to make certain, but the very effort means that you are not ready for surrender.

If you are absolutely certain before you surrender that this man is going to lead you somewhere — to a paradise — and then you surrender, it is not a surrender at all. You have not surrendered. Surrender is always to the unknown. When everything is known, there is no surrender. You have already checked that this is going to happen and that two and two are going to make four. Then there is no surrender. You cannot say "I surrender" because the four is already made certain.

In uncertainty, in insecurity, is the surrender. So it is easy to surrender to God because, really, there is no one to whom you are surrendering, and you remain the master. It is difficult to surrender to a living Master because then you are no longer a master. With God you can go on deceiving, because no one is going to ask you.

I was reading a Jewish anecdote. One old man was praying to God, and he said, "My neighbor 'A' is very poor, and last year also I prayed to you and you have not done anything for him. My other neighbor 'B' is crippled, and I prayed last year also. But you have not done anything." And so on and so forth, he continued. He talked about all the neighbors, and then in the end he said, "Now I will pray again this year. If you forgive me, I can also forgive you."

But he was talking alone. Every talk with the Divine is a monologue; the other is not there. So it is up to you: what you are doing is up to you, and you remain the master. That is why there is so much insistence in tantra to surrender to a living Master: because then your ego is shattered. And that shattering is the base. That shattering is the base, and only then something can arise out of it.

But do not ask me what you can do to surrender. You cannot do anything. Or, you can do only one thing: be aware of what you can do by doing, what you have gained by doing: be aware! You have "gained much": you have gained many miseries, anguish, nightmares. You have "gained"! That is what you have gained through your own effort. This is what ego can gain. Be aware of it — of the misery that you have created — positively, actively, without surrendering. Whatsoever you have done to your life, be aware of it. That very awareness will help you one day to throw it all and to surrender. And remember that you will be transformed not by surrender to a particular Guru, but by surrender itself.

So the Guru is irrelevant; he is not the point. People go on coming to me, and they say, "I want to surrender, but to whom ?" That is not the point: you are missing the point. It is not a question of "to whom". Just the surrendering helps, not the person to whom you have surrendered. He may not be there or he may not be authentic or he may not be an Enlightened One. He may just be a rogue; that is not the point. It is irrelevant! You have surrendered: that helps because now you are vulnerable, open. You have become feminine. The male ego is lost, and you have become a feminine womb.

The person you have surrendered to may be bogus or he may not be. That is not the point! You have surrendered; now something can happen to you. And many times it has happened that even with a false master disciples have become Enlightened. You may be surprised: even with a false master disciples have become Enlightened!

It is reported of Milarepa that he went to a Teacher and he surrendered. Milarepa was a very faithful man, very trusting. So when the Teacher said, "You will have to surrender to me, and only then can I help," he said, "Okay, I surrender." But many persons were jealous. The old followers of that master were jealous of Milarepa because Milarepa was such a different type of man. He was a very magnetic force. They became afraid that if this man remained there he would become the chief disciple, the next Guru. So they said to their teacher, "This man seems to be false, so first check whether his surrender is real."

The master said, "How should we examine him ?" They said, "Tell him to jump from this hill" (they were sitting on a hill). So the master said, "Milarepa, if you have really surrendered, jump from this hill." So he did not wait even to say yes. He jumped. The disciples thought he would be dead. Then they went down. It took hours for them to go to the valley. He was just sitting under a tree meditating, and he was happy — as happy as he had never been.

So they gathered, and the disciples thought it must be a coincidence. The master was also surprised. How could this happen! So he asked Milarepa privately, "What did you do? How did it happen?" He said, "When I surrendered, there was no question of MY doing. YOU have done something."

The master knew well that he had not done anything, so he tried again. One house was on fire, so he told Milarepa to go in and sit there and only to come out when the whole house became ashes. Milarepa went in. He stayed there for hours. Then the house was just ashes. When they reached there, he was just buried in the ashes — but as alive and as blissful as ever. Milarepa touched his master's feet and said, "You are doing miracles."

So the master said, "It is difficult to think that it is again a coincidence." But the followers said, "This is nothing but a coincidence. Try again. At least three trials are needed."

They were passing through a village and the master said, "Milarepa, the boat has not yet come and the ferryman has not kept the promise, so you go — walk on the waters, go to the other bank, and tell the ferryman to come." Milarepa walked, and then the master really thought it was a miracle. He walked and went to the other bank and brought the ferry.

The master said, "Milarepa, how are you doing it?" He said, "I just take your name and go on. It is your name, Master, that helps me." So the master thought, "If my name helps so much..." He tried to walk on the waters also, but he drowned — and no one has ever heard about him again.

How did it happen? Surrender is the thing — not the master, not the thing to which you surrender. The statue, the temple, the tree, the stone — anything will do. If you surrender, you become vulnerable to the Existence. Then the whole Existence takes you into its arms.

This story may be just a parable, but the meaning is that when you surrender the whole Existence is for you. The fire, the hill, the river, the valley — nothing is against you because you are not against anything. The enmity is lost.

If you fall from a hill and your bones are broken, it is the bones of your ego. You were resisting; you didn't allow the valley to help you. You were helping yourself. You were thinking yourself more wise than the Existence. Surrender means you come to realize that whatsoever you do will be stupid, foolish. And you have done many stupid things for many lives.

Leave it to the Existence itself. YOU cannot do anything! You have to realize that you are helpless. This realization that "I am helpless" helps the surrender to happen.

15
From Sound To Inner Silence

January 28, 1973, Bombay, India

SUTRAS:

21.   *Silently intone a word ending in 'AH'. Then in the 'HH',
effortlessly, the spontaneity.*

22.   *Stopping ears by pressing and the rectum by contracting,
enter the sound.*

23.   *Enter the sound of your name and, through this sound,
all sounds.*

Tantra is not a philosophy. Rather, it is a science with one difference: science is objective, tantra is subjective. But still, it is a science and not a philosophy. Philosophy thinks about the Truth, the unknown, the Ultimate; science tries to discover what is. Science enters the immediate; philosophy thinks of the Ultimate. Philosophy is always looking toward the sky; science is more down to earth.

Tantra is not concerned with the Ultimate. It is concerned with the immediate, the here and now. Tantra says the Ultimate is hidden in the immediate, so you need not worry about the Ultimate. By worrying about the Ultimate you will miss the immediate, and the Ultimate is hidden in the immediate. So by thinking about the Ultimate you will miss both. If the immediate should be missed, because of it you will miss the Ultimate also. So philosophy is just smoke. The approach of tantra is scientific, but the OBJECT is different from that of so-called science.

Science tries to understand the object, the objective world, the reality that is before your eyes. Tantra is the science of the reality that is behind your eyes, the subjectivity, but the approach is scientific. Tantra doesn't believe in thinking: it believes in experimenting, in experiencing. And unless you can experience, everything is just a wastage of energy.

I am reminded of one incident. Mulla Nasrudin was crossing a street. Just in front of a church he was knocked down by a hit-

and-run driver. He was an old man, and a crowd gathered. Some-one was saying that that man cannot survive. The priest of the church ran out. He came near and he found out that the old man was just going to die, so he prepared to administer the last rites. He came near and asked the dying Mulla, "Do you believe in God the Father? Do you believe in God the Son? Do you believe in God the Holy Ghost?" Mulla opened his eyes and said, "My God! I am dying and he is asking me puzzles!"

All philosophy is like this: it is asking puzzles while you are dying. Every moment you are dying, every moment everyone is on his deathbed — because death can occur at any moment. But philosophy goes on asking and answering puzzles. Tantra says it is good for children to philosophize, but those who are wise will not waste their time in philosophy. They should try to know — not to think, because through thinking there is no knowledge. Through thinking you go on webbing words, creat-ing patterns of words. It leads nowhere. You remain the same: no transformation, no new insights. The old man just goes on gathering dust.

Knowing is a different phenomenon. It does not mean "think-ing about". It means going deep into the Existence itself in order to know, moving into the Existence. Remember this, that tantra is not a philosophy. It is science — a subjective science. The approach is scientific and non-philosophic. It is very down to earth, concerned with the immediate. The immediate is to be used as a door to the Ultimate. The Ultimate happens if you enter the immediate. It is there, and there is no other way to reach to it.

Philosophy is not a way in the eyes of tantra. It is a false way! It only appears that this is a way. It is a door which is not: it simply appears to be the door. It is a false door. The moment you try to enter it, you come to know that you cannot enter. It is just a painted door. There is no door in reality. Philosophy is a painted door. If you sit by its side and go on thinking and thinking, it is good. If you try to enter it, it is a wall.

So every philosophy is good for philosophizing. For experiencing, every philosophy is impotent. That is why so much insistence on technique in tantra — SO MUCH insistence on technique: because a science can do nothing but give technology, whether of the outside world or of the inside. The very word "tantra" means technique. The very word "tantra" MEANS technique! That is why, in this small and yet one of the greatest and deepest books, only techniques are given — no philosophy: just 112 techniques to reach the Ultimate through the immediate.

The ninth technique (concerning sound): *"Silently intone a word ending in 'AH'. Then in the 'HH', effortlessly, the spontaneity."*

"Silently intone a word ending in 'AH' ": any word that ends in "AH". Intone it silently. Emphasis should be given to the ending "AH". Why? Because the moment this sound "AH" is intoned, your breath goes out. You may not have observed it, but now you can observe: whenever your breath goes out you are more silent, and whenever your breath comes in you are more tense — because the outgoing breath is death and the incoming breath is life. Tension is part of life, not of death. Relaxation is part of death. Death means total relaxation. Life cannot be totally relaxed; it is impossible.

Life means tension, effort. Only death is relaxed. So whenever a person becomes absolutely relaxed, he is both — alive outwardly and dead within. You can see in the face of a Buddha both life and death simultaneously. That is why so much silence and calm. They are part of death. Life is not relaxation. You relax in the night when you are asleep. That is why the old traditions say that death and sleep are similar. Sleep is a temporary death and death is permanent sleep. That is why night relaxes you. It is the outgoing breath. The morning is the incoming breath.

The day makes you tense and the night relaxes you. Light makes you tense, darkness relaxes you. That is why you cannot sleep when there is light. It is difficult to relax because light is similar to life: it is anti-death. Darkness is similar to death: it is pro-death.

So darkness has deep relaxation in it, and those who are afraid of darkness cannot relax. Impossible, because every relaxation is dark and darkness surrounds your life on both the sides: before you are born you are in darkness; when life ceases you are again in darkness. Darkness is infinite, and this light and this life is just a moment in it, just a wave arising and then falling back. If you can remember the darkness that surrounds both the ends, you will be relaxed here and now.

Life, death — they both are two sides of existence. The incoming breath is life, the outgoing breath is death. So it is not that you die someday. You are dying with every breath. That is why the Hindus have been counting life in breaths. They do not count life in years. Tantra, yoga, all the old Indian systems, they count life in breaths: in how many breaths you are going to live. So they say if you breathe very fast, with too much breathing in a short time you will die very soon. If you breathe very slowly and your breaths are less in an interval, you will live very long. And this is so.

If you go and observe animals, those animals whose breathing is very slow live long. Take the elephant: the elephant lives long; the breath is very slow. Then there is the dog: the dog dies soon; the breath is very fast. Whenever you find an animal in which the breath is fast, any animal, the animal will not have a long life. A long life is always with slow breath.

Tantra and yoga and other Indian systems count your life in breaths. Really, with every breath you are born and with every breath you are dying. This mantra, this technique, uses the outgoing breath as the method, the medium, the vehicle, to go deep into silence. It is a death method. "Intone silently a word ending in 'AH'." The breath has gone: that is why a word ending in "AH".

This AH is meaningful because when you say AH it completely empties you. The whole breath has moved out; nothing remains within. You are totally empty — empty and dead. For a single moment, for a very small interval, life has moved out of you. You are dead — empty. This emptiness, if Realized, if you can become aware of it, will change you completely. You will be a different man.

Then you will know well that this life is not your life and this death is also not your death. Then you will know something which is beyond the incoming and outgoing breath — the witnessing soul. And this witnessing can happen easily when you are empty of breath, because life has subsided and with it all tensions have subsided. So try it. It is a very beautiful method. But the ordinary process, the ordinary habit, is to emphasize the incoming breath, never the outgoing breath.

We always take the breath in. We ALWAYS take it in, but we never throw it out. We take it in and THE BODY throws it out. Observe your breathing and you will know. We take it in. We never exhale: we only inhale. The exhaling is done by the body because we are afraid of death: that is the reason. If it was in our power, we would not exhale at all. We would inhale and then control it within. No one emphasizes exhaling: inhaling is emphasized. Because we HAVE to do exhaling after inhaling, that is why we go on "suffering" it. We tolerate it because we cannot inhale without exhaling.

So exhaling is accepted as a necessary evil, but basically we are not interested in exhaling. And this is not only about breath: this is our whole attitude toward life. We cling to everything that comes to us; we will not leave it. This is the miserliness of the mind.

And, remember, there are many implications in it. If you are suffering from constipation, this will be the basic cause: you always inhale and never exhale. The mind which never exhales but just inhales will suffer from constipation. The constipation is the other end of the same thing. He cannot exhale anything. He goes on accumulating, he is afraid. The fear is there. He can only accumulate, but anything that is accumulated becomes poisonous.

If you only inhale and do not exhale, your very breath becomes poison to you; you will die because of it. You can turn a life-giving force into poison if you behave in a miserly way, because the exhaling is absolutely necessary. It throws all the poisons out of you.

So, really, death is a purifying process and life is a poisoning process. This will look paradoxical. Life is a poisoning process because to live you have to use many things — and the moment you have used them they turn into poison: they are converted into poisons. You take a breath in, you use oxygen, and then what remains becomes poison. It was life only because it was oxygen, but you have used it. So life goes on changing everything into a poison.

Now there is a great movement in the West — Ecology. Man has been using everything and turning it into poison, and the very Earth is just on the verge of dying. Any day it can die because we have turned everything into poison. Death is a purifying process. When your whole body has become poisonous, death will relieve you of the body. It will renew you; it will give you a new birth. A new body will be given to you. Through death, all the accumulated poisons are dissolved back into nature. You are given a new mechanism.

And this happens with every breath. The outgoing breath is similar to death: it takes poisons out. And when it is going out, everything ebbs within. If you can throw the whole breath out, completely out so that no breath remains within, you touch a point of silence that can never be touched while the breath is in.

It is just like the ebb and tide: with every breath a tide of life comes to you; with every exhalation, everything ebbs — the tide has gone. You are just a vacant, empty shore. This is the use of this technique. "Silently intone a word ending in 'AH'." Emphasize the exhaling breath. And you can use it for many changes in the mind. If you are suffering from constipation, forget intaking. Just exhale and do not inhale. Let the body do the work of inhaling; you just do the work of exhaling. You force the breath out and do not inhale. The body will inhale by itself; you need not worry about it. You are not going to die. The body will take breath in. You just throw out and let the body take in. Your constipation will go.

If you are suffering from heart disease, just exhale: do not inhale. Then you will not suffer from heart disease. If while just going upwards on a staircase, or anywhere, you feel tired — very much tired, suffocated, breathless — simply do this: just exhale; do not inhale. Then you can climb up any amount of steps, and you will not be tired. What happens? When you go with an emphasis on exhaling, you are ready to let go, you are ready to die. You are not afraid of death; that makes you open. Otherwise you are closed: fear closes you.

When you exhale, the whole system changes and accepts death. There is no fear. You are ready to die. And one who is ready to die can live. Really, only one who is ready to die can live. He alone becomes capable of life — because he is not afraid.

One who accepts death, welcomes it, receives it as a guest, lives with it, goes deep into life. Exhale, do not inhale, and that will change your total mind. Because of simple techniques tantra never appeals, because we think, "My mind is such a complex thing." It is not complex — just foolish. And fools are very complex. A wise man is simple. Nothing is complex in your mind. It is a very simple mechanism. If you understand, you can change it very easily.

If you have not seen anybody dying, if you have been protected from seeing death as Buddha was protected, you cannot understand anything about it. Buddha's father was afraid because some astrologer said that "This boy is going to be a great sannyasin: he will renounce the world". The father asked, "What is to be done to protect him from doing such a thing?" So those astrologers thought and thought, and then they concluded and they said, "Do not allow him to see death, because if he is not aware of death he will never think of renouncing life."

This is beautiful — very meaningful. That means all religion, all philosophy, all tantra and yoga, is basically death oriented. If you are aware of death, only then does religion become meaningful. That is why no animal except man is religious: because no animal is aware of death. They die, but they are not aware. They cannot conceive or imagine that there is going to be death.

When one dog dies, other dogs never imagine that death is going to happen to them also. Always someone else dies, so how can a dog imagine that "I am going to die" ? He has never seen himself dying. Someone else, some other dog dies, so how can he connect that "I am going to die" ? No animal is aware of death; that is why no animal renounces. No animal can become a sannyasin. Only a very high quality of consciousness can lead you to renounce — when you become aware of death. And if even by being a man you are not aware of death, you belong to the animal kingdom; you are not yet a man. You become a man only when you encounter death. Otherwise there is no difference between you and the animal.

Everything is similar; only death makes the difference. With death encountered, you are no more an animal. Something has happened to you which never happens to an animal. Now you will be a different consciousness.

So Buddha's father protected him from seeing any type of death — not only man's death, but the death of animals and even of flowers. So the gardeners were appointed not to allow the child to see a dead flower, a pale flower dying from the branch, a pale leaf, a dry leaf. No, nowhere should he come to realize that something dies. He may infer from it that "I am going to die", and you do not infer it even seeing your wife dying, your mother, your father, your child. You weep for them, but you never conceive that this is a sign that "I am going to die".

But the astrologers said, "The boy is very, very sensitive, so protect him from any type of death." And the father was over-conscious. He would not allow even an old man or an old woman to be seen because oldness is just death heard from a distance: death is there from a distance, just coming. So Buddha's father would not allow any old man or old woman to be seen by the child. If Buddha suddenly became aware that just by stopping the breath a man could die, it would be very difficult for him.

"Just because no breath is coming in, how can a man die?" he would wonder. "Life is such a big, complex process."

If you have not seen anyone dying, even you cannot conceive that just by stopping the breath a man will die. Just by stopping the breath? Such a simple thing! And how can such a complex life die? The same is with these methods. They look simple, but they touch the basic reality. When the breath is going out, when you are completely emptied of death, you touch death: you are just near it, and everything becomes calm and silent within you.

Use it as a mantra. Whenever you feel tired, whenever you feel tense, use any word which ends in "AH". "Allah" will do — any word that brings your total breath out so that you exhale completely and you are emptied of breath. The moment you are emptied of breath you are emptied of life also. And all your problems belong to life: no problem belongs to death. Your anxiety, your anguish, your anger, your sadness, they all belong to life.

Death is non-problematic. Death never gives any problem to anyone. And even if you think that "I am afraid of death and death creates a problem", it is not death that creates the problem but your clinging to life. Only life creates problems; death dissolves all problems. So when the breath has moved completely out, "AH," you are emptied of life. Look within at that moment when the breath is completely out. Before taking another breath in, go deep down in that interval and become aware of the inside calm, the silence. In that moment you are a Buddha.

If you can catch that moment, you have known a taste of what Buddha might have known. And once known, you can detach this taste from the incoming-outgoing breath. Then the breath can go on coming in, going out, and you can remain in that quality of consciousness that you have come to know. It is always there; one has just to discover it. And it is easier to discover when life is emptied out.

"Silently intone a word ending in 'AH'. Then in the 'HH', effortlessly, the spontaneity": and when the breath goes out,

"HH", everything is emptied. "Effortlessly": in this moment, there is no need to make any effort. "The spontaneity": just be aware, be spontaneous, be sensitive, and realize this moment of death.

In this moment you are just near the door, just near the door — very, very near to the Ultimate. The immediate has moved out, the superfluous has moved out. In this moment you are not the wave: you are the ocean — just near, just near! If you can become aware you will forget that you are a wave. Again the wave will come, but now you can never be identified with it. You will remain the ocean. Once you have known that you are the ocean, you can never again be the wave.

Life is waves, death is the ocean. That is why Buddha so much insists about his Nirvana that it is deathlike. He never says you will attain life immortal. He says you will simply die totally. Jesus says, "Come to me and I will give you life, and life abundant." Buddha says, "Come to me to realize your death. I will give you death totally." And both mean the same thing, but Buddha's terminology is more basic. But you will become afraid of it. That is why Buddha had no appeal in India; he was uprooted completely. And we go on saying that this land is a religious land, but the most religious person couldn't get roots here.

What type of religious land is this! We have not produced another Buddha; he is incomparable. And whenever the world thinks India to be religious, the world remembers Buddha — no one else. Because of Buddha, India is thought to be religious. What type of religious land is this? Buddha has no roots here; he was totally uprooted. He used the language of death — that is the cause, and Brahmins were using the language of life. They say "the Brahman" and he says "Nirvana": "Brahman" means life, life, infinite life, and "Nirvana" means just cessation, death — total death.

Buddha says, "Your ordinary death is not total: you will be born again. It is NOT total! you will be born again! I will give you a total death, and you will never be born again." A total death means now no birth is possible. So this so-called death, Buddha says, is not death. It is just a rest period. You will become alive again. It is just a breath gone out. You will take the breath in again, you will be reborn. Buddha says, "I will give you the way so that the breath will go out and will never come again — total death, Nirvana, cessation."

We become afraid because we cling to life. But this is the paradox: the more you cling to life, the more you will die, and the more you are ready to die, then the more you become deathless. If you are ready to die, then there is no possibility of death. No one can give you death if you accept it, because through that acceptance you become aware of something within you which is deathless.

This incoming breath and outgoing breath are the life and death of the body, not of "me". But "I" do not know anything other than the body; "I am identified" with the body. Then it will be difficult to be aware when the breath comes in, easy to be aware when the breath goes out. When the breath is going out, for that moment you have become old, dying, emptied completely of the breath: you are dead for a moment.

"In the 'HH', effortlessly, the spontaneity": Try it! Any moment you can try it. Just riding in a bus or travelling in a train or moving to the office, whenever you have time intone a sound like "Allah" — any sound ending with "AH". This "Allah" helped so much in Islam — not because of any Allah there in the sky, but because of this "AH". This word is beautiful. And then the more one goes using this word "Allah, Allah", it becomes reduced. Then what remains is "lah, lah". Then it is reduced further; then it remains as "ah, ah". It is good, but you can use any word that ends in "AH" — or just — "AH" will do.

Have you observed that whenever you are tense you will sigh "AH", and you will feel relaxed. Or whenever you are in joy, overjoyed, you say "AH", and the whole breath is thrown out and you feel within a tranquillity that you have never felt. Try this: When you are feeling very good, take the breath in and then see what you feel. You cannot feel that well-being that comes with "AH". It is coming because of the breath.

So languages differ, but these two things never differ. All over the world, whenever someone feels tired he will say "AH". Really, he is calling for death to come and relax him. Whenever one feels overjoyed, blissful, he says "AH". He is so overfilled with joy that he is not afraid of death now. He can relieve himself completely, relax completely.

And what will happen if you go on trying it, trying it? You will become fully aware of something within you — the spontaneousness of your being: of *sahaj* — of being spontaneous. That you are already, but you are too much engaged with life, too much occupied with life. You cannot become aware of the being which is behind.

When you are not occupied with life, with the incoming breath, the being behind is revealed; there is a glimpse. But the glimpse will become, by and by, a realization. And once it is known you cannot forget it — and this is not something which you are creating. That is why it is spontaneous: it is not something you are creating. It is there: you have simply forgotten. It is a remembrance! It is a rediscovery!

Try to see children, very small children, taking their breaths. They take them in a different way. Look at a child sleeping. His belly comes up and down, not the chest. If you are sleeping and you are being observed, your chest comes up and down: your breath never goes down to the belly. The breath can go down to the belly only if you exhale and do not inhale. If you inhale and do not exhale, the breath cannot go down to the belly. The reason why breath goes to it is that when one exhales, the whole breath is thrown out and then the BODY takes in. And the body takes only that amount which is needed — never more, never less.

The body has its own wisdom, and it is more wise than you. Do not disturb it. You can take more: then it will be·disturbed. You can take less: then it will be disturbed. The body has its own wisdom. It only takes that much amount which is needed. When more is needed, it creates the situation. When less is needed, it creates the situation. It never goes to the extreme: it is always balanced. But if YOU inhale, it is never balanced because you do not know what you are doing, you do not know what is the need of the body. And the need changes every moment.

Allow the body! You just exhale, you just throw out, and then the body will take breath in — and it will take it deeply and slowly, and the breath will go down to the belly. It will hit the exact navel point, and your belly will go up and down. If you inhale, then, really, you never exhale totally. Then the breath is in and you go on inhaling, so the breath which is already in will not allow your breath to go down to the very bottom. Then just shallow breathing happens. You go on taking in, and the poisonous breath is there, filled in.

They say that you have six thousand holes in your lungs and only two thousand are touched by your breath. The four thousand are always filled with poisonous gases which need to be exhaled, and that two-thirds portion of your chest creates much anxiety, much anguish and misery in the mind, in the body. A child exhales: he never inhales. Inhaling is done by the body itself.

When the child is born, the first thing he is going to do is cry. With that cry his throat opens. With that cry comes the first "AH": the oxygen and air that had been given by the mother is exhaled. This is his first effort with breathing. That is why, if a child is not crying, then the doctor will become uneasy: because he has not shown the sign of life. He still feels dependent on the mother. He must cry! That cry shows that now he is becoming an individual; the mother is not needed. He will take his own breath. And the first thing is that he is going to cry in order to exhale that which was given by the mother, and then his body will start functioning, inhaling.

A child is always exhaling, and when the child starts inhaling, when the emphasis moves to inhaling, be aware. He has already become old; he has learned things from you: he has become tense. Whenever you are tense, you cannot take a deep breath. Why? Your stomach becomes rigid. Whenever you are tense, your stomach becomes rigid: it won't allow breath to go down. Then you have to take shallow breaths.

Try with "AH". It has a beautiful feeling around it. Whenever you feel tired, "AH": throw the breath. And make it a point to emphasize exhaling. You will be a different man, and a different mind will evolve. With the emphasis on breathing in, you have developed a miser mind and a miser body. With exhaling, that miserliness will disappear and with it many problems. Possessiveness will disappear.

So tantra will not say leave possessiveness. Tantra says change your system of breathing. You cannot possess then. Observe your own breathing and your moods, and you will become aware. Whatsoever is wrong is always associated with the emphasis that is given to the incoming breath and whatsoever is good, virtuous, beautiful, true is always associated with exhaling. Whenever you are speaking a lie, you will hold your breath in. Whenever you speak truth, you never hold the breath. You fear that "I am speaking a lie", so you hold the breath. You are afraid something may go out with it — the outmoving breath. Your hidden truth may be revealed, so you are afraid.

Go on trying this "AH" more and more. You will be more healthy in body, more healthy in mind, and a different quality of calm, at-easeness, tranquillity will develop.

The tenth sound method: *"Stopping ears by pressing and rectum by contracting, enter the sound."*

We are not aware of the body even or how the body functions and what is its Tao — what is its way. But if you observe, then you can become very easily aware. If you stop your ears and pull your rectum up, contract your rectum, everything will stop for you. It will be as if the whole world has become non-moving — as if everything has become static, stopped. Not only movements: you will feel as if time has stopped.

What happens when you pull the rectum up, contract it? What happens? When the ears are closed simultaneously, with closed ears you will hear a sound within. But if the rectum is not pulled up, that sound is released by the rectum. That sound is very subtle. If the rectum is pulled up, contracted, and the ears are closed, you will see within you a pillar of sound — and that sound is of silence. It is a negative sound. When all sounds have ceased, then you feel the sound of silence or the sound of soundlessness. But it will be released from the rectum.

So close the ears and pull the rectum up. Then you are closed from both the sides, and your body becomes closed and just filled with sound. This feeling of being filled with sound gives a deep fulfillment. So we will have to understand many things around it. Only then will it become possible for you to have the feeling of what happens.

We are not aware of the body: that is one of the basic problems for a seeker. And the society is against becoming aware of the body because society is afraid of the body. So we train every child not to be aware of the body. We make every child insensitive. We create a distance between the child's mind and the body, so he is not very much aware of the body because body awareness will create problems for the society.

Many things are implied. If the child is aware of the body, he will become aware of sex sooner or later. And if he is too much aware of the body, he will feel too much sexual, sensuous. So we have to kill the very root. He should be "made dull" about his body, insensitive so he never feels it. You do not feel your body. You feel it only when something wrong happens, when something goes wrong.

You have a headache in the head, then you feel your head. Some thorn is there, then you feel your leg, your feet. When your body aches, you feel that you have a body. You feel it only when something goes wrong, and then too not right away. You are never aware of your diseases immediately. You become aware only when a period has passed and when the disease goes on knocking at your consciousness that "I am here". Only then do you become aware. So no one really goes to the doctor in time. Everyone reaches there late, when the disease has entered deep and has done much wrong.

If a child has grown up with sensitivity he will become aware of the disease even before the disease happens. And now, in Russia particularly, they are working on the theory that a disease can be known even six months before its happening if someone is very deeply sensitive about his body, because subtle changes start long in advance. They prepare the body for the disease. The impact is felt even six months before.

But never mind disease! We never become aware even of death! If you are going to die tomorrow, you are not aware even today. A thing like death which may happen the next moment, and you are not aware this moment. You are totally dead to your body, insensitive. This whole society, the whole culture up to now, creates this dullness, this deadness, because it has been against the body. You are not allowed to feel it. Only in accidents can you be pardoned, forgiven for being aware of it; otherwise "do not be aware of the body".

This creates many problems, particularly for tantra, because tantra believes in deep sensitivity and knowledge of the body. You go on, move on, and your body goes on doing many things and you are unaware. Now much work is being done on body language. The body has its own language, and psychiatrists and psychologists and psychoanalysts in particular are being trained for body language because they say you cannot believe the modern man. Whatsoever he says cannot be believed. Rather, one must observe his body. That will give a more true clue.

A man enters a psychiatrist's office. The old psychiatry, Freudian psychoanalysis, will talk and talk with the man to bring out whatsoever is hidden in his mind. Modern psychiatry will observe his body because that gives clues. If a man is an egoist, if ego is his problem, he stands in a different way than a humble man. His neck has a different angle than a humble man, his spine is not flexible, but dead, fixed. He looks wooden, not alive. If you touch his body it has a wooden feeling, not the warmth of a living body. He is like a soldier just moving to the front.

Look at the soldier moving to the front. He has a wooden shape, a wooden feeling, and that is needed by a soldier because he is going to die or to kill. He must not be much aware of the body, so his whole training is to create a wooden body. Soldiers marching look like toys, like dead toys marching.

If you are humble, you have a different body. You sit differently, you stand differently. If you feel inferior, you stand differently; if you feel superior, you stand differently. If you are always in fear, you stand in such a way as if you are protecting yourself from some unknown force. That is always there. If you are not afraid, you are just like a child playing with his mother. There is no fear. Wherever you go you are unafraid, at home with the universe around you. The man who is afraid is armoured. And when I say armoured, it is not only symbolically. Physiologically he is armoured.

Wilhelm Reich was working very much on body structure, and he came to see some deep associations between mind and body. If a man is afraid, his stomach is not flexible. You touch his stomach, and it is like a stone. If he becomes fearless, his stomach relaxes immediately. Or if you relax the stomach, then the fear disappears. Massage the stomach to relax, and you will feel more fearless, less afraid.

A person who is loving has a different quality of body and warmth: he is warm bodily. A person who is not loving is cold: physiologically he is cold. Cold and other things have moved into your body and they have become barriers. They do not allow you to know about your body. But the body goes on working in its own way and you go on working in your own way: a rift is created. That rift has to be broken.

I have seen that if someone is suppressive, if you have suppressed your anger, then your fingers, your hands, have the sensation of a suppressed anger. And a person who knows how to feel it can feel just by touching your hand that you have suppressed anger. And why in the hand? Because anger has to be released by hand. If you have suppressed anger, then in your teeth, in your gums, it is suppressed — and it can be felt by touching. It gives a vibration that "I am suppressed here".

If you have suppressed sex, then in your erotic zones it is there. If a person has suppressed sex, then if you touch his erotic zone you can feel it. With any erotic zone touched, sex is there if it has been suppressed. The zone will become afraid and will withdraw from your touch. It will not be open. Because the person inside is withdrawing, the part of the body will withdraw. It will not allow you to bring about an opening.

Now they say that fifty percent of women are frigid, and the reason is because we teach girls to be more suppressive than boys. So they have suppressed, and when a girl suppresses her sexual feelings up to the age of twenty, it has become a long habit — twenty years of suppression. Then when she will love, she will talk about love, but her body will not be open: the body will be closed. And then an opposite, a diametrically opposite phenomenon happens: two currents oppose each other. She wants to love, but her body is repressive. The body withdraws; it is not ready to come closer.

If you see a woman sitting with a man, if the woman loves the man she will be inclining toward him. The body will be inclining. If they are sitting on a sofa, both of their bodies will be inclining toward each other. They are not aware, but you can see it. If the woman is afraid of the man, her body will be inclining to the opposite direction. If a woman loves a man, she will never cross her legs when sitting near him. If she is afraid of the man, she will cross her legs. She is not aware; this is not done consciously. It is body armour. The body protects itself and works in its own ways.

Tantra became aware of this phenomenon; the first awareness of such deep body feeling, sensitivity, was with tantra. And tantra says that if you can use your body consciously, the body becomes the vehicle to move to the spirit. Tantra says it is foolish, absolutely idiotic, to be against the body. Use it! It is a vehicle! And use its energy in such a way that you can go beyond it.

Now, "Stopping ears by pressing and rectum by contracting, enter the sound." Many times you have been contracting the rectum and sometimes the rectum is released even without your consciousness. If you suddenly become afraid, the rectum is released. You may defecate in fear, you may urinate in fear. Then you cannot control it. If a sudden fear grips you, your bladder will relax, your rectum will relax. What happens? In fear, what happens? Fear is a mental thing, so why do you urinate in fear? Why is the control lost? There must be some deep connecting root.

Fear happens in the head, in the mind. When you are un-afraid this never happens. The child really has no mental control over his body. No animal controls his urine, bladder or anything. Whenever the bladder is full it is released. No animal controls it, but man has to control it of necessity. So we force a child to control when he should go to the bathroom and when not. We tell him he has to control; we give timings. So the mind takes over the control of a function which is non-voluntary. That is why it is so difficult to train the child for the toilet. And now psychologists say that if we stop toilet training, humanity will very much improve.

Toilet training is the first repression of the child and its natural spontaneity, but it seems difficult to listen to these psychologists. We cannot listen to them because then the children will create many problems. We have to train them of necessity. Only a very, very rich, affluent society will be able not to bother. Poor societies have to manage. We cannot afford it. If the child urin-ates anywhere, we cannot afford it. If he urinates on the sofa we cannot afford it, so we have to train. This training is mental. The body really has no built-in program for it. The body has NO built-in program for it!

Man is an animal as far as body is concerned, and the body knows no culture, no society. That is why, when you are in deep fear, the control mechanism that you have imposed on the body is relaxed. You are not in control; you are thrown off control. You can control only in normal conditions. In emergencies you cannot control because for emergencies you have never been trained. You have only been trained for the normal, day-to-day routine world. In an emergency the control is lost. Your body starts functioning in its own animal way. But one relationship can be understood, that with a fearless man this will never happen. So this has become a sign of a coward.

If in fear you urinate or defecate, this shows you are a coward. A fearless man will not behave in this way, because a fearless man is taking deep breaths. His body and his breathing system are related; there is no gap. With a man who is a coward there is a gap, and because of that gap he is always overburdened with urine and defecation. So whenever an emergency comes, that overburdenedness has to be thrown: he has to be unburdened. And it has a reason in nature. A coward who is unburdened can escape more easily with his stomach relaxed, can run more easily. A burdened stomach will become a hindrance, so it is helpful for a coward to be relaxed.

Why am I talking about this? I am just saying this, that you have to be aware of your mental processes and your stomach processes. They are deeply related. Psychologists say that fifty to ninety percent of your dreams are because of your stomach processes. If you have taken a very heavy meal you are bound to see nightmares. They are not related with the mind. It is just that the heavy stomach creates them.

Many dreams can be created by outside tricks. If you are sleeping, your hands can be crossed on your chest and immediately you will start dreaming some nightmare. A pillow can be put on your chest, and you will dream that some demon is sitting on your chest just going to kill you. And this has been one of the problems. Why such a burden from the small weight of a pillow? If you are awake, there is no weight; you do not feel anything heavy. But why is it that a small pillow placed on you in the night when you are sleeping is felt as being so heavy that it is as if you have been burdened with a big stone or a rock? Why is so much weight felt?

The reason is this: when you are aware, when you are awake, your mind and body are not correlated; the gap is there. You cannot feel the body and its sensitivity. While asleep, the control, the culture, the conditioning, dissolves; you have again become a child and your body has become sensitive. Because of that sensitivity, a small pillow is felt as a rock. It is magnified because of sensitivity: the sensitivity magnifies it. So body-mind processes are deeply related, and if you know what happens you can use this.

Rectum closed, pulled upwards, contracted, creates a situation in the body in which sound can be felt if present. You will feel a pillar of sound in silence within the closed space in your body. Close the ears and pull up the rectum, and then just remain with what is happening inside you. Just remain in that vacant state which is created by these two things. Your life energy is moving within and it has no way to go out. Sound goes out either from your ears or from your rectum. Those are the two doors from where the sound can move out. If it is not moving out, you can feel it more easily.

And what will happen when you feel this inner sound? With the very phenomenon of hearing the inner sound, your thoughts dissolve. Just try it anytime during the day: just pull up the rectum and put your fingers in the ears. Press the ears and pull up the rectum. You will feel that your mind has stopped. It will not be functioning; thoughts will have stopped. That constant flow of thoughts is not there. It is good! And if one goes on doing it whenever there is time, in the day if you can do it for five or six times, within three or four months you will become an expert in it. And then such a well-being flows out of it!

And the inner sound, once heard, remains with you. Then you can hear it the whole day. The market is noisy, the road is noisy, the traffic is noisy, but if even in that noise you have heard the inner sound, you will feel the still small voice that goes on inside. And then nothing will disturb you. If you can feel your inner sound, then nothing from the outside can disturb you.

You remain silent; whatsoever happens around you makes no difference.

The last sound technique: *"Enter the sound of your name and, through this sound, all sounds."*

"Enter the sound of your name and, through this sound, all sounds": your own name can be used as a mantra very easily, and it is very helpful because your name has gone very deep into your unconscious. Nothing else has gone so deep. If we all here are sitting, and we all fall asleep and someone comes and calls "Ram", no one will listen except the person whose name is Ram: he will listen to it; he will be disturbed in his sleep. No one will listen to the sound "Ram", but why does this man listen? It has gone down deep; it is not conscious now. It has become unconscious.

Your name has gone very deep within you, but there is a very beautiful phenomenon about your name. You never call it: others call it. Others use it: you never use it.

I have heard that in the First World War, for the first time in America rationing was created. Thomas Edison was a very great scientist, but he was very poor so he had to stand in the queue for his ration card. And he was such a great man that no one ever used his name before him. There was no need to use his name for himself, and no one else would use his name because he was so much respected. Everyone would call him "Professor", so he had forgotten what was his name.

He was standing in the queue, and when his name was called, when it was asked who "Thomas Alva Edison" was, he just started blankly. Again the name was called, then someone who was a neighbour to Edison said to him, "Why are you standing? Your name is being called. It is your name, Professor." Then he became aware and he said, "But how can I recognize it? No one calls me 'Edison'. It has been so long. They just call me 'Professor'."

You never use your own name. Only others use it: you have heard it used by others. But it has gone deep, very deep. It has penetrated like an arrow into your unconscious. If you yourself

use it, then it becomes a mantra. And for two reasons it helps:
one, when you use your own name, if your name is "Ram" and
you use "Ram-Ram-Ram", suddenly you feel as if you are using
someone else's name — as if it is not yours. Or, if you feel that
this IS yours, you feel that there is a separate entity within you
which is using it. It may belong to the body, it may belong to
the mind, but he who is calling "Ram-Ram" becomes a witness.

You have always called others' names. When you call your
own name it looks as if it belongs to someone else, not to you,
and it is a very revealing phenomenon. You can become a witness to your own name, and with the name your whole life is
involved. Separated from the name, you are separated from
your whole life. And this name has penetrated deep within you
because everyone has called you this from your very birth. You
have always heard this. So use this sound, and with this sound
you can go to the very depths to which the name has gone.

In the old days we gave everyone a name of God — everyone.
Someone was Ram, someone was Narayan, someone was Krishna,
someone was Vishnu, or something like that. They say all the
Mohammedan names are the names of God — ALL the Mohammedan names! And all over the world that was the practice —
to give a name which is really a name of God.

This was for good reasons. One reason was this technique:
because if your name can be used as a mantra it will serve you
a double-purpose. It will be YOUR name — and you have heard
it so much, so many times, and all your life it has penetrated
deep. Then also, it is the name of God. So go on repeating it
inside, and suddenly you will become aware that "This name
is different from me". Then by and by this name will have
a sanctity of its own. You will remember any day that
"Narayan" or "Ram", this is God's name. Your name has turned
into a mantra.

Use it! This is very good! You can try many things with
your name. If you want to be awakened at five o'clock in the
morning, no alarm is so exact as your own name. Just repeat
thrice inside, "Ram, you have to be awake by five o'clock

sharp." Repeat it three times, and then just fall to sleep. You will be awakened at five o'clock because "Ram", YOUR name, is very deep in the unconscious.

Call your name and tell yourself that at five o'clock in the morning, "Let me be awakened." Someone WILL awaken you. And if you continue this practice, one day you will suddenly realize that at five o'clock someone calls you and says, "Ram, be awake." That is your unconscious calling you.

This technique says, "Enter the sound of your name and, through this sound, all sounds." Your name becomes just a door for all names. But enter the sound. First, when you repeat "Ram-Ram-Ram", it is just a word. But it means something when you go on repeating "Ram-Ram-Ram". You must have heard the story of Valmiki. He was given this mantra "Ram", but he was an ignorant man — uneducated, simple, innocent, childlike. He started repeating "Ram-Ram-Ram", but he was repeating so much that he forgot completely and reversed the whole thing. Instead he was chanting "mara-mara". He was chanting "Ram-Ram-Ram" so fast that it became "mara-mara-mara", and he achieved the goal through "mara-mara-mara".

If you go on repeating the name fast inside, soon it will not be a word: it will become a sound, just meaningless. And then there is no difference between "Ram" and "mara" — no difference! Whether you call "Ram" or "mara" makes no sense. They are not words. It is just the sound, just the sound that matters. Enter the sound of your name. Forget the meaning of it; just enter the sound. Meaning is with the mind, sound is with the body. Meaning is in the head, sound spreads all over the body. So forget the meaning. Just repeat it as a meaningless sound, and through this sound you will enter all sounds: this sound will become the door to all sounds, and "all sounds" means all that exists.

This is one of the basic tenets of Indian inner search, that the basic unit of the Existence is sound and not electricity. Modern science says that the basic unit of the Existence is electricity, not sound, but they also say that sound is a form of electricity.

Indians, however, have always been saying that electricity is nothing but a form of sound.

You may have heard that through a particular *raga* — a particular sound, fire can be created. It can be created — because this is the Indian idea, that sound is the basis of all electricity. So if you hit sound in a particular frequency, electricity will be created.

On long bridges, if a military is passing, they are not allowed to march because many times it has happened that because of their march the bridge falls. It is because of sound, not because of their weight. They will be passing anyhow, but if they pass marching, then the particular sound of their feet breaks the bridge.

In old Hebrew history, the city of Jericho was very protected by great walls and it was impossible to break those walls by guns. But through a particular sound the walls were broken, and that sound was the secret of the breaking of those walls. If that sound is created before walls, the walls will give way.

You have heard the story of Ali Baba: a particular sound and the rock moves. These are allegories. Whether they are right or not, one thing is certain: if you can create a particular sound so continuously that meaning is lost, mind is lost, the rock at your heart will be removed.

16
Tantra—The Path Of Surrender

January 29, 1973, Bombay, India

QUESTIONS:

1. *Do these techniques belong to yoga or actually to the central subject matter of tantra?*

2. *How to make sex meditative and should any special sexual positions be practised?*

3. *Is "anahat nada" a sound or soundlessness?*

The first question: *"Bhagwan, please explain whether the techniques you have discussed so far from 'Vigyana Bhairava Tantra' belong to the science of yoga instead of to the actual and central subject matter of tantra. What is the central subject matter of tantra?"*

This question arises to many. The techniques that we have discussed also belong to yoga. They are the same techniques, but with a difference: you can use the same techniques with a very different philosophy behind it. The framework, the pattern, differs — not the technique. You may have a different attitude toward life — just the contrary to tantra.

Yoga believes in struggle; yoga is basically the path of will. Tantra does not believe in a struggle; tantra is not the path of will. Rather, on the contrary, tantra is the path of TOTAL SURRENDER. Your will is not needed. For tantra your will is the problem — the source of all anguish. For yoga, your surrender, your "will-lessness", is the problem.

Because your will is weak, that is why you are in anguish, suffering — for yoga. For tantra, because you have a will, because you have an ego, an individuality, that is why you are suffering. Yoga says bring your will to absolute perfection and you will be Liberated. Tantra says dissolve your will completely, become totally emptied of it, and that will be your Liberation. And both are right; this creates the problem. For me, both are right.

But the path of yoga is a very difficult one. It is just impossible, nearly impossible, that you can attain to the perfection of the ego. It means you become the center of the whole universe. The path is very long — arduous. And, really, it NEVER reaches to the end. So what happens to the followers of yoga? Somewhere on the path, in some life, they turn to tantra.

Intellectually yoga is conceivable; existentially it is impossible. If it IS possible, you will reach by yoga also, but generally it never happens. Even if it happens, it happens very rarely, such as to a Mahavir. Sometimes centuries and centuries pass, and then a man like Mahavir appears who has achieved through yoga. But he is rare, an exception, and he breaks the rule.

But yoga is more attractive than tantra. Tantra is easy, natural, and you can attain through tantra very easily, very naturally, effortlessly. And because of this, tantra never appeals to you as much. Why? Anything that appeals to you appeals to your ego. Whatsoever you feel is going to fulfill your ego will appeal to you more. You are gripped in the ego. Yoga thus appeals to you very much.

Really, the more egoistic you are, the more yoga will appeal to you, because it is pure ego effort. The more impossible, the more it is appealing to the ego. That is why Mt. Everest has so much appeal. There is so much attraction to reach to the top of a Himalayan peak because it is so difficult. And when Hillary and Tensing reached Mt. Everest, they felt a very ecstatic moment. What was that? It was because ego fulfills. They were the first.

When the first man landed on the moon, can you imagine how he felt? He was the first in all history. And now he cannot be replaced; he will remain the first in all the history to come. Now there is no way to change his status. The ego is fulfilled deeply. There is no competitor now and there cannot be. Many will land on the moon, but they will not be the first. But many can land on the moon and many can go to Everest. Yoga gives you a higher peak. And the more unreachable the end, the more there is the perfection of the ego — pure, perfect, absolute ego.

Yoga would have appealed to Nietzsche very much because he felt that the energy which is working behind life is the energy of will — the will to power. Yoga gives you that feeling. You are more powerful through it.

The more you can control yourself, the more you can control your instincts, the more you can control your body and the more you can control your mind, then the more you feel powerful. You become a master inside. But this is through conflict; this is through struggle and violence. And it always happens more or less that a person who has been practising through yoga for many lives comes to a point where the whole journey becomes drab, dreamy, futile, because the more ego is fulfilled, the more you will feel it is useless. Then the follower of the path of yoga turns to tantra.

But yoga appeals because everyone is an egoist. Tantra never appeals in the beginning. Tantra can appeal only to the higher depths — to those who have worked on themselves, who have REALLY been struggling through yoga for many lives. Then tantra appeals to them because they can understand. Ordinarily, you will not be attracted by tantra. And if you are attracted, you will be attracted by the wrong reasons, so try to understand them also.

You will not be attracted by tantra in the first place because it asks you TO SURRENDER, not to fight. It asks you to float, not to swim. It asks you to move with the current, not to go upstream. It tells you nature is good. Trust nature; do not fight it. Even sex is good. Trust it, follow it, flow into it; do not fight it. NO-FIGHT is the central teaching of tantra. Flow, let-go!

It cannot appeal. There is no fulfillment of your ego through it. In the first step it asks for your ego to be dissolved. In the very beginning, it asks you to dissolve it.

Yoga also asks you, but at the end. First it will ask to purify it. And if it is purified completely, it dissolves; it cannot remain. But that is the last in yoga, and in tantra that is the first.

So tantra will not appeal generally. And if it does appeal, it will appeal for wrong reasons. For example, if you want to indulge in sex, then you can rationalize your indulgence through tantra. That can become the appeal. If you want to indulge in wine, in women, in other things, you can feel attracted toward tantra. But, really, you are not attracted to tantra. Tantra is a façade — a trick. You are attracted to something else which you think tantra allows you. So tantra always appeals for wrong reasons.

Tantra is not to help your indulgence. It is to transform it. So do not deceive yourself. Through tantra you can deceive yourself very easily. And because of this possibility of deception, Mahavir would not describe tantra. This possibility is always there. And man is so deceptive that he can show one thing when he really means another. He can rationalize.

For example, in China, in old China, there was something like Tantra — a secret science. It is known as Tao. Tao has similar trends to tantra. For example, Tao says that it is good, if you want to be freed of sex, that you should not stick to one person — to one woman or one man. You should not stick to one if you want to be freed. Tao says that it is better to go on changing partners.

This is absolutely right, but you can rationalize it; you can deceive yourself. You may just be a sex maniac and you can think that "I am doing tantra practice, so I cannot stick to one woman. I am to change." And many Emperors in China practised it. They had big harems only for this.

But Tao is meaningful if you look deep down into human psychology. If you know only one woman, sooner or later your attraction for that woman will wither away, but your attraction for women will remain. You will be attracted by the other sex. This woman, your wife, will really not be of the opposite sex. She will not attract you, she will not be a magnet for you. You will have become accustomed to her.

Tao says that if a man moves amidst woman, MANY women, he will not only be beyond one: he will go beyond the opposite 'sex. The very knowledge of many woman will help him to transcend. And this is right, BUT DANGEROUS, because you would like it not because it is right but because it gives you license. That is the problem with tantra.

So in China also that knowledge was suppressed; it had to be suppressed. In India, tantra was also suppressed because it said many dangerous things — dangerous only because you are deceptive. Otherwise they are wonderful. Nothing has happened to the human mind that is more wonderful and mysterious than tantra; no knowledge is so deep.

But knowledge always has its dangers. For example, now science has become a danger because it has come to know many deep secrets. Now it knows how to create atomic energy. Einstein is reported to have said that if he is again given a life, rather than being a scientist he would like to be a plumber, because as he looks back his whole life has been futile — not only futile, but dangerous to humanity. And he has given one of the deepest secrets, but to man who is self-deceptive.

I wonder, the day may come soon when we will have to suppress scientific knowledge. There are rumours that there are secret thoughts amid scientists whether to disclose more or not — whether they should stop the search or whether they should go further — because now it is dangerous ground.

Every knowledge is dangerous; only ignorance is not dangerous. You cannot do much with it. Superstitions are always good — never dangerous. They are homeopathic. If the medicine is given to you, it is not going to harm you. Whether it is going to help you or not depends on your own innocence, but one thing is certain: it is not going to harm you. Homeopathy is harmless; it is a deep superstition. If it works, it can only help. Remember, if something can ONLY help, then it is deep superstition. If it can do both, help and harm, then only is it knowledge.

A real thing can do both — help and harm. Only an unreal thing can just help, but then the help never comes from the thing. It is always a projection of your own mind. So, in a way, only illusory things are good. They never harm you.

Tantra is science, and it is deeper than atomic knowledge because atomic science is concerned with matter and tantra is concerned with you, and you are always more dangerous than any atomic energy. Tantra is concerned with the biological atom, with you — the living cell, with life consciousness itself and how its inner mechanism works.

That is why tantra became so much interested in sex. One who is interested in life and consciousness will automatically become interested in sex because sex is the source of life, of love, of all that is happening in the world of consciousness. So if a seeker is not interested in sex, he is not a seeker at all. He may be a philosopher, but he is not a seeker. And philosophy is, more or less, nonsense — thinking about things which are of no use.

I have heard that Mulla Nasrudin was interested in girls, but he had very bad luck with girls. No one would like him. He was going to meet a certain girl for the first time, so he asked a friend, "What is your secret ? You are wonderful with women. You simply hypnotize them and I am always a failure, so give me some clue. I am going on a date for the first time with a girl, so give me some secrets."

The friend said, "Remember three things: always talk about food, family and philosophy." "Why about food ?" Mulla asked. The friend said, "I talk about food because then the girl feels good — because every woman is interested in food. She is food for the child. For the whole humanity she is food, so she is basically interested in food."

Mulla said, "Okay. And why family ?" So the man said, "Talk about her family so your intentions look honourable." Then Mulla said, "And why about philosophy ?" The man said, "Talk about philosophy. That makes the woman feel that she is intelligent."

So Mulla rushed. Immediately, when he saw the girl, he said, "Hello, do you like noodles ?" The girl was startled and said,

"No!" Then the Mulla asked the second question: "Have you got two brothers?" The girl was even more startled and wondered, "What type of date is this!" She said, "No!" So for a moment Mulla was at a loss. He wondered, "How to start talking about philosophy?" Just for a moment he was at a loss, and then he asked, "Now, if you had a brother would he like noodles?"

Philosophy is more or less nonsense. Tantra is not interested in philosophy; tantra is interested in actual existential life. So tantra never asks whether there is a God or whether there is *Moksha* (Liberation) or whether there is hell or heaven. Tantra asks basic questions about life. That is why so much interest in sex and love. They are basic. YOU ARE through them; you are part of them.

You are a play of sex energy and nothing less. And unless you understand this energy and transcend it, you will never be anything more. You are, right now, nothing but sex energy. You can be more, but if you do not understand this and you do not transcend it, you never will be more. The possibility is just there as a seed. That is why tantra is interested in sex, in love, in natural life.

But the way to know it is not through conflict. Tantra says you cannot know anything if you are in a fighting mood because then you are not receptive. Then, BECAUSE you are fighting, the secrets will be hidden from you. You are not open to receive. And whenever you are fighting, you are always outside. If you are fighting sex, you are always outside. If you surrender to sex, you reach the very inner core of it; you are an insider. If you surrender, then many things become known.

You have been in sex, but always with a fighting attitude behind it. That is why you have not known many secrets. For example, you have not known the life-giving forces of sex. You have not known because you cannot know. That needs an "insider".

If you are really flowing with sex energy, totally surrendered, sooner or later you will arrive at the point where you will know that sex cannot only give birth to a new life: sex can give YOU more life. To lovers sex can become a life-giving force, but for that you need a surrender. And once you are surrendered, many dimensions change.

For example, tantra has known, Tao has known, that if you ejaculate in the act, then it cannot be life-giving to you. There is no need to ejaculate; ejaculation can be totally forgotten. Tantra and Tao both say ejaculation is because you are fighting; otherwise there is no need of it.

The lover and the beloved can be in a deep sexual embrace, just relaxing into each other with no hurry to ejaculate, with no hurry to end the affair. They can just relax into each other. And if this relaxation is total, they both will feel more life. They both will enrich each other.

Tao says a man can live for 1,000 years if he is not in any hurry with sex, if he is deeply relaxed. If a woman and man are deeply relaxed with each other, simply melting into each other, absorbed into each other, not in any hurry, not in any tension, many things happen — alchemical things happen — because the life juices of both, the electricity of both, the bio-energy of both, meet. And just by this meeting (because they are "anti" — one is negative, one is positive: they are anti-poles), just by meeting with each other deeply, they invigorate each other, make each other vital — more alive.

They can live for a long time and they can live never becoming old. But this can only be known if you are not in a fighting mood. And this seems paradoxical. Those who are fighting sex, they will ejaculate sooner, because the tense mind is in a hurry to be relieved of the tension.

New research says many surprising things, many surprising facts. Masters and Johnson, they have worked scientifically for the first time with what happens in deep intercourse. They have come to realize that 75% of men are premature ejaculators — 75% ! Before there is a deep meeting, they have ejaculated and the act is finished. And 90% of women never have any orgasm;

they never reach to a peak, to a deep fulfilling peak: 90% of women !

That is why women are so angry and irritated, and they will remain so. No meditation can help them to be peaceful and no philosophy, no religion, no ethics, will make them at ease with the men with whom they are living. They are in frustration, in anger, because modern science and old tantra both say that unless a woman is deeply fulfilled orgasmically, she will be a problem in the family. That which she is lacking will create irritations and she will be always in a fighting mood.

So if your wife is always in a fighting mood, think again about the whole thing. It is not simply the wife: you may be the cause. And because women are not achieving orgasm, they become anti-sex. They are not willing to go into sex easily. They have to be bribed; they are not ready to go into sex. Why should they be ready if they never achieve any deep bliss through it ? Rather, they feel after it that the man has been using them, that they have been used. They feel like a thing which has been used and then discarded.

The man is satisfied because he has ejaculated. Then he moves and goes to sleep, and the wife goes on weeping. She has been just used, and the experience has not been in any way fulfilling to her. It may have relieved her husband or lover or friend, but it has not been in any way fulfilling to her.

Ninety percent of women do not even know what orgasm is. They have never known it; they have never reached a peak of such a blissful convulsion of the body that every fibre vibrates and every cell becomes alive. They have not reached it, and this is because of an anti-sexual attitude in the society. The fighting mind is there, and the woman is so repressed that she has become frigid.

The man goes on doing the act as if it is a sin. He feels it as guilt: "it is not to be done." And while he is making love to his wife or beloved, he is thinking of some *mahatma* (so-called saint) — of how to go to the *mahatma* and how to transcend this sex, this guilt, this "sin".

It is very difficult to get rid of the *mahatmas*. They are already there even while you are making love. You are not two; one *mahatma* must be there. If there is no *mahatma*, then "God" is watching you doing this "sin". The concept of God in people's minds is just that of a Peeping Tom: He is always watching you. This attitude creates anxiety. And when anxiety is there, ejaculation comes soon.

When there is no anxiety, ejaculation can be postponed for hours — even for days. And there is no need of it. If the love is deep, both parties can invigorate each other. Then ejaculation completely ceases, and for years two lovers can meet with each other without any ejaculation, without any wastage of energy. They can just relax with each other. Their bodies meet and relax; they enter sex and relax. And sooner or later, sex will not be an excitement. It is an excitement right now. Then it is not an excitement: it is a relaxation — a deep let-go.

But that can happen only if you have first surrendered inside to the life energy — the life force. Only then can you surrender to your lover or beloved. Tantra says this happens, and it arranges HOW it can happen.

Tantra says never make love while you are excited. This seems very absurd because you want to make love when you are excited. And, normally, both partners excite each other in order that they can make love. But tantra says that in excitement you are wasting energy. Make love while you are calm, serene, meditative. First meditate, then make love, and when making love do not go beyond the limit. What do I mean by "do not go beyond the limit"? Do not become excited and violent, in order that your energy will not be dispersed.

If you see two persons making love you will feel that they are fighting. If small children sometimes see their father and mother, they think the father is going to kill the mother. It looks violent; it looks like a fight. It is not beautiful; it looks ugly.

It must be more musical — harmonious. The two partners must be as if they are dancing, not fighting — as if singing one harmonious melody, just creating an atmosphere in which both may dissolve and become one. And then they relax. This is what tantra means. Tantra is not sexual at all. Tantra is the least sexual thing and yet it has so much concern with sex. And if through this relaxation and let-go nature reveals to you its secrets, it is no wonder. Then you begin to be aware of what is happening. And in that awareness of what is happening many secrets come to your mind.

Firstly, sex becomes life-giving. As it is now, it is death-giving. You are simply dying through it, wasting yourself, deteriorating. Secondly, it becomes the deepest natural meditation. Your thoughts cease completely. When you are totally relaxed with your lover, your thoughts cease. The mind is not there; only your heart beats. It becomes a natural meditation. And if love cannot help you into meditation, nothing will help because everything else is just superfluous, superficial. If love cannot help, NOTHING WILL HELP!

Love has its own meditation. But you do not know love; you know only sex and you know the misery of wasting energy. Then you get depressed after it. Then you decide to take a vow of *brahmacharya* (celibacy). And this vow is taken in depression, this vow is taken in anger, this vow is taken in frustration. It is not going to help.

A vow can be helpful if taken in a very relaxed, deeply meditative mood. Otherwise you are simply showing your anger, your frustration, and nothing else, and you will forget the vow within twenty-four hours. The energy will have come again, and just as an old routine you will have to release it.

Tantra says sex is very deep because it is life, but you can be interested in it for the wrong reasons. Do not be interested in tantra for wrong reasons, and then you will not feel that tantra is dangerous. Then tantra is life transforming.

Some tantric methods have been used by yoga also, but with a conflict — a fighting attitude. Tantra uses the same methods, but with a very loving attitude — and that makes a great difference. The very quality of the technique changes. The technique becomes different because the whole background is different.

It has been asked, "What is the central subject matter of tantra?" The answer is YOU! You are the central subject matter of tantra — what you are right now and what is hidden in you that can grow, what you are and what you can be. Right now you are A SEX UNIT, and unless this unit is understood deeply, you cannot become a spirit; you cannot become a spiritual unit. Sexuality and spirituality are two ends of one energy.

Tantra starts with you AS YOU ARE; yoga starts with what your possibility is. Yoga starts with the end; tantra starts with the beginning. And it is good to start with the beginning. It is ALWAYS good to begin with the beginning, because if the end is made the beginning, then you are creating unnecessary misery for yourself. You are not the end — not the ideal. You have to become a god, the ideal, and you are just an animal. And this animal goes berserk because of the ideal of the god. It goes mad; it goes crazy.

Tantra says forget the god. If you are the animal, understand this animal in its totality. In that understanding itself, the god will grow. And if it cannot grow through that understanding, then forget it; it can never be. Ideals cannot bring your possibilities out; only the knowledge of the real will help. So you are the central subject matter of tantra, as you are and as you can become — your actuality and your possibility; they are the subject matter.

Sometimes people get worried. If you go to understand tantra, God is not discussed, *Moksha* (Liberation) is not discussed, Nirvana is not discussed. What type of religion is tantra? Tantra discusses things which make you feel disgusted, which you do not want to discuss. Who wants to discuss sex? Everyone thinks he knows about it. Because you can reproduce, you think you know.

No one wants to discuss sex and sex is everyone's problem. No one wants to discuss love because everyone feels he is a great lover already. And look at your life ! It is just hatred and nothing else. And whatsoever you call love is nothing but a relaxation, a little relaxation, of the hatred. Look around you, and then you will know what you know about love.

Baal Shem, a fakir, went to his tailor every day for his robe, and the tailor took six months to make a simple robe for the fakir. The poor fakir ! When the robe was ready and the tailor gave it to Baal Shem, Baal Shem said, "Tell me, even God had only six days to create the world. Within six days God created the whole world and you took six months to make this poor man's robe ?"

Baal Shem remembered the tailor in his memoirs. The tailor said, "Yes, God created the world in six days, but look at the world — at what type of world it is ! Yes, he created the world in six days, but look at the world !"

Look around you; look at the world YOU have created. Then you will come to know that you do not know anything. You are just groping in the dark. And because everyone else is also groping in the dark, it cannot be that you are living in light. If everyone else is groping in the dark, you feel good because then you feel there is no comparison.

But you are also in the dark, and tantra starts with you as you are. Tantra wants to enlighten you about basic things which you cannot deny. If you try to deny them, it is at your own cost.

The second question : *"How can one convert the sex act into a meditative experience ? Should one practise any special positions in sex ?"*

Positions are irrelevant; positions are not very meaningful. The real thing is the attitude — not the position of the body, but the position of the mind. But if you change your mind you may want to change your positions, because they are related. But they are not basic.

For example, the man is always on the woman — on top of the woman. This is an egoist posture because the man always thinks he is better, superior, higher. How can he be below the woman ! But all over the world, in primitive societies, the woman is above the man. So in Africa this posture is known as the missionary posture because for the first time, when missionaries — Christian missionaries — went to Africa, the primitives just could not understand what they were doing. They thought it would kill the woman.

The man-on-top posture is known in Africa as the missionary posture. African primitives say this is violent, that man should be on top of the woman. She is weaker, delicate, so she must be on top of the man. But it is difficult for man to think of himself lower than woman — under her.

If your mind changes, many things will change. It is better that the woman should be on top, for many reasons. If the woman is on top she will be passive, so she is not going to do much violence; she will simply relax. And the man under her cannot do much. He will have to relax. This is good. If he is on top he is going to be violent. He will do much, and nothing is needed to be done on her part. For tantra you have to relax, so it is good that the woman should be on top. She can relax better than any man. The feminine psychology is more passive, so relaxation comes easy.

Positions will change, but do not be bothered about positions much. Just change your mind. Surrender to the life force; float in it. Sometimes, if you are really surrendered, your bodies will take the right position that is needed in that moment. If both partners are deeply surrendered, their bodies will take the right posture that is needed.

Every day situations change, so there is no need to fix postures beforehand. That is a problem — that you try to fix beforehand. Whenever you try to fix, this is a fixing by the mind. Then you are not surrendering.

If you surrender, then you let things take their own shape. And that is a wonderful harmony — when both partners have surrendered. They will take many postures or they will not take them and will just relax. That depends on the life force, not on your cerebral decision beforehand. You need not decide anything beforehand. Decision is the problem. Even to make love, you decide. Even to make love, you go and consult books.

There are books on how to make love. This shows what type of human mind we have produced. You consult books even on how to make love. Then it becomes cerebral; you think everything. Really, you create a rehearsal in the mind and then you enact it. Your action is a copy; it is never real then. You are enacting a rehearsal. It becomes acting; it is not authentic.

Just surrender and move with the force. What is the fear? Why be afraid? If you cannot be unafraid with your lover, then where will you be unafraid? And once you have the feeling that the life force helps by itself and takes the right path that is needed, it will give you a very basic insight into your whole life. Then you can leave your whole life to the Divine. That is your beloved.

Then you leave your WHOLE life to the Divine. Then you do not think and you do not plan; you do not force the future according to you. You just allow yourself to move into the future according to Him, according to the Total.

But how to make the sex act a meditation? Just by surrendering it becomes so. Do not think about it; let it happen. And be relaxed; do not move ahead. This is one of the basic problems with the mind: it always moves ahead. It is always seeking the result, and the result is in the future. You are never in the act; you are always in the future seeking a result. That seeking of a result is disturbing everything; it damages everything.

Just be in the act. What is the future? It is to come; you need not worry about it. And you are not going to bring it with your worries. It is already coming; it HAS already come. So you forget about it. You just be here and now.

Sex can become a deep insight into being here and now. That is, I think, the only act now left into which you can be here and now. You cannot be here and now while in your office; you cannot be here and now while you are studying in your college; you cannot be here and now anywhere in this modern world. Only in love can you be here and now.

But even then you are not. You are thinking of the result. And now many modern books have created many new problems. You read a book on how to make love, and then you are afraid over whether you are making it rightly or wrongly. You read a book on how a posture is to be taken — or what type of posture is to be used, and then you are afraid of whether you are taking the right posture or not.

Psychologists have created new worries in the mind. Now they say the husband must remember whether his wife is achieving orgasm or not, so he is worried over it. And this worry is not going to help in any way. It is going to become a hindrance.

The wife is worried whether she is helping the husband to relax totally or not. She must show that she is feeling very blissful. Then everything becomes false. Both are worried about the result. And because of this worry the result will never come.

Forget everything. Flow in the moment and allow your bodies their expression. Your bodies know well; they have their own wisdom. Your bodies are constituted of sex cells. They have a built-in program; you are not asked at all. Just leave it to the body, and the body will move. This leaving it to nature together, both together, this let-go, will create meditation automatically.

And if you can feel it in sex, then you know one thing: that WHENEVER you surrender you will feel the same. Then you can surrender to a Master. It is a love relationship. You can surrender to a Master, and then, while you are putting your head at his feet, your head will become empty. You will be in meditation.

Then there is even no need of a Master. Then go out and surrender to the sky. You know HOW to surrender; that is ALL. Then you can go and surrender to a tree. But it looks foolish because we do not know how to surrender. We see a person — a villager, a primitive man — going to the river, surrendering himself to the river, calling the river the Mother, the Divine Mother, or surrendering himself to the rising sun, calling the rising sun a great god, or going to a tree and putting his head at the roots and surrendering.

For us it looks superstitious. You say, "What nonsense he is doing! What will the tree do? What will the river do? They are not goddesses. What is the sun? The sun is not a god." Anything becomes a god if you can surrender. So your surrender creates Divinity. There is nothing Divine; there is only a surrendering mind which creates Divinity.

Surrender to a wife and she becomes Divine. Surrender to a husband and he becomes Divine. The Divinity is revealed through surrender. Surrender to a stone and there is no stone now. That stone has become a statue, a person — alive.

So just know how to surrender. And when I say "how to surrender", I do not mean to know a technique; I mean you have a natural possibility of surrendering in love. Surrender in love and feel it there. And then, let it spread all over your life.

The third question: *"Please explain whether the 'anahat nada' (soundless sound) is a type of sound or whether it is total soundlessness. And also explain how the state of total soundfulness can be equal to total soundlessness."*

Anahat nada is not a type of sound. It is soundlessness, but this soundlessness is heard. To express it is difficult because then the logical question arises of how soundlessness can be heard.

Let me explain it: I am sitting on this chair. If I go away from this chair, will you not see my absence in the chair? It cannot be seen by one who has not seen me sitting here. He will simply see the chair. But a moment before I was here and you have seen me sitting here. If I move away and you look at the chair, you will see two things: the chair and my absence. But that absence will be seen only if you have seen me and you have not forgotten me — that I was there.

We are hearing sounds; we only know sounds. So when that soundlessness comes, *anahat nada*, we feel that every sound has disappeared, and absence is felt. That is why it is called *anahat nada*. It is also called *nada*; *"nada"* means sound. But *"anahat"* changes the quality of the sound. *"Anahat"* means uncreated, so it is uncreated sound.

Every sound is a created sound. Whatsoever sounds you have heard, they are all created. That which is created will die. I can clap my hands; a sound is created. It was not there before and now it is no more. It was created and it has died. A created sound is known as *"ahat nada"*. Uncreated sound is known as *"anahat nada"* — the sound that is always. Which is that sound that is always ? It is not really a sound. You call it a sound because the absence is heard.

If you live by a railway station and one day the railway union goes on a strike, you will hear something no one can hear. You will hear the absence of the trains coming and going and moving.

I was travelling in the past for at least three weeks every month. In the beginning it was very difficult to sleep in the train, and then it became difficult to sleep at home. When I was no longer sleeping only in trains, the sound of the train was missed. Whenever I would reach home, it would be difficult because I would miss and I would feel the absence of the railway sounds.

We are accustomed to sounds. Every moment is filled with sound. Our heads are constantly filled by sounds and sounds and sounds. When your mind goes away, moves up or down, goes beyond or below, when you are not in the world of sounds, you can hear the absence. That absence is SOUNDLESSNESS.

But we have called it *anahat nada*. Because it is heard, we call it *"nada"* — sound, and because it is not really a sound we call it *"anahat"* — uncreated. "Uncreated sound" is contradictory. Sound IS created; "uncreated" contradicts. So all deep experiences of life have to be expressed in contradictory terms.

If you go and ask a Master like Eckhart or Jacob Boehme, or Zen Masters like Hui Hai or Huang Po or Bodhidharma or Nagarjuna, or Vedanta and the Upanishads, everywhere you will find two contradictory terms whenever a deeper experience is talked about. The Vedas say, "He is and He is not" about God.

You cannot find a more atheistic expression: "He is and He is not." He is far away and He is near. He is far away and He is ALSO near. Why contradictory statements ? Upanishads say,

"You cannot see Him, but unless you see Him you have not seen anything." What type of language is this?

Lao Tse says that "Truth cannot be said" and he is saying it. This too is a saying. He says that "Truth cannot be said — if it is said it cannot be true", and then he writes a book and says something about the Truth. It is contradictory.

One student came to a great old sage. The student said, "If you can forgive me, Master, I want to relate to you something about myself. I have become an atheist; now I do not believe in God."

So the old sage asked, "For how many days have you been studying scriptures? For how many days?" So the man, the seeker, the student, said, "Near about twenty years I have been studying the Vedas — the scriptures." So the old man sighed and said, "Just twenty years and you have the nerve to say that you have become an atheist?"

The student was puzzled. What was this old man saying? So he said, "I am puzzled. What are you saying? You make me more confused than when I came here." The old man said, "Go on studying the Vedas. In the beginning one says God is. Only in the end does one say God is not. To become an atheist you will have to travel much into theism. God is at the beginning; God is not at the end. Do not be in a hurry." He was even more puzzled.

"God is and God is not" has been uttered by those who know. "God is" is uttered by those who do not know and "God is not" is also uttered by those who do not know. Those who know, they utter both simultaneously: "God is and God is not."

"*Anahat nada*" is a contradictory term, but used with much consideration — with deep consideration. It is meaningful. It says the phenomenon is felt as a sound and it is not a sound. It is felt as a sound because you have only felt sounds. You do not know any other language. You know only the language of sounds; that is why it is felt as sound. But it is silence, not sound.

And the question further says, "Explain in which way the state of soundfulness can be equal to total soundlessness." It is always so. The zero and the absolute both mean the same!

For example, if I have a jar which is completely empty and I have another jar which is completely filled, both are COMPLETE. One is completely empty, another is completely filled. But both are complete, both are perfect. If the jar is half-filled, it is half-filled and half-empty. You can call it half-empty, you can call it half-filled. But whether it is completely empty or completely filled, one thing is common to both: COMPLETENESS !

Soundlessness is complete. You cannot do anything more to make it more soundless. Understand this: it is complete; nothing can be done. You have come to a point beyond which there is no movement possible. And if a sound is total you cannot add anything to it. You have come to another limit; you cannot go beyond it. This is common and this is what is meant.

One can say it is soundlessness because no sound is heard; everything has become absent. You cannot reduce anything further from it; it is complete. Or, you can say it is a complete sound, a full sound, absolute sound; nothing can be added to it. But in both the cases the indication is for perfection, absoluteness, wholeness.

It depends on the mind. There are two types of minds and two types of expressions. For example, if you ask Buddha, "What will happen in deep meditation ? When one achieves Samadhi what will happen ?" he will say, "There will be no *dukkha* — there will be no pain." He will never say there will be bliss, he will simply say there will be no pain — just painlessness. If you ask Shankara, he will never talk about pain. He will simply say, "There will be bliss — absolute bliss."

And both are expressing the same experience. Buddha saying "no pain" refers to the world. He says, "All the pains I have known are not there. And whatsoever IS there, I cannot relate it in your language." Shankara says, "There is bliss — absolute bliss." He never talks about the world and its pain. He is not referring to your world; he is referring to the experience itself. He is positive; Buddha is negative.

But their indications are toward the same moon. Their fingers are different, but what their fingers indicate is the same.

Rajneesh Meditation Centers in the United States

Bodhitaru, 7231 S.W. 62nd Place, Miami, Florida 33143.

Sarvam, 6412 Luzon Avenue, Washington, D.C. 20012. 202-726-1712

Geetam, Box 576, Highway 18, Lucerne Valley, California 92356. 714-248-6163

Paras, 4301 24th Street, San Francisco, California 94122. 415-664-6600

Premsagar, P.O. Box 2862, Chapel Hill, North Carolina 27514.

Rajneesh Yoga Institute, 3910 El Cajon Blvd., San Diego, California 92115

Batohi c/o Esalen Institute, Big Sur, California 93920. 408-667-2335

Dhyanataru, 375A Huron Avenue, Cambridge, Massachusetts 02138

Shantiduta, P.O. Box 52911, Houston, Texas 77052. 713-527-9039

Devagar, 310 Petit Brule, Ste. Madeleine de Regand, P.O. J0P 1P0